MAKING WAVES

Greenpeace has a policy of complete political independence and shuns all political and corporate affiliations. Greenpeace will not endorse any commercial products or services anywhere in the world.

Greenpeace New Zealand
Private Bag, Wellesley Street,
Auckland 1

Title page: Rainbow Warrior, Rongelap 1985.

Published by Reed Books, a division of Octopus Publishing Group (NZ) Ltd,
39 Rawene Road, Birkenhead, Auckland.
Associated companies, branches and representatives throughout the world.

This book is copyright. Except for the purpose of fair reviewing, no part of this publication may be reproduced or transmitted in any form or by any means, electronic or mechanical, including photocopying, recording, or any information storage and retrieval system, without permission in writing from the publisher. Infringers of copyright render themselves liable to prosecution.

ISBN 0 7900 0230 2
Copyright © 1991 Greenpeace New Zealand
First published 1991

Design and production by Paradigm, Auckland
Printed in Singapore on environmentally friendly paper

To Elaine Shaw,
an ordinary person
who did extraordinary things

Acknowledgments

This book was made possible through the collective effort of many people. For their inspiration, perspiration and patience, my thanks go first of all to Elaine Shaw, Jem Bates, Stephanie Mills, Carol Stewart, Jude Seaboyer, Naomi Petersen, Irene Petersen, Martin Gotje, Bunny McDiarmid, Bev Cormack, Owen Wilkes, Bette Johnson, David Robie, Bengt and Marie-Thérèse Danielsson, Margaret Baker, John Ringer and Mark Derby.

Also special thanks to Rien Achterberg, George Armstrong, Lucinda Androu, Tony Atkinson, Ken Ballard, Jacqui Barrington, Jim Boyack, Paul Bruce, Pip Burch, Joan Cavaney, Ron Cavaney, Karen Cauty, Alain Connan, Jane Cooper, Derek Craig, Arani Cuthbert, Janet Dalziell, Yvonne Dasler, Steve Dawson, Maj De Poorter, Keith Dignan, Mike Donoghue, Lorette Dorreboom, Leith Duncan, Davey Edward, Bruce Gabites, Vicki Getz, Roger Grace, Graham Gulbransen, Henk Haazen, Nicky Hager, Mike Hagler, Kirsty Hamilton, Gil Hanly, Tracey Harbutt, Sebia Hawkins, Alice Heather, Alan Hemmings, Mabel Hetherington, Tea Hirshon, Kurt Horn, Anna Horne, Gene Horne, Gordon Jackman, Rebecca Johnson, Richard King, Renate Kroesa, Pene Lefale, Dorothy Levy, Tony Lilleby, Tony Lindsay, Pauline Macdonald, Alison McCulloch, Raewyn Mackenzie, David McTaggart, Julie Miles, Margaret Mills, David Moodie, Michele Nanni, Susi Newborn, Richard Northey, Susan-Jane Owen, Remi Parmentier, Diana Pipke, Philip Pupuka, Libby Giles, Mike Rann, Kelly Rigg, Chris Robinson, Ted Rutter, Sara Saunders, Steve Sawyer, Giselle Shaw, Joanne Soper, Maurice Shadbolt, Peter Smith, Elizabeth Slooten, Orietta Sloth, Manu Smith, Joel Stewart, Lesley Stone, Didi Swete, Bob Tait, Mike Taylor, Jess Tooker, Jacinda Torrance, Jay Townsend, Anneke Ursem, Ann van Leeuwen, Meriel Watts, Steve Whitehouse, Bill Wieben and Roger Wilson.

During the course of writing I found the following to be invaluable sources and have in some instances drawn directly from them: Michael Brown and John May's *The Greenpeace Story*, Bengt and Marie-Thérèse Danielsson's *Poisoned Reign: French Nuclear Colonialism in the Pacific*, Jane Dibblin's *Day of Two Suns: US Nuclear Testing and the Pacific Islanders*, various editions of *Greenpeace News* and the Greenpeace New Zealand magazine, David McTaggart and Robert Hunter's *Greenpeace III: Journey into the Bomb*, Tom Newnham's *Peace Squadron*, and David Robie's *Eyes of Fire* and *Blood on their Banner: Nationalist Struggles in the South Pacific*.

Contents

Part One: Origins

CHAPTER ONE	Moruroa, Mon Amour	1
CHAPTER TWO	Fri Spirit	21
CHAPTER THREE	The Odyssey	37

Part Two: Sea Changes

CHAPTER FOUR	Whale Soundings	57
CHAPTER FIVE	Rocking the Boat	73
CHAPTER SIX	Private Bag, Wellesley St	91
CHAPTER SEVEN	Exodus – the Final Voyage	109
CHAPTER EIGHT	L'Affaire Greenpeace	127

Part Three: Riding the Wave

CHAPTER NINE	Pasifik Talkstory	147
CHAPTER TEN	Beneath the Surface	163
CHAPTER ELEVEN	The Rolling Snowball	177
CHAPTER TWELVE	You Can't Sink a Rainbow	199
CHAPTER THIRTEEN	Turning the Toxic Tide	215
CHAPTER FOURTEEN	New Horizons	235

Photo credits	251
Further reading	253
Directory	255
Index	257

Introduction

ON THE NIGHT of 9 July 1962 the sky over the South Pacific was suffused with a sullen orange glow. Most New Zealanders who saw it didn't know then that they were witnessing an artificial aurora, as thousands of miles to the north, above the US nuclear test site on Johnston Atoll, a giant thermonuclear bomb exploded in the upper atmosphere.

When he was reading early drafts of this book, Owen Wilkes recalled that it was seeing this man-made sun that had first alerted him to the nuclear threat. Others, such as David Lange, Elsie Locke and Wilf Foote, have recently made similar claims. Another who was watching the sky that night and credits it as a turning point in her life was a young Auckland nurse. Elaine Shaw, to whom we dedicate this book, would become one of the founders of Greenpeace New Zealand, and continued to be a driving force until her death in 1990. How many more New Zealanders were affected by this aurora, and is it too far-fetched to wonder if it played a part in turning New Zealand into such an extraordinary nation of anti-nuclear campaigners?

From the heady days of the early Pacific voyages by our peace boats to confront the French Navy off Moruroa through to the setting-up of the World Park Antarctica base, New Zealanders have followed Greenpeace's exploits with a sympathetic and proprietorial interest. This is of course no accident. Greenpeace and New Zealand share an orientation towards the sea, but there's another, more fundamental link: New Zealanders have long been characterised – by friend and foe – as a stubbornly independent lot, who stand up for what they believe in, no matter how formidable the odds. Perhaps we recognise something of ourselves in the David and Goliath images of Greenpeace on our television screens.

As awareness of the threat posed by unrestrained industrial growth and military escalation has increased, so has the importance of Greenpeace as a focus for anti-nuclear and environmental activism. We now have more than four million supporters worldwide, the Auckland office forming part of a network of twenty-three national offices from Russia to Costa Rica. Yet nowhere does the level of support equal that in this country, where today one in twenty New Zealanders is a paid-up Greenpeace supporter.

As both our supporters and detractors agree, Greenpeace has always been skilled at grabbing a headline. From our beginnings nearly twenty years ago, it was recognised that our strength lay in the power of the few to alert the many. A Greenpeace inflatable in front of a whaler's harpoon might save one

Greenpeace swimmers and inflatable blocking path of the Japanese whaler *Nisshin Maru No 3*, Tasman Sea 1991.

animal, but a newspaper headline or a television story broadcast around the world could help save a species from extinction as people are galvanised into demanding action from their elected representatives.

An active, adventurous and theatrical approach to campaigning has contributed greatly to the organisation's effectiveness. The activists we see on our television screens are those who sail the Greenpeace ships, climb smokestacks, hang from bridges, block pipes and chain themselves to ships, trains, trucks and buildings. But direct action is only a part of the work we do, and *Making Waves* looks as well at the hidden work of the lobbyists, scientists and administrators.

Greenpeace has always focused on international environmental issues. What makes us different is that each national office draws on a global network of resources to highlight an international issue, rather than simply duplicating the work of other national groups. So though this is the story of a New Zealand organisation, it also features many non-New Zealanders and takes us on journeys far from these shores. The balanced international mix of those who work for GPNZ and the global focus of the campaigns is an essential part of our strength, just as the perspectives of people like David Moodie, Bette Johnson and Martin Gotje have enriched the vision and work of the New Zealand office.

Ironically the success Greenpeace enjoys today is a source of unease among some of its long-time supporters. 'When it has been traditional for pressure-group resources to be honourably threadbare, there is something unsettling about all this slickness, this level of organisation,' comments one local magazine. As this book makes clear, the same debate has been taking place within GPNZ for years. The idealists in the organisation are concerned that today's professionals are losing touch with their grassroots origins, while the pragmatists point to the undeniable practical benefits of a highly developed resource base. Certainly there have been ructions over style and philosophy, but there is rarely disagreement over what needs to be done. And it is the creative tension between a fierce personal commitment to righting wrongs and a hard-headed, calculated approach to achieving goals, between what one contributor calls 'the passion and the professionalism', that has made GPNZ the broad-based and highly effective organisation that it is today.

The bombing of the *Rainbow Warrior* in Auckland in 1985 and better known international campaigns in the Pacific and Antarctica have given Greenpeace a higher profile than most other local environmental groups. But Greenpeace does not take all the credit for two decades of successful peace and environmental campaigning, much of which belongs to other groups who share our concerns, including Friends of the Earth, CND, Forest and Bird, ASOC, Project Jonah, Peace Movement Aotearoa, the Peace Squadrons and ECO. This book, however, is the story of Greenpeace New Zealand, and while it pays tribute to the work of others, it does not purport to tell their stories.

Making Waves is the story of only one important element in New Zealand's peace and environmental movement. It does not present an 'official line' for GPNZ or for its supporters, since there will always be as many points of view as people to express them. It is above all a personal chronicle, told largely by those who were and are in the thick of things – the sailors, scientists, students, hippies, lawyers, potters, engineers, journalists, office workers, labourers and children who have seen the dangers we face and have been prepared to do something. We hope you enjoy their story.

Keith Dignan,
Chair,
Greenpeace New Zealand Board

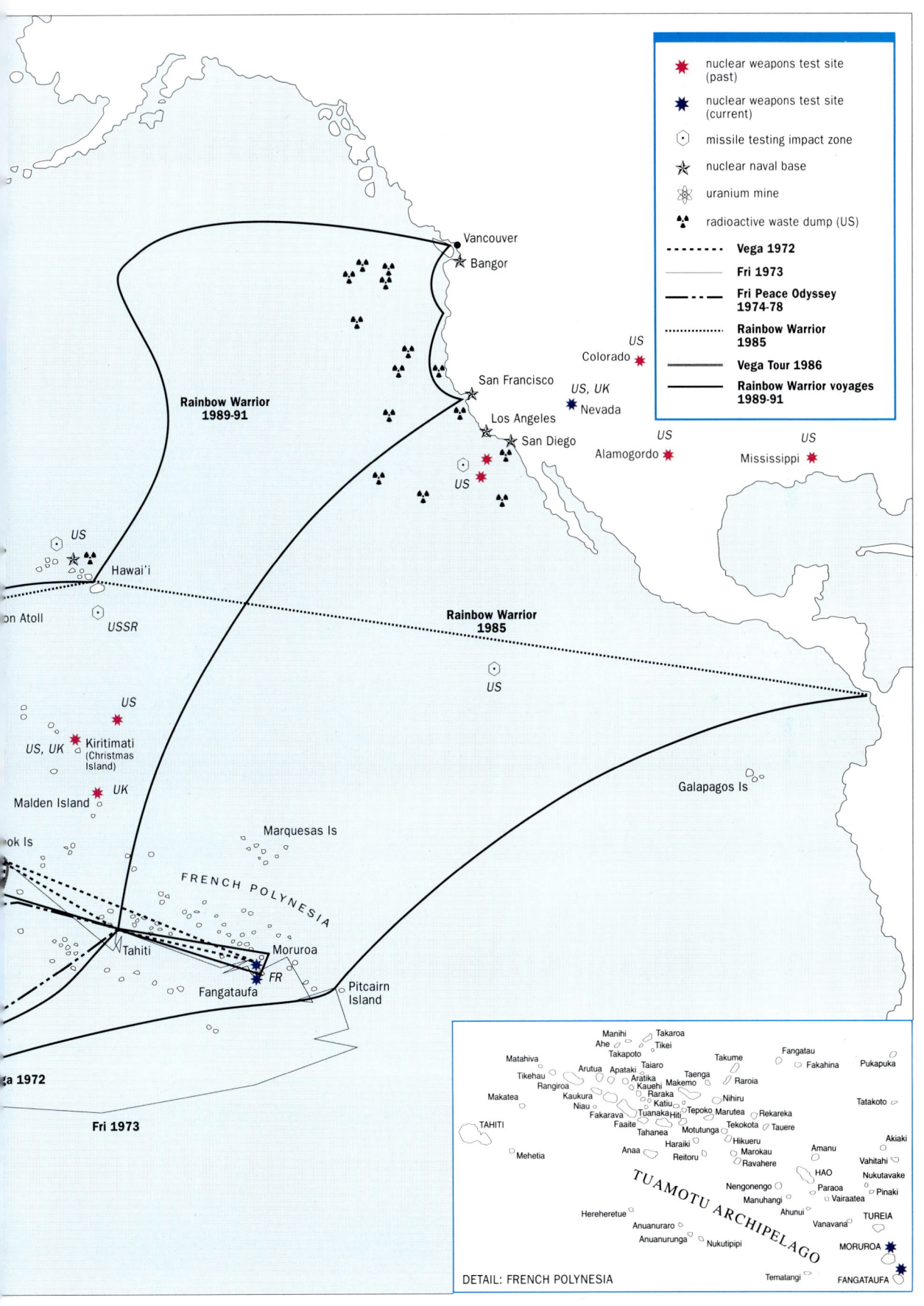

PART ONE
Origins

CHAPTER ONE

Moruroa, Mon Amour

'It is difficult to describe the magnitude of the South Pacific to anyone accustomed to living on land. Looking over the charts, ordered and subdivided by lines of latitude and longitude, the great blanks of the Pacific covered with islands and atolls and peppered with depth soundings, it all appears so reassuringly organised and tamed.'

'On the surface of the ocean, you can see no more than ten miles to the horizon in any direction. The hull of Vega *pulses, as if alive, with the repeated angry concussions of the sea, and everything is in constant motion. Beneath the hull, perhaps two and a half miles down, mountains and canyons sit in still darkness, while above your head the skies seem to stretch forever.'*

'Our most constant companion is the deserted sea and the unhappy thought of the Bomb at the end of our voyage.'

David McTaggart, excerpts from Vega log, 3 June 1972

THE 'DESERTED SEA', the Pacific Ocean, is where the story of Greenpeace New Zealand really began, nearly twenty years ago and hundreds of miles beyond sight of land. *Vega*, a small yacht with an international crew of five, set out in 1972 on the first-ever protest voyage from New Zealand against nuclear weapons testing. The voyage ended abruptly and violently when the yacht was rammed by a French warship, and the tests were delayed by only a few days. Yet *Vega* succeeded in drawing the spotlight of international attention to France's abuse of the Pacific environment and the people of the region. French testing was already an issue in New Zealand, having occupied the Campaign for Nuclear Disarmament (CND) in particular since 1962. Two months after *Vega* set out, a flotilla of three more small boats, assembled by CND and the recently formed Peace Media, built on *Vega*'s pioneering initiative. It was from these existing New Zealand peace groups that Greenpeace New Zealand grew. And it is with France's nuclear testing programme in the Pacific that the story of Greenpeace New Zealand is most intimately linked.

From a small yacht at sea level, the Pacific appears truly a deserted ocean. Its thousands of small islands are scattered across such vast expanses that the Pacific has been described as 'a continent of water'. Yet the idea of emptiness is misplaced, for the ocean itself teems with infinitely varied life forms, its islands and atolls hosting an exuberant range of human, animal and plant

Opposite: Moruroa and the nuclear test balloon, as seen from the deck of a French frigate.

populations. Where the European traveller may see an immense, desolate emptiness, Polynesians, the prodigious navigators of the Pacific, see an elaborate network of bounteous pathways.

The very remoteness of many Pacific communities from one another has led over centuries to an astounding diversity of cultures and tongues: more than 1,200 languages and dialects, reflecting both its indigenous and colonial heritage, are spoken in the region. But in recent years the Pacific's great landless reaches have provided the justification for a terrible new intrusion from the colonial powers far to the north.

The United States began to explode nuclear bombs above the Marshall Islands of Bikini and Enewetak, in the northern Pacific, in 1946, a year after unleashing the unimaginable horror and devastation of two crude atomic bombs on the civilian populations of Hiroshima and Nagasaki. Britain's nuclear tests were held on the island of Monte Bello off the coast of Western Australia, at Emu Fields and Maralinga in the South Australian desert, then on Kirimati (Christmas) and Malden Islands in the central Pacific before moving to the US testing site in Nevada in 1963. The United States used Kirimati and Johnston Islands for atmospheric nuclear tests between 1957 and 1963, then moved to the Aleutian Islands and finally fell back on their Nevada test site, which had been used in the 1950s. In each case the nuclear state paid little or no regard to the welfare of the local people or the environmental consequences of their activities.

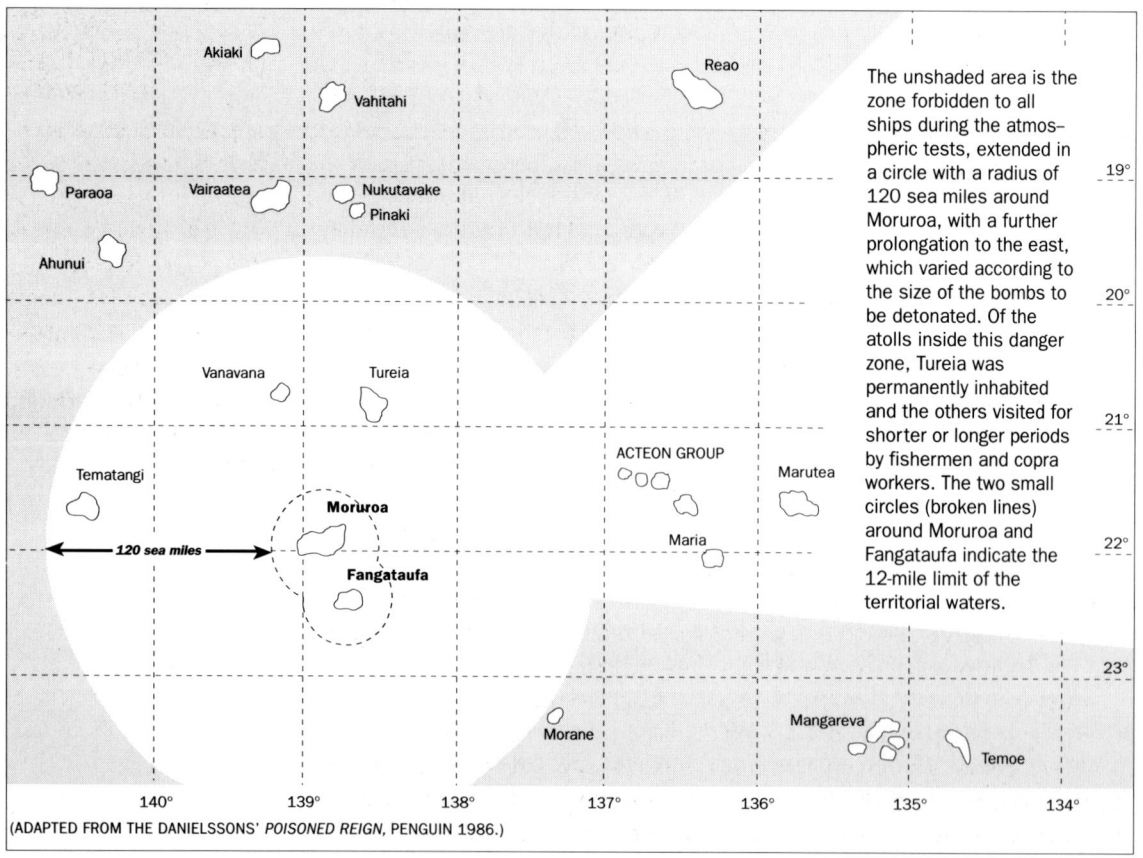

The danger zone during the atmospheric testing season, 1966–74.

The unshaded area is the zone forbidden to all ships during the atmospheric tests, extended in a circle with a radius of 120 sea miles around Moruroa, with a further prolongation to the east, which varied according to the size of the bombs to be detonated. Of the atolls inside this danger zone, Tureia was permanently inhabited and the others visited for shorter or longer periods by fishermen and copra workers. The two small circles (broken lines) around Moruroa and Fangataufa indicate the 12-mile limit of the territorial waters.

(ADAPTED FROM THE DANIELSSONS' *POISONED REIGN*, PENGUIN 1986.)

The United States and Britain ceased testing in the atmosphere in 1963. Significantly, the move away from atmospheric testing was made not in response to the objections of Pacific peoples, but because the radioactive isotope strontium-90 began to show up in children's milk teeth in the Northern Hemisphere. That same year, President de Gaulle announced his intention of moving the French testing programme from Algeria, where France had suffered military defeat after a bloody war of independence, to a new site in the South Pacific. Following a hasty rummage through her remaining overseas territories, France had decided to shift the tests to Moruroa and Fangataufa, two coral atolls in the Tuamotu Archipelago. 'French' Polynesia, Te Ao Maohi to its indigenous people, was chosen, de Gaulle would later inform a sceptical Tahitian audience, as 'a tribute to her loyalty to France'. Polynesian contingents had fought for France in two world wars; in the Second World War one in three of the 300 Tahitians who fought in Europe and North Africa was killed.

The first French Legionnaires were shipped into Tahiti in 1963 to build the new Centre d'Expérimentations Nucléaires du Pacifique (CEP), the nuclear testing centre, on Moruroa. Eight thousand military personnel, followed by 3,000 technicians, civil servants and ancillary staff, constituted an extraordinary invasion of the fragile society of French Polynesia, whose entire population then numbered less than 85,000. Some local people initially welcomed this transformation. Employment opportunities associated with the massive construction projects required by the CEP lured thousands of young men away from their traditional subsistence lifestyle on the outer islands. Some brought their families with them; most came alone. Once their jobs came to an end, many had little economic choice but to stay on in Papeete rather than return to their home islands. On the depopulated outer islands fishing and the cultivation of food crops declined and the traditional life was permanently undermined. Within a few years, with the decline in work opportunities and increasing economic disruption, slums sprawled behind Papeete, and stories of poisoned fish and strange illnesses began to spread.

The first atmospheric test above Moruroa, codenamed Aldébaran, took place on 2 July 1966. A tethered helium balloon was towed into position above the lagoon, the nuclear device suspended beneath it. The force of the explosion was three times that of the bomb dropped on Hiroshima.

That May, as was to become the norm before the testing season each year, the CEP had unilaterally declared a 120-mile exclusion zone around the atoll. The zone contained no less than seven inhabited atolls. In the Territorial Assembly, the local parliament in Tahiti, Deputy John Teariki asked, 'If this zone is declared dangerous and prohibited for sailors and pilots throughout the world, why would it not be equally so for the inhabitants?' In time the CEP acknowledged its mistake and adjusted the radius of the zone, yet the island of Tureia remained inside the zone, and generally no effort was made to warn or evacuate its inhabitants, though on one occasion the entire population was secretly spirited away to Tahiti for a three-month 'holiday'.

Even before the French nuclear industry's invasion of Polynesia, local political leaders in the Tahitian Territorial Assembly had predicted many of the negative consequences for their society. From the outset the French testing

'No government has ever been honest enough nor had the cynical frankness to admit that its nuclear testing entails health hazards. No government has ever hesitated to expose other peoples – particularly if they are small and defenceless – to these dangers.' *John Teariki, September 1966*

Atmospheric nuclear test above Moruroa.

'Not a single particle of radioactive fallout will ever reach an inhabited island.'
Governor Grimald, 1963

facility was widely opposed throughout the South Pacific, the issue rapidly becoming a unifying force for the people of the region. Within a short time of the establishment of the test centre, serious health problems were linked with the contamination of the surrounding islands and marine life.

United opposition from South Pacific governments and regional organisations failed to influence the French authorities, who insisted that the tests were harmless and routinely lied to the local people about the nature of the tests. On one occasion military and scientific experts from the French Atomic Energy Commission (CEA), which conducted the tests, assured local people there was no danger because the bombs only became dangerous once 'armed' in France. That visiting French ministers viewed the people of Polynesia as a *quantité négligeable* was always abundantly clear. It took only a little longer for other South Pacific communities to discover that France viewed their health and welfare with a similar callous disregard.

In 1963 New Zealand's Prime Minister Keith Holyoake, under growing public pressure, expressed 'deep regret' at France's intention to establish its nuclear testing centre in the South Pacific in the face of overwhelming opposition from the United Nations and Pacific states. The National Government's politely worded diplomatic protests over the next ten years settled into a pattern that would cause France little anxiety.

The first active protests by New Zealanders took the form of street marches and petitions organised by CND and the Labour Party. As public concern grew, the need for more emphatic and direct action came to be recognised especially by younger New Zealanders. Richard Northey, later an Auckland

Labour MP, remembers how in 1965 he and others from CND helped support an early Australian protest voyage from Sydney to Moruroa, which was ultimately abandoned by the inexperienced crew in Rarotonga.

In the following years the Vietnam War came to eclipse the anti-nuclear issue, diverting the energies of peace activists towards opposing United States and New Zealand intervention there. Only in the early 1970s, with the US military's retreat from Vietnam and the withdrawal of New Zealand troops, did the New Zealand peace movement's focus shift back to the Pacific. Now, though, a resurgence of anti-militarism and internationalism gave the movement a new dynamism and urgency.

Anti-testing campaigns had meanwhile sprung up in other parts of the world. When the United States began testing nuclear weapons on the Aleutian island of Amchitka in 1971, a group of Canadians and expatriate Americans formed the 'Don't Make a Wave' Committee in Vancouver to organise opposition. Inspired by the 1958 protest voyages to the US nuclear test site at Bikini Atoll by two American Quaker boats, *Phoenix* and *Golden Rule*, a new generation took up the Quaker philosophy of bearing witness. The *Phyllis Cormack*, a 25-metre rustbucket of a fishing boat, sailed from Vancouver to Amchitka in 1971 in a bid to halt the tests – and Greenpeace was born.

> 'Those who claim these tests are harmless are liars.'
> Dr Albert Schweitzer, in a letter to John Teariki, 1964

The strategy of non-violent direct action has roots in New Zealand reaching back to the great Maori leader Te Whiti at Parihaka in the 1880s, though it is probably more commonly associated even here with Gandhi's anti-British civil disobedience campaigns in India decades later. It has since become widely established as a potent method of popular protest. A person bearing witness must accept responsibility for being aware of an injustice. That person may then choose to do something, or stand by, but may not turn away in ignorance. The Greenpeace ethic is to not only bear witness to abuses of the environment, but to take action to prevent them.

The full story of the *Phyllis Cormack*'s voyage is told in Robert Hunter's *The Greenpeace Chronicle*. Eventually the ship was seized and turned back by the US Coastguard, and the nuclear test proceeded on schedule on 6 November 1971. It was, nonetheless, the last test to be carried out on Amchitka. The saga had attracted enormous publicity across Canada and the United States, which put pressure on the US Government to justify the tests, and a few months later the Department of Energy wound up its testing programme in the Aleutians (the site is now a bird sanctuary), falling back on the Nevada test site. Stopping the Amchitka programme deprived the United States of a site for its largest, dirtiest tests, which could not be effected at Nevada, where the test site is too close to population centres. The action was therefore an important tactical victory for the environmentalists. It had also shown the fledgling Greenpeace Foundation of Canada the publicity value of the strategy of direct action. They were anxious, therefore, to build on this initial success by dispatching another protest boat, this time to Moruroa. So began the chain of events leading to the pioneering *Vega* voyage and the eventual formation of Greenpeace New Zealand.

In 1971 no Greenpeace organisation existed in New Zealand, so the

Vancouver-based group contacted New Zealand CND and asked them to launch a media appeal for a boat and crew to sail from New Zealand to Moruroa on Greenpeace's behalf. CND were already grappling with the idea of a Moruroa protest when they were contacted out of the blue from Canada. 'We made an appeal that appeared on the front page of the New Zealand Herald,' says Mabel Hetherington, then secretary of CND. Mabel belonged to an earlier generation of peace campaigners. She had been a peace activist in England and when she moved to New Zealand after the war she helped organise NZCND. The dedicated work of Mabel, Alison Duff, Pat Denby and others carried CND in Auckland through the 1960s.

In another, entirely coincidental Canadian connection, David McTaggart sailed into Auckland Harbour on board his ketch, *Vega*. McTaggart had set out on a Pacific voyage after quitting his timber and tourism business in Vancouver. In Auckland he met nineteen-year-old New Zealand student Anna Horne, who took him home to meet her parents. Just a few days earlier CND's appeal for a protest ship had appeared in the national press. Anna recalls, 'My father Gene said, "Oh, you're from Vancouver, I suppose you know that group Greenpeace I read about in the paper."' David admitted he didn't. At that stage he knew and cared little about politics. Indeed, he had just sailed across the South Pacific unaware that a vast area of French Polynesian waters had been closed to sailors like himself while France tested its weapons there.

As Anna remembers it, 'The truth was that none of us had ever given much thought to the nuclear tests. Even as students our major concerns were the Vietnam War and Woodstock!' For her father the issue was simple: 'It was as if the French were invading the area. Why did they have to test their bombs in the Pacific? It couldn't be safe; if it were, they would have been doing it in France.'

At first McTaggart thought the idea of sailing a boat thousands of miles to Moruroa and back just to make a protest was ludicrous. At thirty-nine, he joked, he was too old for protesting. But his curiosity was aroused. Later that day he noticed a CND poster in a shop window. He wrote down their phone number and called Mabel Hetherington to find out more about the proposed protest. Once convinced of his seriousness, she gave him Greenpeace's telephone number in Canada, and McTaggart was soon speaking long-distance to Greenpeace chairman Ben Metcalfe, a veteran of the Amchitka trip, who reassured him that Greenpeace was indeed a group of 'ordinary' people dedicated to stopping nuclear testing. A day or so later David quietly told Anna, 'I'm going into that test zone.'

Why McTaggart finally decided to go is hard to pin down. The decision marked a watershed in his life – a time of reassessment – and it would be unfair to deny a place for idealism in his motivation. But as a sailor he was infuriated by France's arbitrary annexation of international waters, and saw the issue as a yachting as well as a personal challenge. He was also hard-headed and stubborn – exactly the wrong sort of man for the French to provoke, as they would learn.

The weeks following the decision to go were a blur of activity for Anna. 'We were overwhelmed by the help we received. It came in the form of food,

> 'When the bomb was detonated ... all the water in the lagoon basin was sucked up into the air, and then rained down. The islets on the encircling reef were all covered with heaps of irradiated fish and clams, whose slowly rotting flesh continued to stink for weeks.'
> *La Dépêche de Tahiti*,
> 18 June 1971

money, time and work. So many people wanted to be on the crew we set up a phone to deal with the flood of calls... It was an exciting time. I hesitate now to say we were in the right place at the right time, because the events surrounding the two voyages *Vega* made to Moruroa in 1972 and 1973 turned out to be traumatic... The 1972 trip also served as a crash course in politics as the National Government threw one obstacle after another in our way in an effort to stop *Vega* leaving.'

After announcing the voyage through the media, a joint CND-Greenpeace Vancouver fund was set up. Richard Northey and CND arranged an office at Auckland University with shifts of students and other volunteers to help organise the effort. For David McTaggart it was an introduction to a different world. In Canada he had been a successful sportsman and business entrepreneur with no background in political activism. 'The people I met were serious and intelligent. I had to admit I felt moved, even though a bit embarrassed, by their warmth. I hadn't worked with a voluntary group before and I was astonished by their discipline and the amount of work they got through – for nothing but the honour of helping.'

Vega at anchor

Appeals broadcast by Radio Hauraki brought to the jetty a steady flow of volunteers and wellwishers with food and other supplies. A twelve-metre solid kauri ketch built in Whangarei in 1948 by top New Zealand boatbuilder Allan Orams, *Vega* was one of the busiest yachts in the harbour that summer. As McTaggart remembers it, 'Sailors, students, housewives, whole families came just to look at the boat that would go out to face the Bomb on their behalf... The hard core of workers came down to perhaps twenty. These were people, mostly channelled through CND, who were adamantly opposed to the Bomb, and yachtsmen and sailors disgusted by France's arbitrary seizure of 100,000 square miles of ocean in international waters. Almost all were Kiwis ashamed that their own Government was more concerned with selling butter and cheese in France than it was with the possibility of genetic damage to the next generation, let alone with matters of principle or international law.'

McTaggart selected his own crew: Nigel Ingram, a 26-year-old English navigator who had been an officer in the Royal Navy and had spent the last couple of years skippering racing yachts in the South Pacific; Roger Haddleton, another ex-Royal Navy sailor; New Zealander Grant Davidson; and Ben Metcalfe of the Canadian Greenpeace Foundation. Nigel Ingram recalls that during those weeks of preparation it seemed as if every possible bureaucratic obstacle was thrown up in their path. 'We were visited in turn several times by the police, Customs, the Marine Department – just about everyone came down to check on us, and they all had one reason or another why they thought *Vega* shouldn't go.'

On 27 April 1972, at sunset, *Vega* – renamed *Greenpeace III* for the voyage – left Auckland Harbour and glided past Rangitoto Island, while Radio Hauraki broadcast messages of goodwill and cars along the waterfront flashed their headlights to farewell the crew on their long voyage around the curve of the planet.

After a spell of bad weather *Vega* rested up for a few days at Rarotonga, where two of the crew left. Haddleton was forced to leave with a tropical fever. Tension had grown rapidly between McTaggart and Metcalfe, who suddenly announced he was flying to Peru to help arrange a second protest boat. He headed off and nothing more was heard of this venture.

In Rarotonga sacks of tropical oranges and other fresh fruit were loaded on board by the Cook Islanders who flocked down to the wharf to wish *Vega* well. The crew of three set off again, sailing into ever stronger seas, undermanned, uncomfortable and increasingly weary. For David this was the toughest leg of the voyage, as restored harmony on board was offset by the increased workload.

After weathering a particularly violent seventy-knot gale, and as they approached the test zone, they were joined periodically by several French surveillance ships and aircraft. They at last sighted Moruroa and moved into position outside the twelve-mile territorial limit. On 10 June, six weeks after leaving Auckland, they picked up a BBC broadcast announcing that the tests would proceed on schedule. Reconnaissance aircraft ensured that the French military were always aware of *Vega*'s position. A small boarding party was finally sent over to them from the minesweeper *La Bayonnaise* with a curt message ordering them to leave the area. *Vega*'s crew replied that they had no intention of leaving, that unlike their reception party they were entirely within their rights under international law, and that they did not recognise the French military's attempt to arbitrarily cordon off a large tract of the Pacific Ocean.

Vega was positioned squarely downwind of the atoll. On 16 June, after a golden sunset, David was climbing into the cockpit to take his turn on watch

Suspended from a helium-filled balloon, a nuclear device is towed by barge into position for detonation over Moruroa's lagoon.

when an unusual shape directly over Moruroa caught his eye. It was the zeppelin-shaped balloon from which the bombs were suspended for detonation above the atoll; scientists in Auckland had warned them that if they could see the balloon, they were too close. The crew slept uneasily that night in the shadow of the Bomb.

The next morning the three men could clearly see, etched on the horizon, the outline of the nuclear device slung beneath the balloon. Fighting their anxiety, they resolved to move in closer and place themselves well within the blast area. They had already agreed that if the bomb were detonated, two of them would remain below deck while the third would stay topside wrapped in oilskins. He would have to motor the boat out of the danger zone, keep washing the deck over with seawater and keep the sails down to minimise the fire risk. As they prepared *Vega* for the blast, images filled their minds of scorching heat, blinding light and shock waves shooting molten rocks across the water. David recalls how worried they were about the blinding effects of the nuclear flash: 'We started wearing sunglasses just in case. Each of us developed the habit of squinting automatically when looking in the direction of the balloon, already half-consciously protecting our eyes in case the thing suddenly went off.' In desperation they sent a cable over the radio, unsure if the outside world even knew they were there: BALLOON RAISED OVER MORUROA LAST NIGHT STOP GREENPEACE III SIXTEEN MILES NORTHEAST STOP SITUATION FRIGHTENING STOP PLEASE PRAY.

But the next day passed without incident, the scheduled test evidently delayed. It wasn't until a Radio Australia broadcast that evening announced that the French Government had given a public assurance of the safety of *Vega*'s crew that their mood changed. Over the next few days they played cat and mouse with the French warships. Sensing that the tests would be held regardless of their presence, the three men readied themselves for boarding.

On 18 June *La Bayonnaise* bore down on them, sweeping by just a few metres off and leaving *Vega* rolling dangerously in its wake. For the next two days the minesweeper shadowed *Vega*'s every move. On 21 June an inflatable brought across an unequivocal directive: Leave the test zone immediately. The French had evidently lost patience with these troublesome protesters, who had not only confounded their expectations by daring to sail into the testing zone but now showed every intention of staying there.

The large cruiser *De Grasse* and a tug, *La Hippopotame*, arrived the next day and, together with the minesweeper, began making close passes to within a few metres of *Vega*. '*La Bayonnaise* came in alone and parallel to our port side, a scant fifteen metres from us, her huge grey hull rising up and down, the force of her displacement churning the small space of water between us into a maelstrom… Behind us, *La Hippopotame* was crowding in on our starboard quarter and for a moment or two we rode like that, under full sail, crashing along at about eight knots,' recalled David.

'I looked up to the bridge of *La Bayonnaise* and there was no pity on the face of the man who clung to the railing, glaring down at me. It was not just machismo, although there was plenty of that. It was hate. The look on the man's face said: Look out, I'm gonna get you… Then he turned and rapped out an order, and *La Bayonnaise* began to edge in closer.' *Vega*'s crew were

Vega photographed from the French minesweeper *La Paimpolaise*.

badly shaken. They shouted across to the warships, calling on them to keep clear, but no concessions were made.

During the next eight days these tactics were replayed endlessly, with planes buzzing them overhead and the night sky lit by helicopter searchlights. Too tired to think about the bomb, it never occurred to them that they were winning, that every day they held out the bomb tests had to be delayed. On 25 June a military aircraft began to make a series of low passes over the yacht, deafening the crew. It wasn't until several days later, after hearing another news report, that they realised this had been a ploy to cover the noise of the first nuclear test of the series, now some twenty-five miles away. Barred from testing a fully armed nuclear weapon, the CEP had set off a smaller trigger device.

The French Government was now putting out the story that *Greenpeace III* (*Vega*) had sailed out of the zone a week earlier, and had not been sighted since. Fabricated news reports were to become a familiar feature of the French response to the anti-nuclear movement, 'disinformation' being a recognised function of the colonial authorities in Polynesia. Realising they had been tricked, the crew raised *Vega*'s sails and made straight for the test zone. If this was only the first test of the series, perhaps it was still possible to stop the others. The minesweeper *La Paimpolaise* made several attempts to block her way until darkness interrupted the chase.

During the following days the radio carried further reports that *Vega* had long since sailed away from the zone, a story that isolated the yacht from

La Paimpolaise, moments after ramming *Vega*.

potential New Zealand and international support. An interview with New Zealand's Prime Minister John Marshall particularly annoyed the crew: 'Well,' Marshall observed, 'the boys on the Greenpeace III have sailed out [of the zone], which is good. Discretion is the better part of valour.' Convinced that he had been responsible for the harassment that had delayed their departure from New Zealand, the *Vega* crew were infuriated by Marshall's smug tone.

Finally, early on 1 July, they heard the low, rending sound of far-away thunder from the direction of Moruroa and raised their sails once more. *La Paimpolaise* was again in close pursuit, this time flying a 'Do Not Proceed' flag. Changing course was really not an option for *Vega* in the tight space available as the French ship closed in astern. While the yacht tried to manoeuvre out of the ship's path, the wind suddenly dropped and the 4,000-tonne warship smashed into *Vega*'s stern, hurling splintered wood into the air. *La Paimpolaise*'s bow buried itself in the rigging and for a moment *Vega* tilted over dangerously. The crew were flung down as the minesweeper reversed engines and backed away in a boiling sea, the yacht's rigging still tangled in its bow. McTaggart's whole body was shaking. 'Unable to form words, I looked at the others. The blood had run from their faces and I could see they were trembling... *Vega*'s mainsail flopped uselessly, like a broken wing. But the deck still felt solid beneath my bare feet. *Vega*, I thought, you're still alive!'

They had little option but to agree to being towed to Moruroa for repairs. David recorded a vivid impression of this once-lush and palm-covered atoll:

Moruroa, in the Maohi language of Polynesia 'the place of the great secret', is officially spelt Mururoa as the result of a nineteenth-century French cartographer's mistake. Greenpeace and other opponents of French nuclear colonialism prefer to use the original spelling.

David McTaggart (left) and Nigel Ingram flank CEP commander Admiral Claverie, their 'gallant host'.

'Our first glimpse of Moruroa revealed a moonlike stretch of grey rock, perfectly flat, without a single shrub or blade of grass breaking through. In order to enter the lagoon, the tug towed us in past Ground Zero. Until then it had not occurred to me what a perfect name this was for the point of detonation: the earth had been reduced to absolutely nothing. I found myself automatically shrinking away, for it was like nothing so much as a vision of the end of the world. It came as no surprise that the first two structures we saw were concrete blockhouses, as though an attempt had been made to colonise a lifeless planet. The overall impression was that we had arrived in a land where Armageddon was already history. Two helicopters came skittering overhead like giant mutant insects.'

To the crew's amazement the CEP commander, Admiral Claverie, personally invited them to take a swim in the lagoon before joining him for lunch. They declined the offer but, in their innocence, thought the meal might offer a useful opportunity for debate. During the meal they were surreptitiously photographed, the pictures subsequently released to the international media with another extraordinary story: *Greenpeace III* had run into trouble at sea, the crew had called for help and were rescued by their gallant hosts, with whom they were now on the best of terms! 'I was indeed naive,' recalls David wryly. 'I had completely lost track of the reality that there were legions of cynical news editors sitting out there waiting for the slightest opportunity to write the voyage off as the work of radicals and frauds.'

Forty-eight hours later, after minimal repairs, Davidson, Ingram and McTaggart set off on the long haul back to New Zealand filled with a sense of anger and failure. Yet the reality was that they had held up the testing

programme for weeks and, more importantly, had drawn the attention of the world to the controversial issue of atmospheric nuclear testing. And even as *Vega* limped downwind to Rarotonga, other protest boats were closing in on Moruroa to take over their lonely vigil.

In New Zealand, after the first reports that *Vega* had been disabled, the Peace Media organisation had hastily organised three more vessels to sail to Moruroa. Co-ordinated by Barry and Jacqui Mitcalfe, Peace Media emerged from an anti-Vietnam War conference held in Wellington in 1971. Barry, who died in 1985, shortly after the *Rainbow Warrior* bombing, was an inspiration to many in those days. A former lecturer in Polynesian studies, a poet, a writer and an idealist, Mitcalfe was above all an enormously energetic organiser whose drive and determination were crucial for the peace movement. As chairman of the Wellington Committee on Vietnam he had been a central figure in the anti-Vietnam War movement, before he switched to opposing French testing in 1972.

Owen Wilkes knew him well. 'He was full of bullshit, but Mitcalfe bullshit was prodigiously effective as a fertiliser of ideas and actions. His first idea for a Moruroa action – to charter a dirty great ship and fill it with dozens or hundreds of protesters – was typical Mitcalfe. The way he ran the Committee on Vietnam was that he'd say, "Right, we're gonna have a demo tomorrow," and he'd ring up the *Dominion* and say, "We're having a march from Courtenay Place to Parliament grounds… We're expecting 5,000 to turn up." Next morning people would read in the *Dom* about the gigantic demo planned for that afternoon, and it would sound so big and impressive that, sure enough, 5,000 people would show up!'

Opposition within New Zealand to the French testing programme was nothing new. As soon as they had learned, in October 1962, that France intended to establish a nuclear testing site in the South Pacific, the New Zealand Campaign for Nuclear Disarmament had petitioned the Government to lodge a strong complaint in Paris. The first official New Zealand protest was made on 28 May 1963. In 1964 a campaign tagged 'No Bombs South of the Line' was launched by CND, members of which regularly called on the French Embassy and visited French warships to deliver protests. CND also urged the Government to take up the issue at the United Nations, and it was this group that first suggested sending a New Zealand frigate into the testing area as a protest. A 1963 CND petition against French testing had produced more than 80,000 signatures, the most collected since the votes for women petition in the 1890s. The Holyoake Government rejected this plebiscite, but the gulf between the Government's and the public's views on the issue continued to grow.

While the Government soft-pedalled on the issue, Peace Media, CND and other groups sought to harness the frustration of growing numbers of New Zealanders. Mitcalfe now saw Peace Media's mission in terms of channelling people's indignation about the testing into active protest. 'Positive action might be effective through sending ships – preferably government ships – into the international waters where the French bomb tests were scheduled,' wrote Mitcalfe. 'Our aim was partly to shame the New Zealand Government into action, but it was also practical, in that sufficient public concern and support for a peace fleet from the countries around the Pacific could see an end to French nuclear testing by popular demand... We tried to show that ordinary people do matter, that we do have the power to affect events, that not everything must be decided for us, that the world is not yet too big to be changed – a little.'

In June 1972 Peace Media launched a public appeal on radio and through newspaper advertisements, which brought an immediate offer of a boat and $1,000 from Bay of Plenty orchardists Willem and Ann van Leeuwen, recent immigrants from Malaysia. The van Leeuwens' trawler, *Boy Roel*, named after their son, was gratefully snapped up for the peace flotilla. Some people were amazed at this generosity, but Wim saw it as a wise investment in his own future. 'I have thought about it very deeply, and I think that the things at stake at the moment continue far beyond any particular life. This involves the future of humankind, and that is the reason why I do not see it in the perspective of my own particular life-savings or livelihood. So I have no hesitation in putting up those things I possess for what may be the welfare of future generations.' One of *Boy Roel*'s crew, Brett Cooper, summed up the mood of those days: 'Government is ineffectual, so far as I can see. Basically, the politicians are thinking of themselves, of their position in government, and this restricts them. The time has come for direct action. Ordinary, everyday people can do this, if only they realised it...'

'The Government had underestimated the strength of popular concern, had failed to understand the depth of feeling against the nuclear bomb,' recalled Mitcalfe. 'Some of the uglier things said and implied about Peace Media were part of an attempt to discredit an impulse that had found an appropriate response. I think we touched the hearts of many New Zealanders. There were of course many who thought we were crazy, or at least presumptuous; but judging by the support we received from the people of Tauranga, there were more who believed in us and our cause.'

Tauranga proved an ideal place to prepare for *Boy Roel*'s voyage – big enough to provide the necessary support framework but small enough for it to be done on a human scale. From the day Peace Media arrived, a cross-section of the community – schoolkids, local journalists, small businesses, pensioners, seamen and professional people – lined up at the wharf to offer help.

Radio Hauraki and Radio Waikato helped publicise the plans and co-ordinate volunteer help, and while some things did not go quite according to plan (the planners were hopelessly optimistic in allowing just a few days' preparation for a voyage lasting months), communication with the public was one of Peace Media's key successes. The crews were amazed by the enthusiastic support they received in a provincial area not noted for supporting public protests.

Peace Media had announced their plans for a peace flotilla on 26 June. A week later *Boy Roel*, an eleven-metre sloop called *Tamure*, and another yacht, *Magic Isle*, were confirmed participants. On Saturday 1 July, while *Vega* was still defying the French Navy off Moruroa, a small crowd of supporters gathered in the drizzle to farewell *Boy Roel* from Tauranga wharf. Barry Mitcalfe had made a last-minute television appeal, calling for Prime Minister

John Marshall to send New Zealand naval vessels into the illegally declared French exclusion zone.

Best-selling writer Maurice Shadbolt was one of hundreds who volunteered to sail with the Peace Media flotilla. Like the van Leeuwens, he had responded to Barry Mitcalfe's broadcast appeal in late June, and soon afterwards he joined *Tamure* in Auckland. Angered by the Government's refusal to act forcefully against the tests, Shadbolt had scorned it for 'twitching perceptibly in response to public pressure, then sending another of those melancholy diplomatic messages to France, but never in language too strong, in case the French blocked sale of our butter and lamb within the Common Market after 1977'.

'So we behave like lambs and talk like butter: such protests have become a charade to placate the people of New Zealand. In other words, for the sake of some dubious trade advantage, we are evidently willing to accept more and more strontium-90 in our milk, and more poison in the atmosphere and the bones of our children... We propose, then, to do what our feeble and fearful Government cannot bring itself to do.' If governments appeared powerless, most individuals felt doubly so, and it was this feeling of powerlessness – 'the feeling that as an individual I was able to do nothing to halt the slow slide of the human race towards extinction, and that as a writer I was doing no more than stand a passive doomwatch' – that Shadbolt sought to escape when he joined *Tamure*'s crew.

In the aftermath of the 1960s Shadbolt had begun to develop his own personal view of politics, rejecting the traditional politics of right and left. Instead he described a new polarity between the politics of human survival and human disaster. As he saw it, 'New Zealand's current right-wing National Government has thought inertia an adequate stance. But our world, like the new politics, now admits no compromise: there are only diverse degrees of collaboration with disaster. Yet it is all too conceivable that a Labour Government would be no less inert. For me the voyage to Moruroa, beyond all moral measure, represents a small attempt to engage in the politics of survival.'

Tamure left Marsden Wharf, Auckland, a fortnight after *Boy Roel*, at noon on 15 July with a crowd of several hundred to see them off. As a gesture of support from the people of Auckland, Mayor Sir Dove-Myer Robinson had donated a plaque of the city's coat of arms and a New Zealand ensign for the yacht to fly. Also crewing on the *Tamure* was Jim Cottier, a Manxman who would maintain close links with Greenpeace for the next two decades. Cottier, who had worked at sea for years as a chief officer, had been compelled after the death of his wife to take work ashore in order to look after their two young children.

The days passed slowly as *Tamure* motored eastwards, the slap of the waves punctuated by the occasional appearance of a lone albatross or a curious whale. After three weeks at sea the crew were astonished to hear a radio report that the nuclear tests had been called off early that year. 'The news comes faintly on our radio one night at ten, just as I am about to relieve Jim Sharp on watch,' wrote Shadbolt in a letter to Barry Mitcalfe. 'Jim and I wake the other two. We are a handful of days short of Moruroa, running just south

'Our world now admits no compromise: there are only diverse degrees of collaboration with disaster.'
Maurice Shadbolt

of the Austral Islands. Over hot soup we agree that we should now take our protest to Tahiti itself, where the French nuclear test fleet will soon converge; we also propose taking a protest letter from Auckland's mayor to Papeete's mayor.'

Five days later the distinctive peaks of Tahiti appeared above the horizon at sunrise to greet them, the rich scent of the tropics in the warm air. The last time Shadbolt had been here, five years earlier, 'la Bombe' was talked about like a new toy. Tahiti was then flush with French francs, with many Polynesians employed on military construction work at Papeete port and Moruroa Atoll. But the prosperity had been fleeting and the Bomb had become an object of fear. Now he heard stories of radiation sickness, of fish dying in the lagoons, of people falling strangely ill and of a mysterious disease of the coral carried by fish, called ciguatera.

The leisurely voyage of the yacht *Magic Isle* contrasted with the rigours experienced by the other crews. In the crew of five were Michel Caillard, a French citizen living in New Zealand, and Matiu Rata, an experienced seaman who was then Labour MP for Northern Maori. Making good time out of Whangarei under sail, *Magic Isle* raced ahead of the motorised *Tamure,* despite the latter's two-day headstart. After a 1,300-mile easterly leg the yacht turned northwards towards the Australs. As they approached Rarotonga, Michel, who had been listening to the news on Radio Noumea, suddenly let out a yell. 'They've finished!' he shouted. Michel, too, had heard the report of the early wind-up of the testing season.

A few days later they put in at Avarua, where the Cook Islands Government placed a house at the crew's disposal and provided for all their requirements. Mat Rata recorded his impressions: 'People were extremely kind. We didn't have a single moment to ourselves, for we were invited – and went as a group – to many house functions. Both people and Government showed their admiration and respect for our endeavour. Talks with [Cook Islands Prime Minister] Mr Henry and his cabinet ministers made this quite clear. They were all totally opposed to the tests and were anxious that more should be done by New Zealand to reflect their concern. People in the Cook Islands had more faith in the symbolic value of our protest than in New Zealand officialdom – but, in truth, many in official positions were sympathetic too. We represented small people, small countries, who felt powerless in the face of events beyond the comprehension of our Government. Rarotonga looked to New Zealand to take the initiative, hoping that New Zealand would project the feelings of the Cook Islanders – so close to the testing zone – onto the wider screen of world opinion.'

Boy Roel's voyage had been dogged by technical failures. On 4 July the crew heard a news broadcast that the French were considering a withdrawal from Moruroa and an end to the tests there, an announcement they interpreted (rightly, as events would prove) as a ruse to put off the protest boats. After a radio breakdown, *Boy Roel*'s progress was checked by a flat battery just five days from Rarotonga, where she wallowed in the waves, cut off from the world and with all systems dead. As they continued slowly under sail, the crew's morale was buoyed only by the thought of the other boats still headed for the test zone.

Back in New Zealand, Peace Media had organised a protest that saw 2,000 people march on Parliament. A delegation seeking a meeting with the Prime Minister was informed that the Government would take no further action over the current test series. On 14 July, France's Bastille Day, Labour leader Norman Kirk pledged in Parliament that if Labour won the upcoming general election, he would send one of New Zealand's four frigates to Moruroa as a 'silent accusing witness'. Peace Media, meanwhile, had reported *Boy Roel* missing.

The Government's decision not to launch an immediate search and rescue mission provoked angry reactions from family and friends of the crew. Ultimately the whole episode became a political embarrassment, and under mounting public pressure the cabinet met and agreed to mount a full-scale search immediately, a week after the yacht had first been reported missing. Finally, a month after the yacht went off the air, Radio Hauraki announced that contact with *Boy Roel* had been regained.

Their voyage had been an ordeal: one crew member, Warren Graham, was hospitalised after collapsing from nervous exhaustion; another, Torres Bonnevie, left the boat to rest up with friends in Apia. But despite their failure to reach Moruroa the *Boy Roel* had maintained media attention on the issue – ironically, because of its having lost contact with the outside world. The *Auckland Star* ran front-page stories; radio bulletins kept the public abreast of events; the *Dominion* and Radio Hauraki carried Maurice Shadbolt's message from *Tamure* appealing to the Government to send out a search and rescue

The distinctive sloping roof of the Moruroa blockhouse (right), the control centre for the tests – as seen from Moruroa lagoon.

Tahitian pirogue in Papeete harbour.

mission. The *Sunday Times* ran an editorial that asked, 'What sort of government would allow political considerations to sway normal humanitarian instincts? Mr Marshall has chosen a bad year to express contempt for the nuclear protest movement. He will live to regret his extraordinary behaviour over the missing protest ship *Boy Roel* – politically, and we hope, personally. If anything happens to the *Boy Roel* and its brave crew, the Prime Minister will be asked whether he treated the *Boy Roel*'s disappearance differently from the way marine disappearances have been treated in the past. He will be asked if such discrimination was influenced in any way by the fact that the protesters were risking their lives to act where his Government should have acted.'

Several other vessels had initially been put forward for the 1972 Peace Media flotilla. The high dropout rate and the all-too-frequent equipment breakdowns have sometimes been attributed to covert sabotage by French military agents. Despite the public and published boasts of former French intelligence officers and plenty of local hearsay, Greenpeace has no reliable evidence to confirm such speculation.

Reflecting on those tiring weeks, Barry Mitcalfe wrote: 'The *Boy Roel* saga touched many New Zealanders, arousing opinion against French nuclear testing to such an extent that, according to opinion polls, though not to the Prime Minister, it became a significant election issue. Politically it was necessary for the Government to belittle *Boy Roel* to obscure the real issue: the

Government's failure to act effectively on a matter of public concern.'

Over the winter months of 1972 sympathetic Labour MPs tabled motions calling on the Government to send the Prime Minister to Paris to complain personally to French President Georges Pompidou. Marshall rejected this suggestion and dismissed the idea of sending a frigate into the test zone. However, contrary to the Prime Minister's prediction, it seemed that French nuclear testing had become an election issue in 1972, and in November Norman Kirk's Labour Party was swept to power by a wide margin. In the future, broad-based popular opposition to the tests could not be ignored by the Government of the day.

The 1972 testing season was unusually brief – just three small-scale tests – and there is no doubt that it was cut short by the protests. Around the world, opposition to the French tests was stronger than ever before. Resolutions at the United Nations condemned them, the 1972 Stockholm Conference on the Human Environment had voted for a halt, and trade unions across the Pacific and in Europe boycotted suppliers to the testing centre. In New Zealand, Peace Media were determined to keep up the pressure with their own brand of direct popular politics.

CHAPTER TWO

Fri Spirit

IN EARLY 1971, among the cruise liners and millionaires' yachts lining the wharves of Honolulu harbour, a battered ketch lay up on a boat-yard ramp. Looking like a relic of the last century, the *Fri*, a forerunner of the *Rainbow Warrior*, was about to be drafted into the service of the New Age and was soon to become the best-known peace ship in the world, to be superseded only by the *Rainbow Warrior* herself.

The *Fri* was an old Baltic trader whose new owners were David Moodie, a confident young long-haired American, his partner Emma Young, and his two brothers. The Moodies, who came from a wealthy East Coast family, had grown up with a love of the sea. In March 1971 they bought the *Fri* in San Francisco, and set about planning a voyage across the Pacific to New Zealand. After a brief diversion to run water supplies for a group of Native Americans struggling to win back the prison island of Alcatraz in San Francisco harbour, *Fri* set sail into the Pacific in 1971.

In Honolulu the elderly vessel was on the ramp for several weeks for repairs. David Moodie was hanging from her stern in a bosun's chair, rebuilding her rudder, when he first heard of Greenpeace over a local radio station. It was a news report on the Amchitka protest: 'Greenpeace atom protesters... Amchitka underground tests... faultline... earthquake and tidal wave danger...' He was particularly intrigued by the organisation's name. 'Those two evocative words instantly struck a chord with me.' At that stage, however, the Moodies' primary concern was to take *Fri* out to sea to avoid the tidal wave some were predicting would follow the Amchitka bomb tests. Within a year they and their ship would be facing the same dangers at much closer range.

The scattered atolls and islands of the Line and Cook groups became *Fri*'s stepping stones from Hawai'i to New Zealand. Within days of her arrival in Auckland in April 1972, and before David McTaggart and *Vega* had made their first appearance there, *Fri*'s crew were approached by Mabel Hetherington and Barry Mitcalfe and sounded out on the idea of a trip to Moruroa. It was the first time the Moodies had heard of the atoll, or of the French atmospheric tests. They had been at sea for seven months, the old boat was in need of a refit and a change of crew (David's brothers had returned to shore life), and there wasn't enough time for the necessary preparations, so with some regret David declined. Yet the germ of an idea had been planted.

Above: Captain David Moodie.

Opposite: Fri running with the wind for Moruroa, 1973.

Fri was built in 1912 in Svendborg, Denmark, as a traditional coastal trading vessel. An all-timber ship, she is thirty-two metres long with a gaff rig, hand winches, and traditional rope and canvas sails.

That New Zealand protest boats would return to Moruroa was never in doubt so long as the nuclear tests continued. Peace Media were determined to go back in 1973, this time applying lessons from the previous year's experience. Their first priority was to find seaworthy boats capable of safely reaching eastern Polynesia. In their search for vessels, new players were drawn in and plans developed for a fresh approach to the campaign. Public support for the protests was still high from the first voyages. Two circumstances in particular now helped their cause – a change of government in New Zealand and growing international pressure against the tests. The French authorities would soon be on the defensive as the mood of the anti-testing lobby became more confident and determined.

Fri attracted young alternative lifestylers wherever she went. Naomi Petersen, a twenty-one-year-old university student in Auckland with an interest in social justice issues, heard of the boat through the student network. On her way to university she used to enjoy cycling past *Fri*'s berth at Marsden Wharf, almost exactly where the *Rainbow Warrior* would be bombed thirteen years later. Eventually Naomi plucked up the courage to ask if extra crew were needed, and as soon as her exams were over she joined as a deckhand and cook, working in the galley with Emma. With several local crew members assembled, *Fri* soon became associated with the hippie, back-to-the-land movement around the Hauraki Gulf. They hauled building supplies, fishing equipment, friends and fruit trees to communal farms around the Gulf, and carried hand-processed potter's clay from Coromandel to sell to potters in Auckland. At the same time, the crew kept track of the *Boy Roel*'s story and *Vega*'s sorties into the test zone.

One clear, moonlit night in June, *Boy Roel*'s owner, Wim van Leeuwen, tracked down the *Fri* at anchor on the Waihou River, near Thames, her masts towering over the surrounding paddocks. He hailed the crew from the river bank and was welcomed aboard. Peace Media needed more ships for the forthcoming expedition, he told them. Were they willing to go? David certainly was, but said help would be needed to prepare and provision his ship. The crew agreed to think about it and to stay in touch.

By November 1972 the legal status of *Fri*, and particularly her foreign crew members, was tenuous. Immigration applications had been denied, and a six-month extension to their visas would only see the crew through the coming hurricane season. Their plans were to sail to the New Hebrides and the Solomon Islands with a cargo of treadle sewing machines, but they still lacked sufficient funds for the project. Peace Media, on the other hand, offered a small but dedicated support community and the means to maintain, provision and crew the ship. For both practical and idealistic reasons it made sense to rally to the anti-testing campaign. Indeed, *Fri*'s crew were starting to feel that a journey into the nuclear test zone was their fate.

As the pohutakawa burst into summer flower, *Fri* was beached at Parua Bay in Northland, where four tonnes of Coromandel clay were offloaded. In fact, she had become stranded on a sandbank, but the crew made the most of the situation by working on the ship and at Yvonne Rust's pottery nearby, and floated her off again on the next spring tides. It was here that they finally submitted to fate and wrote to Barry Mitcalfe to arrange a January meeting in

Whangarei. There it was agreed that *Fri* would act as the mother ship to a fleet of twenty or so smaller yachts in a new peace flotilla of boats from around the Pacific. It was a grandiose plan, but Peace Media now boasted branches all round New Zealand and contacts in France, Fiji, Western Samoa and Peru. *Fri* would be ideal for such a voyage: she could stay on station for months at a time, and she was large enough to carry a big crew. The fact that her owners had no qualms about risking damage to the vessel, when insurance against nuclear blast or military assault was rather hard to come by, was also an advantage.

David Moodie was concerned that *Fri* might not be up to another trip through the Roaring Forties, so they hauled the ship onto the hard at Whangarei to get an independent surveyor's opinion. Planking and caulking were found to be in good order and the voyage was confirmed. Mitcalfe agreed that Peace Media would take responsibility for finding crew, volunteers, provisions and the means for an overhaul on her return. As a start, he arranged a meeting between David and Peter Yeates, an enterprising potter and ex-seaman based in Opua in the Bay of Islands. David drove up to Opua and was collected by Peter in an open boat for the fifteen-minute trip to his home at Rum Point, where they laid plans late into the night around the campfire beside Peter's bamboo geodesic dome.

Peter was excited by the plan, and by the next morning he had agreed to sail as mate while Patchouli, his pregnant partner, was half-persuaded to go as – you guessed it – cook! The ship was then brought up to Opua for the estimated six-week conversion to a protest mother ship. Here *Fri* became a focus for the local alternative communities – Maori and Pakeha – but especially for the young hippies converging on Opua from further afield.

Through the glorious Northland summer days, this strange assortment of sympathisers worked away on *Fri* to the amplified rhythms of the Rolling Stones, their morale further boosted by a telegram of support from John Lennon and Yoko Ono. Some of *Fri*'s crew already lived in the Bay of Islands; others came from further afield. Some were enthusiastic amateurs; others were qualified and experienced seafarers. As Barry Mitcalfe remembered it, 'From Opua to Whangarei, the people of Northland responded in ways that were direct, personal and characteristically generous. Volunteer workers and crew came from all over New Zealand, and from Britain, the Netherlands, the United States and France.' Fundraising concerts were organised, and the local Maori community would come down to share their kai with the '*Fri* circus'. Wherever *Fri* called in along the coast around Opua, she received warm local support. A strong and popular feeling against the nuclear tests had taken root around the country, bringing rural conservatives alongside long-haired radicals in the communal effort.

There were those, even in Peace Media, who doubted that such a motley collective could be sufficiently

'We wanted *Fri* to represent a cross-section of the community – young and old, men and women, different nationalities. Nuclear weapons and fallout don't respect those distinctions.' – *David Moodie*

Peace Media organiser Barry Mitcalfe unloading ballast from *Fri*, summer 1974.

organised for the task. Kurt Horn, a former Vancouver Greenpeacer who had taken part in the Amchitka protest and was a recent immigrant to New Zealand, was enlisted by Mitcalfe to maintain a semblance of order among the crew. Kurt was a sailor who believed in a strong captain and maritime discipline. By contrast, David Moodie's mellow, relaxed style invited participation and shared responsibility rather than hierarchical control and accountability.

Fri's navigator, the piratical Martini Gotje.

David felt strongly that the only way his colourful crew could work together successfully was by developing a sense of individual responsibility based on their convictions. The rigorous demands of life at sea, David believed, could be relied upon to instil the discipline necessary for survival. And since the crew were the ones putting their lives on the line, it was only reasonable that they carry out the wishes of their supporters in their own way. That Kurt Horn eventually opted not to sail with Fri was a final signal of Peace Media's trust in David's judgment.

All that remained was to find a navigator. Back in Whangarei one morning, less than a week before departure, David looked up on the dock at a very long, thin pair of legs poured into tight red trousers and attached to a figure who 'looked like he'd stepped off the Dutch Masters cigar box'. Another crew member, Rua Paul, remarked that the tall stranger looked 'as cool as a martini', and Martini he became. A fully qualified navigator and sailor, Martin Gotje had emigrated to New Zealand from the Netherlands just two weeks before and was job-hunting when he spotted Peace Media's appeal for skilled crew in the newspaper. Between Whangarei and Moruroa, across the vast reaches of the South Pacific, Martini taught David all he knew of astral navigation.

For Martini, this was the start of an association with Greenpeace that continues nearly twenty years later. Now living and working in Auckland, employed by the organisation's international Marine Division and the Pacific campaign, he is a veteran of several Moruroa voyages, linking the early days

Preparing for departure – Fri at the Town Basin, Whangarei, March 1973.

Fri in heavy seas.

of *Fri* and Peace Media with Greenpeace's later campaigns, including the *Rainbow Warrior*'s visits to the Marshall Islands to protest against the United States nuclear testing programme. The rest of *Fri*'s crew comprised Naomi Petersen, Patchouli Yeates, Peter Yeates, Rua Paul, engineer Ted Rutter, ship's medic Colin Marshall, Graeme Marrett, film-maker Alister Barry who would make a documentary of the voyage, Murray Glue and Gilbert Nicolas, with the relief crew of Bernard Rhodes, Hugh Monroe, Peter Martin, Ray Wilson and Elsa Caron.

On 21 March 1973 *Fri* sailed down the Whangarei Channel and out to sea. Two days out both ship and crew were straining under a south-westerly gale, the old timber hull taking in 3,000 litres of water an hour. For the largely novice crew, most of them suffering from varying degrees of seasickness, it was a harsh introduction to life at sea. One week out, the tiller snapped. Two failed repair efforts later, Peter Yeates and engineer Ted Rutter succeeded in constructing a serviceable replacement from a jumble of on-board odds and ends.

As a low-impact, energy-efficient vessel, *Fri* was exemplary. The crew collected fresh rainwater in a specially slung sail, set up a small wind-power generator in the rigging and constructed a bicycle generator too. The constantly leaking bilges were pumped out every hour by muscle power, the crew taking turns at the pump on a strict rotation. Nearly all solid waste was recycled. Their diet included fresh tuna and hapuka, with sweet-smelling, yeasty doughnuts and bread baked in the galley's wood range. They carried no refrigerator on board. On sunnier days the deck would be draped with

Deckhand Naomi Petersen rinses the beansprouts!

laundry as crew members fought a losing battle with the relentless damp of the ship's wooden hull.

'The ship passed through the swelling waves of the Roaring Forties,' recalls Naomi. 'These days I wouldn't take too much notice of such seas, but sick as I was, the waves and the night sky still seemed magical to me, weaving with the old ship and her tarry smells a web that made me want to be in no other place in the world for the next seven years.' *Fri*'s crew began as strangers and (mostly) inexperienced sailors. Thrust together on the pitching ship, they evolved a practical system of working together, relying on the interdependence of their diverse strengths, and proved David right in his conviction that a widely disparate group of people could, with commitment, successfully unite around a common task.

Fri was not alone on her voyage to Moruroa that year. In fact, up to twenty-five other vessels from across the Pacific were said to be preparing to make the voyage. From New Zealand were the *Spirit of Peace, Bluenose, Barbary, Arakiwa, Tanea* from Tauranga and two other vessels out of Wellington and Christchurch. As well, there were the *Malaguena* and *Warana* from Australia, a handful of canoes from Fiji, at least one Peruvian vessel with governmental representatives, *Carmen* from Tahiti and a boat from Western Samoa. One yacht due to leave Hawai'i was prevented from leaving by United States authorities, and the *Arakiwa* was turned back at Rapa Island after French harassment. In the event, despite this impressive list, only *Fri* and the *Spirit of Peace* would complete the journey.

Yvonne and Clive Dasler had supported the 1972 flotilla with prayers and donations. This year Clive decided to go himself to Moruroa. As committed Christian pacifists, the Daslers' determination to protest was so strong that they sold their home to raise funds for a yacht. Auckland Peace Media organiser Bill Ralston eventually found them a fourteen-metre Bermudan ketch, which they renamed the *Spirit of Peace.*

In Auckland Joan and Ron Cavaney took food down to the wharf each weekend to share amongst the helpers on the *Spirit of Peace* and the other Peace Media boats. 'I suppose we were squares compared with everyone on *Fri*,' says Joan, 'but I began to learn that if you share what you have with others, you get more back in the long run.' The atmosphere surrounding the boats generated enough energy and money to support them through the long winter months of 1973. Seventeen thousand dollars was raised by Peace Media in New Zealand during that year to support *Fri*, the *Spirit of Peace* and *Bluenose*, while another $9,000 came from French peace groups.

The Daslers and the Cavaneys represented a different strand in Peace Media – 'conventional' Kiwis by comparison with the wild young *Fri* trippers – and the *Spirit of Peace* became a focus for this group. Dedicated though he was, Clive had the notion that it might even be fun to spend the New Zealand winter cruising around the South Pacific. He couldn't have been more wrong. *Spirit* was to stay in the test zone longer than any other protest vessel before or since, and yet, perhaps because her crew was not as obviously colourful as some of the others involved, and was never arrested, the boat did not receive the same level of publicity as the others.

On board the *Spirit* with Clive were captain Bernard Rhodes, an expat-

Bounty Bay, Pitcairn Island. The flying fox, which carried fresh supplies to *Fri*.

Crew coming ashore in the Pitcairn longboat.

riate Englishman and an experienced Pacific sailor, who would later skipper the *Fri* and play a prominent part in the Auckland Peace Squadron, French Canadian Mark Roumieu and radio operator Peter Martin, a young Taranaki dairy farmer. Leaving Auckland at the end of April, *Spirit* had a swift and trouble-free passage across the southern Pacific, and in late May they began their long vigil at Moruroa, standing off the twelve-mile limit, all the time

Rendezvous in the zone – *Spirit of Peace* crew cross to *Fri*.

Prime Minister Norman Kirk farewells HMNZS *Otago*, on her way to the zone.

wondering what the French military might do and just how long they could endure the isolation and limited diet.

Fri, meanwhile, had broken her outward journey at Pitcairn Island, just 500 miles short of Moruroa, arriving on 7 May. Here the crew enjoyed a few days' rest on land while they took on fresh supplies, and also gathered information on local increases in radioactivity in rainwater monitored after previous tests. Leaving the remote island, *Fri* was soon in radio contact with the *Spirit of Peace.* On 26 May the two boats finally rendezvoused inside the 120-mile military exclusion zone. It was Clive's birthday and both crews celebrated with a birthday cake conjured up by Naomi. For the crew of the *Spirit,* after their long confinement on such a small boat, it was bliss to be able to walk about, even on *Fri's* narrow deck.

The following weeks were spent tacking back and forth along a fifty-mile course across the trades, downwind of the test site and as close to the twelve-mile territorial limit as they could, on a ritual maritime picket line. The monotony was broken only by the occasional migrating fin whale attracted to the boats. In the often sweltering tropical heat, the humidity constantly sapped the crews' energy. By now it was clear that the other Peace Media vessels were not going to make it. *Bluenose* had turned back after the skipper was injured in a storm, and *Barbary* got no further than 100 miles offshore before succumbing to engine and other problems.

The Labour Governments in New Zealand and Australia, less inclined than their predecessors to rely on gently chiding diplomatic notes to express their opposition, had meanwhile begun proceedings at the World Court, which after several weeks of deliberations issued France with an interim injunction to stop the atmospheric tests. Paris chose to ignore the injunction, de Gaulle's conservative successor, Georges Pompidou, informing the New Zealand Government that the tests would continue regardless of the expressed concerns of Pacific nations or the world community. At this, Norman Kirk kept his promise and dispatched a New Zealand Navy frigate, HMNZS *Otago*, to the zone.

The *Otago*, crewed by volunteers and farewelled by thousands of well-wishers, left Wellington Harbour on 28 June, and the following day the Australian ship HMAS *Supply* rendezvoused with the New Zealand frigate 300 miles north of Auckland. Kirk commented: 'We hope that mobilising world opinion will help persuade France to comply with the International Court's order.' Cabinet Minister Fraser Colman was chosen as the New Zealand Government's representative on the *Otago*. An invitation to the National Opposition to send their own representative was met with derision. The protest, said party leader John Marshall, was 'a futile and empty gesture'.

Within days millions of people around the world watched on television as the ships from two 'friendly' navies converged on Moruroa. Large-scale protests against the French tests were held in a number of countries, in some cases where no organised opposition had previously been evident. Peru, for instance, severed diplomatic relations with France. For some years before Greenpeace opened an official office in England in 1978, an anarchistic collection of supporters operated under the name Greenpeace London. In May this group organised a march from London to Paris, which was blocked by police at the French/Belgian border. The marchers dispersed, to cross the border independently and reconvene near the Eiffel Tower, where one party occupied Notre Dame cathedral and several thousand peaceful protesters were baton-charged by the city's riot police.

New Zealand's neighbours in the Pacific, who had for ten years waged a lonely and unequal struggle against French nuclear colonialism, were delighted by the support from their more influential neighbours. Fijian trade unions organised boycotts and public marches against the testing. An even more extraordinary development for the Tahitian anti-testing activists was the arrival of support from the least expected quarter. In despair over their dealings with the colonial authorities, independence leaders Pouvanaa a Oopa and Francis Sanford sent an open letter to 200 French newspapers and magazines addressing the French people and explaining their plight. A single metropolitan magazine took up the issue – the national weekly *L'Express*, owned by the wealthy Radical MP and writer Jean-Jacques Servan-Schreiber, which ran the full text of the letter. JJSS, as he is known, who led the anti-testing, pro-independence Radical Party, wrote a stinging rebuke of the Government, which had refused to allow any debate or vote in Parliament on nuclear policy in France. Not only did JJSS galvanise a heated national debate on the *force de frappe*, but he went further, organising an extraordinary group of influential Frenchmen into the Bataillon de la Paix, sending some of them along with several of his Radical Party colleagues to Tahiti. On 23 June, six members of the bataillon and several Radical Party MPs joined Tahitian independence leaders to address a crowd of 5,000, gathered in defiance of the colonial authorities. It was the largest-ever public demonstration in Papeete.

Pouvanaa a Oopa fought for France with distinction in the First World War and was among the one hundred Tahitian survivors who waited a year in Europe after the war's end before a hulk was found to take them home. Back in Tahiti they faced the same oppression that had always been their lot in the French colony. Pouvanaa was a natural leader, and his carpentry workshop in Papeete became a meeting-place for disaffected Tahitians. During the Second World War his open criticism of the dictatorial administration in Tahiti led to his imprisonment in the colony's asylum and later his banishment, under a permanent gendarme guard, to his home island of Huahine. In 1950 Pouvanaa formed the Rassemblement Democratique des Populations Tahitiennes (RDPT), an anti-colonial party that swamped the Tahitian Territorial Assembly. In 1959, when he was sixty-four, he was framed on absurdly concocted charges and sent to prison in France, where he spent the next eight years in solitary confinement in the notorious Baumette Prison in Marseilles. He then faced a further fifteen years' exile from Polynesia but was finally released in 1974, by which time his health was broken. Pouvanaa had remained a courageous and consistent champion of his people's rights and was an inspiration for all succeeding Tahitian independence leaders. He died in 1977.

New Zealand's frigate was in no position to enter into a confrontation with the French Navy off Moruroa, and it was left to the peace movement boats to challenge the military zone declared before each atmospheric test. At the same time, Kirk vainly urged the protest yachts to leave the area, in compliance with the request of the International Court that no actions be taken to aggravate the dispute with the French Government. After one month in the exclusion zone, and with no bombs detonated, *Fri* was radioed by Barry Mitcalfe, who had arranged with JJSS for members of the Bataillon de la Paix to join the ship. The group was now on its way via New Zealand to the Cook Islands and would be sailing out to meet her on a chartered resupply yacht, the *Arwen*. *Fri*'s epic voyage was approaching its fifth month.

The French authorities had already dismissed the protests as simply anti-French, so the arrival of these protesters was timely, refocusing attention squarely on the nuclear issue. Altogether five French citizens sailed on board *Fri*: Gilbert Nicolas, a pacifist pastor who had sailed all the way from New Zealand, was now joined by General Jacques Paris de Bollardière, Brice Lalonde, then president of Les Amis de la Terre (Friends of the Earth), Catholic scholar Jean Toulat, and Jean-Marie Muller, an eminent professor of philosophy. General Bollardière, the most highly decorated general in the French Army and once described as the 'Eisenhower of France', had been a key military figure in France's colonial wars in Indochina and Algeria. In recent years he had grown deeply sceptical of the national purpose behind these wars and was strongly opposed to nuclear weapons. His present stand could not be easily dismissed in France.

On 17 July the French Admiralty at Moruroa announced the imposition of the 120-mile exclusion zone, indicating that a nuclear test was imminent. The *Spirit of Peace* was out of the zone at the time, reprovisioning at Rarotonga; only *Fri* with its new French crew members remained. After 118 days at sea,

Fri's crew watched as an inflatable approached them from the minesweeper *Dunkerquoise*. Three French marines delivered a letter instructing the protesters to leave the zone. David Moodie replied that they would not leave, patiently pointing out that they were after all in international waters, and instead inviting the admiral directing the CEP for talks on board *Fri*.

As soon as this reply was delivered, the French warship signalled 'Stop Vessel Immediately'. Within minutes *Fri* was boarded by some thirty marine commandos and sailors from the frigate *Doudart de Lagrée*. Two more inflatables brought across towing gear. As quickly as the marines tried to make fast, Martin Gotje cut the towlines, while Colin Marshall tossed overboard any spare shackles he could find. The crew cheered when a rocket line fired from the tug *Hippopotame* missed *Fri* altogether; the marines smiled at them nervously, unsure how to react to their subversive captives. Gilbert Nicolas and General Bollardière had meanwhile seized the opportunity to address the marines, calling on them to examine their consciences and disobey their orders. Bollardière would later return his Legion d'Honneur in protest and be stripped of his status as a reserve general.

As the tension rose, David Moodie quietly slipped out of his jeans and, without warning, jumped overboard, forcing the marines to send a dinghy after him. He was fished out of the water and tied up to prevent a repeat performance. Next minute, however, Colin Marshall dived over the side. Further attempts to obstruct the tow were summarily dealt with by the marines, *Fri*'s crew offering only passive resistance as they were dragged back repeatedly

'Several alerts woke us up during the night: the lights of ships on the horizon, a plane flying at low altitude, and the boom of the mainsail broken...' (Day 118, 17 July 1973, *Fri Alert*)

Minutes before boarding, the French Navy closes in on *Fri*.

The 23 June anti-testing march in Tahiti. Pouvanaa (seated) leads, with JJSS and Francis Sanford (with glasses) behind him on the left.

from the bow. Finally, with the peace and *Fri* flags hauled down from the mast, the long tow to shore began. Six hours later they arrived at Moruroa and were promptly flown 500 kilometres north to the military base at Hao Atoll.

From Hao Atoll Naomi wrote to her family: 'What a horrible place Moruroa is! Square miles of concrete, tarmac and blockhouses, every conceivable type of warship and combat aircraft, constant noise and khaki. *Fri* sat among all the iron grey like a beautiful bird with its wings clipped. Here at Hao too the wastage of the military and its callousness towards Polynesian culture upsets me. The Tahitian people in the village of Otepa are incredibly generous to us and have plied us with gifts of clothes and food. We are the first English-speaking, non-military people they have seen for a long time and are welcomed as supporters of Polynesian independence. The movement is quite strong even here on Hao.'

From the start of their detention *Fri*'s stronger crew members mounted a hunger strike. After a week the authorities were sufficiently worried by the condition of the hunger strikers to transfer them forcibly to the military hospital in Papeete, where they received supportive visits from local activists like Bengt and Marie-Thérèse Danielsson, and independence politicians John Teariki, Francis Sanford and Oscar Temaru. Before their capture the crew had decided, both to maximise the publicity over the incident and to prevent the confiscation of their ship, not to make it easy for the French simply to deport them. During their tow into Moruroa, Alister Barry had hastily collected and hidden their passports – so well, it seemed, that much though the authorities would have liked to have speedily deported their exasperating 'guests', and despite having virtually trashed the ship in the attempt, the military never found the documents. Within ten days the crew and their allies in Tahiti had secured their and *Fri*'s unconditional release.

When *Fri* was towed out to the twelve-mile limit it was with limited food stocks and no opportunity to repair the damage done to the ship over the previous weeks – she had been roughly covered in plastic sheeting and left in the lagoon during two atmospheric tests. Soon afterwards, a fire in the engine-room badly burned engineer Hugh Monroe, who had joined *Fri* via the *Arwen* shortly before their arrest. The *Otago,* which had proved useful as a radio relay station to facilitate *Fri*'s rendezvous with the *Spirit,* had by now been relieved by HMNZS *Canterbury.* Now, a day out of Moruroa, *Fri* and the *Spirit of Peace* rendezvoused with the frigate and the injured engineer was transferred to the ship. *Fri* and the *Spirit* then sailed on to Papeete to resupply, only to be refused entry. 'If they will not allow you to come to Tahiti,' said leading *Autonomist* Francis Sanford, 'then we will bring Tahiti to you.' The ships waited at the twelve-mile limit, and a fleet of Tahitian pirogues – light outrigger canoes – paddled out carrying baskets of coconuts, papayas, melons, bananas, oranges, meat and eggs, and crates of beer, courtesy of local Tahitian supporters and Bengt and Marie-Thérèse Danielsson.

In the six weeks following *Fri*'s seizure five nuclear tests took place – on 21 and 28 July, and 19, 25 and 28 August. The tests that year were to miniaturise TN60 thermonuclear warheads for submarine- and ground-launched missiles. These warheads, first deployed in 1976, each have a yield of approximately 1,000 kilotons, 100 times the destructive power of the bomb dropped on Hiroshima.

This was not the last of the galling distractions the CEP faced that year. Now *Vega* was back in the zone with David McTaggart and a new crew. Following her deliberate ramming by a French warship the previous year, repairs to *Vega* had run up a bill of around $30,000. The French Government had offered to pay half that sum on condition that *Vega* never return to the zone. This was just the stimulus McTaggart needed! Yet he could not have anticipated the ferocity of the French military's reaction to his return.

This time with McTaggart, Nigel Ingram and New Zealanders Anna Horne and Mary Lornie as crew, *Vega* covered the 3,000-mile voyage from Whangarei in just twenty-one days. It was mid-August when they approached the atoll, to be met by their old adversary *Dunkerquoise,* soon joined by the tug *Hippopotame.* The following day, 15 August, the two ships were joined by a third, which wasted no time in sending over a squad of commandos. 'Mary and I took our stations with the cameras,' remembers Anna, 'and in a flash they were across the back of the boat and just flailing David.'

McTaggart recalls barely having time to tell the commandos not to board his boat. 'Then, because I knew they intended to beat me whatever I did, I brought my arms up in a blocking motion level with the neck of the soldier who was halfway over the railing, and with all my strength I checked him hard.' Quickly two more soldiers jumped onto *Vega,* pulling McTaggart's shirt over his head and pinning him down. Then they began to beat him with their steel-cored batons. 'The first truncheon came down on the back of my head with a weight and force unlike anything I'd ever felt; the second blow came down across my shoulders... With scarcely a pause, the truncheons were flailing again, each blow rattling my teeth so it seemed they'd be

Vega's crew (from right): Anna Horne, Mary Lornie, McTaggart and Ingram.

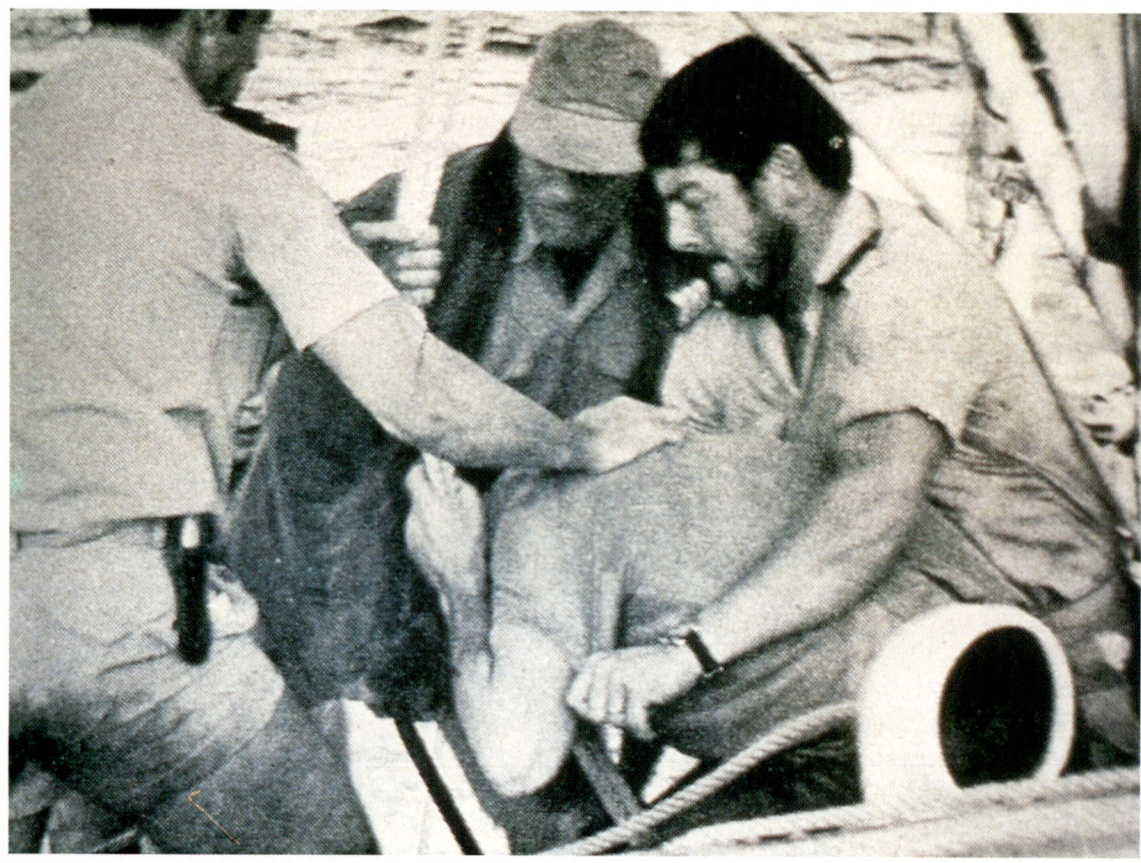

Nuclear diplomacy – French commandos debate the testing issue with Nigel Ingram.

shattered and my spine and ribs and skull would cave in any second. Back, neck, head, kidneys. I writhed and thrashed but was so expertly pinned there was absolutely nothing I could do, not even duck… Something crashed into my right eye with such force it seemed to explode right in the middle of my brain, so I thought that half my head had been torn off. Then everything went black.'

Nigel blacked out after the first couple of truncheon blows to the head. He was brought round by a series of brutal kicks to the groin and ribs as he lay curled up in the corner of the cockpit, before losing consciousness again. Mary had managed to capture this whole episode on her movie camera while Anna had taken still photos. The commandos threw the movie camera overboard, but Anna managed to hide the Nikon on board and fool the marines into seizing a decoy camera. Later she ingeniously smuggled the film past their guards.

David's injuries were so severe he was flown to Tahiti for emergency treatment, while the other three were taken to Hao Atoll. True to form, the French authorities quickly fabricated a cover story for the media. The official account was that McTaggart had tried to throw the commandos into the water and had himself fallen, injuring his eye on a dinghy cleat! 'Our men boarded his vessel unarmed and without striking a single blow…' the statement read. Once the crew members were released, Anna's film was passed to the media by Greenpeace Canada, who used it to maximum effect. On his return to

Canada McTaggart was met by a barrage of reporters, and news of his beating spread around the world.

McTaggart subsequently pursued his claims against the French Government through the civil courts in France. The Paris Civil Tribunal eventually ruled that the French Navy had been guilty of deliberately ramming *Vega* in 1972. On the second, more serious, charge of piracy, however, the court ruled itself unable to judge a case of international law and eventually absolved the French Navy by decreeing that 'matters of state security' such as nuclear testing could not be judged by a civil court.

Meanwhile, after an eighteen-day break on the Polynesian island of Moorea and rest with the Danielssons over the water on Tahiti, *Fri* sailed back against the wind to Moruroa, to find that the tests were concluded for the season, then returned to New Zealand. At home it was once more time to reassess the campaign. *Fri*'s crew were by now convinced that their efforts had most meaning when seen as part of a wider struggle. The protesters had not previously been in contact with the Tahitian independence movement, but over these months the indigenous Maohi people had extended enormous practical support. It was to be the beginning of a network of contacts that Greenpeace built up throughout the Pacific, and it sowed the seeds for important co-operation in years to come.

The protests had scored both a moral and a concrete victory over the French Government. In November 1973, at the United Nations General Assembly, France announced its intention, after thirty-six atmospheric nuclear tests in the atmosphere in the Pacific, to move the testing programme underground in 1975. In the end popular pressure in the Pacific region against the tests, in which the voyages of *Vega*, *Fri* and the other protest boats had played no small part, had proved unstoppable.

Of course, this decision gave only limited cause for celebration – nuclear testing underground remained a potent threat both to the environment and to world peace. Peace Media's and Greenpeace's campaign emphasised the regional environmental effects, yet France's testing programme continued to play a significant role in the arms race. After 1975 there was an inevitable falling away of public concern, many believing that the move underground had eliminated the serious health hazards linked with nuclear testing. For Greenpeace, there was also a tactical problem: the French nuclear authorities were now practically immune from the protest voyagers, who could no longer count on even delaying, let alone halting the individual tests. Nonetheless, their limited success, and the widespread international support for their cause, gave many of those involved the confidence and sense of purpose to look ahead and develop a longer-term approach to the campaign to creating a nuclear-free Pacific.

CHAPTER THREE

The Odyssey

AFTER THE FRENCH Government announced it would stop atmospheric nuclear testing, there was double cause for celebration when *Fri* arrived back at Opua on 11 November 1973. The ship skimmed down to Auckland for a reception organised by the 'Friends of the *Fri*', with music, laughter and rousing speeches from Mayor Robbie and Labour MPs Mike Moore and Jonathan Hunt. Now, riding the wave, David Moodie especially was fired up for a challenge that would lead in new, more positive directions.

There were to be two key developments in the New Zealand peace movement in 1974. The first was the official formation of the Greenpeace Foundation of New Zealand in April through the union of Peace Media, the *Fri* and their supporters. The second was the decision to send *Fri* on an epic voyage around the Pacific carrying the peace message to all the nuclear weapon states. The Pacific Peace Odyssey, a 25,000-mile adventure partially financed and co-ordinated by Greenpeace New Zealand, would last until 1977 and take *Fri* on an extraordinary journey across the Pacific and Indian Oceans.

Martini remembers taking a critical look at a map of the Pacific on *Fri*'s return from Tahiti in 1973 and coming to the realisation that the 'peaceful' ocean was becoming a breeding ground for nuclear weapons. 'We wanted to come up with something positive to do this time, rather than just returning to Moruroa – something that would link all the nuclear weapon states.' Heated arguments between the crew and French military personnel on Moruroa and Hao had time and again thrown up their captors' sensitivity to being 'singled out' to the exclusion of the other nuclear powers. 'Obviously this had not been our intention,' says David. 'The idea of a peace odyssey to all five nuclear powers, France, the United States, the Soviet Union, Britain and China, had been a topic of wishful thinking for some weeks at least, so it seemed a logical thing to do next.'

The ship would return to Tahiti, not in a spirit of confrontation but with a message of peace, and this would be just the first stage in a journey that would include visits to the other nuclear weapon states, three of whom were Pacific Rim nations. They would also undertake to learn first-hand the testimonies of those directly affected by nuclear testing in the Pacific. *Fri* would be an envoy of peace throughout the Pacific to counterbalance the ubiquitous United States nuclear navy and the warships of French Polynesia. A special 'Sowing the Seeds of Peace' postcard was printed, on which New Zealanders

Opposite: Fri in Cook Strait, Hiroshima Day, 1973.

and other friends along the way could write their own personal messages of peace to the governments and people of the nuclear testing states.

Over the weekend of 15 and 16 December 1973 a decisive meeting was held in Carey Park, West Auckland. It was Peace Media's annual general meeting and brought together a range of people concerned about French testing in the Pacific, including Francis Sanford from Tahiti and Peter Hayes, one of the organisers of the London to Paris march. Hayes went on to set up the authoritative US-based Nautilus Research group, renowned for its exposés on military/strategic skulduggery in the Pacific, and was one of the authors of *American Lake: Nuclear Peril in the Pacific*. Naomi Petersen recalls the scene: 'Boat-owners and crew, Peace Media people and others were there. It was the first I heard of the idea that Peace Media should change its name to Greenpeace, to signify the two groups' unity of purpose. Greenpeace was such a good name – it summed up what we were about.' The activists around Peace Media and *Fri* slipped effortlessly into this new identity. During *Fri*'s post-Moruroa refit at Tauranga this informal network was formalised in the creation in April 1974 of the Greenpeace Foundation of New Zealand. Peace Media contributed its network of contacts to help set up the Auckland office. No one at the time guessed the extent to which the change would draw this mostly younger section of the New Zealand peace movement into a broader organisation, with concerns embracing environmental as well as peace issues.

David Moodie has always seen *Fri*'s participation in the 1973 Moruroa protest as an early Greenpeace action, and though he sailed as part of the Peace Media flotilla, even then he proudly wore a Greenpeace T-shirt that Kurt Horn had brought from Canada. 'We all imagined Greenpeace New Zealand would act as an umbrella organisation, and hoped that the positive energy focused on *Fri* and the Moruroa protests would take root.' In practical terms Greenpeace would also co-ordinate the Peace Odyssey's fundraising from Auckland. Taking the seeds of peace idea literally, symbolic peace trees would be planted in each of the five nuclear states or their Pacific colonies.

The Peace Odyssey aimed to develop a network between the people of the nuclear testing nations and the people of the Pacific most directly affected by the testing and the militarisation of their homelands. (It would also come to be remembered as an early effort to spread the anti-nuclear 'New Zealand disease'.) As part of a drive to enlist wider support, Naomi Petersen and Jim Boyack, a former New York journalist now living in New Zealand who had been a helpful contact for *Fri* in Tahiti, addressed a meeting of the Anglican Synod at Hamilton. With the help of Bishop Paul Reeves they persuaded the Synod to support the voyage and encourage individual parishes to distribute and sell the postcards. Greenpeace was already beginning the work of building up a broad-based network of support in New Zealand. In response to the many requests speakers had fanned out from Greenpeace and *Fri*, hitchhiking around the country to give public talks on the Peace Odyssey while catching up with friends and family. Jim Boyack was an especially active and enthusiastic organiser, acting as ad-hoc director of the Foundation during this formative six months. David, Martini and Naomi were the only members of the original Moruroa voyage crew to remain with *Fri*. Emma had by now left the ship to seek a quieter, saner life on shore.

By the time *Fri* reached Wellington in July 1974, five months after the idea was conceived, the momentum for the Peace Odyssey was unstoppable. Every day scores of people converged on the wharf to say hello, sign cards and give money, while substantial donations of goods and food mysteriously appeared on deck. One evening, when David Moodie was discussing the project on a Wellington talkback show, Prime Minister Norman Kirk called up from his sickbed to offer his support. Greenpeace, he said, was on the right track in mounting a people-to-people campaign aiming to give ordinary citizens the opportunity to voice their opposition to the nuclear arms race. While Kirk had done more for the cause of peace than any other world leader at that time, he impressed on David that governments were powerless in comparison to the pressure ordinary citizens could exert. Only the people, he insisted, had sufficient strength to halt the nuclear threat.

Ship of state – Leader of the Opposition Muldoon visits *Fri* in the capital.

Norm Kirk was too sick to visit – he died only weeks later – but the Opposition Leader put in an appearance. In a prophetic piece of photojournalism, readers of the Wellington morning newspaper, the *Dominion,* were treated to the sight of Muldoon beaming at them over their breakfast cereal, standing at the wheel of *Fri*, apparently steering the ship backwards.

Elaine Shaw, Michael Taylor and other Greenpeace supporters from Auckland came down to help with the departure preparations, and literally thousands of kids came to see *Fri* in the capital. On Hiroshima Day, 6 August 1974, hordes of Wellington school children marched to the ship, each throwing a flower into the harbour as they left. Greenpeace had invited ambassadors of all the nuclear weapon states, but as it turned out, only a representative of the Japanese Government showed up.

Fri set sail for Tahiti from Wellington on 11 August 1974 on the first leg of the Pacific Peace Odyssey with a crew of three women, nine men and one child, Italian deckhand Orietta Sloth's eight-year-old son Tobias, representing nine nationalities. In the hold were 12,000 peace cards filled in by people from all over New Zealand. Bernard Rhodes was at the helm, David Moodie opting to take an extended break. Naomi, too, took time out and rejoined the ship in Japan.

After six months, with several thousand dollars raised for the Peace Odyssey, Greenpeace's funds stood at a couple of hundred dollars. Meeting in Auckland, the key movers agreed on the aims of the new organisation as being 'to protect the environment against misuse and destruction and to support *Fri*'s Pacific Peace Odyssey.' Present at those early meetings were, among others, Irene and Hugh Petersen, Bette Johnson, David Moodie, Elaine Shaw, Jim Boyack, Kay Couper, Wendy Armstrong, and Joan and Ron Cavaney.

The Greenpeace support team was then working out of a small office in Queen Street loaned by Auckland barrister Peter Williams, the operation relying solely on the unpaid voluntary work of people like Elaine Shaw, whose long commitment would provide Greenpeace with a thread of continuity over the next sixteen years. In early 1975 Peter Williams reclaimed his office, so until late 1976, when Epicentre opened in the Town Hall, all the work was done from home. Meetings were held at night or on weekends, but activities were hampered by a lack of funds and equipment.

In its embryonic, grassroots stage Greenpeace New Zealand could have evolved in many directions. In April 1974 a Bay of Plenty businessman, Ken Bartrum, was keen to back GPNZ financially as an umbrella organisation to co-ordinate the whole New Zealand peace and environment movement. Long discussions ensued between Bartrum, Mitcalfe, Boyack and Moodie as the prospect of Greenpeace as a big-budget, centralised organisation loomed unexpectedly. But a formal coalition between all these diverse groups was never likely to gel. CND and others were understandably not keen to sacrifice their unique identities and concerns.

The newly gathered core of Greenpeace personnel in Auckland were equally wary of Ken Bartrum's plans, and he in turn was soon put off by their lack of enthusiasm for his ideas. Grassroots fundraising – from street collections, benefit concerts, supporter donations and sales of merchandise – has remained the main method of financing the organisation's activities to the present day. It is doubtful whether GPNZ could have succeeded as a 'top heavy' organisation: many people within Greenpeace now attribute its success to the way it has grown steadily over the years from its grassroots beginnings.

Irene Petersen

Back in Auckland Naomi's mother, Irene Petersen, was by now an active supporter. Irene had grown up in small-town New Zealand. Having spent years learning to downplay her intellect, she had just completed a mature student's degree in psychology and was now relishing the chance to relax. But in a few short months, with Jim Boyack's departure, she was thrust from suburban routine to assuming the role of de facto Greenpeace co-ordinator, taking to her new duties with all the patience and calm she could muster. Irene was now entering the most chaotic and demanding period in her life. *Fri* was already at sea, but money was constantly needed to keep the Odyssey going.

The ship cost just $10,000 a year to run, thanks to her low-tech energy efficiency; it was quite an advantage on remote coastlines far from modern aluminium-welding facilities to be able to obtain a replacement spar or block from the nearest forest. Nonetheless there were crew changes, some unavoidable boat repairs, provisions, publicity – the list went on. With only a small group of volunteers to contribute, life was mayhem. The phone rang constantly; meals were missed or bolted down while the work was done; meetings went on into the night; and there were press releases and interviews to organise. Inexperienced hands were turned to anything from stencilling and duplicating the newsletters to screenprinting T-shirts and posters.

Greenpeace began to totally absorb people, sometimes at the expense of their jobs and home lives. One solution was to involve the whole family. Karen Cauty, another of Irene's daughters, rushed around buying T-shirts and screenprinting them on the kitchen table. Irene recalls the excitement and the pressure of that period: 'We had permanent jobs keeping the Peace Odyssey going, always fundraising, bringing crew home, sending them out, sometimes even shipping food, but always trying to drum up media coverage. We joined with CND and others to organise peace marches. We held dances, jumble sales and film marathons, and sold our T-shirts, posters, books... We rushed around pasting up posters, gave talks and slide shows to schools and any groups who asked us. On top of that there was always the office work, endless letter-writing, mailing out orders and administration, and arranging benefit concerts – we even ran one of the city's nightclubs for one memorable night! Needless to say, all our expenses were met out of our own pockets, as no one was paid by Greenpeace then – we couldn't afford it.'

Karen remembers those as the good old days. She was involved in something she passionately believed in, happy to be working with others who shared her concerns and were prepared to set aside a more conventional lifestyle to work for a cause they felt strongly about. Irene's life from 1974 to 1977 was taken up almost every day with those activities, along with the care of a family and their inconveniently large Birkenhead house. *Fri* crew tended to pass the Petersens' home address to their contacts, and vaguely addressed letters arrived from exotic parts of the world – 'I once had a letter addressed to Mrs Greenpeace!' It was relatively easy to maintain a high level of commitment and energy among the sights and smells and thrills of the voyage, but harder to keep the magic alive back home. The months and years of often monotonous administrative work by Irene Petersen and Elaine Shaw were to provide the solid foundation on which Greenpeace's later successes were based.

Below: Bette Johnson.
Bottom: Elaine Shaw.

Another founding mother of Greenpeace was the ubiquitous Bette Johnson, whose fast and feisty protests, delivered in gravelly Chicago patois, earned her the well-meant nickname of 'the machine-gun for peace'. A longtime civil rights activist who had opposed nuclear weapons since the first tests in the Pacific in the 1950s, Bette was crucial in holding Greenpeace New Zealand together, giving guidance to those unused to campaigning, and providing an invaluable grounding in the art of politics.

Coming from the United States, Bette had a healthy distrust of politicians. In her eyes the New Zealand Labour Government of the early 1970s had little choice, given the strength of public feeling, but to oppose the French tests. She could see, even then, the groundswell of popular feeling against nuclear weapons among New Zealanders, especially after the protest boats started going to Moruroa. 'The French military shot themselves in the foot every time they rammed, boarded and arrested the crews of the protest boats. Even the Brits had the sense to stop nuclear testing in the Pacific in 1962!'

Bette espoused every progressive issue in New Zealand at that time – from women's rights, food co-operatives and Maori language teaching to save the whales and ban the bomb. A compulsive communicator, she dispensed a steady flow of information, wisdom and support to activists all around the Pacific. Bette and her son Giff played an important role in the early years of the Nuclear Free and Independent Pacific (NFIP) movement. Bette was a tireless worker and could often be found sitting in Queen Street, collecting donations and debating the issues with anyone who would listen. But perhaps her most valuable contribution to the peace movement was in cultivating protégés, of whom Elaine Shaw was the first of many. The embryonic

GPNZ group then meeting regularly at her Ponsonby flat were an oddly diverse bunch who thrived on encouragement from Bette and David Moodie.

Bette knew Greenpeace New Zealand would have fizzled out after a few months without the support of a committed group of independently minded people. 'Elaine Shaw was really a key person. Greenpeace New Zealand would not have taken off without her energy, imagination and creativity behind it – and she managed to bring up three kids at the same time!'

Elaine's involvement began in April 1974, when she heard Karen Cauty answering questions about the Peace Odyssey on a radio talkback show. A registered nurse, she was then thirty-five, married, with three young children. It was her first contact with the peace movement, and she became completely involved from day one, at first shy and reserved, but with encouragement she gradually overcame her self-doubt.

Greenpeace was starting to grow, and while many of the early figures in the movement would later move on, Elaine stayed – to become the mainstay of GPNZ for the rest of her life. 'The reason I got involved was simple enough: for my children's future. I had seen the sky turn strange shades of pink after the American bomb tests in the upper atmosphere above Johnston Atoll in the early 1960s. They were visible all over the Pacific. As a nurse and mother, I was concerned about the effects of nuclear fallout on my own and other people's children. Reports had already shown that strontium-90 and other radioactive elements from the explosions were beginning to show up in children's teeth in the Northern Hemisphere. It didn't seem like a particularly pleasant world for my children to grow up in.

'We met and worked in Bette's flat, which had gorgeous tapa cloths all over the walls and newsclips pinned to every inch of wall space left – she was an amazing networker and communicator, forever putting people in touch.'

After 1974 Bette divided her time between Fiji and New Zealand. Elaine and the GPNZ people had the key to her flat while she was away. Elaine learned the story of *Fri* from David Moodie. 'She was dazzled by the new world it opened up for her,' Bette remembers. 'I saw her as a terribly energetic, bright and articulate person. She would shoot off countless telegrams and letters to President Pompidou and other people; she always got things done. It took me a while to realise this was not her natural behaviour.'

Although Elaine never saw herself as an organiser, at that stage Greenpeace needed someone who was ready and willing to grab it and run. 'Things were pretty simple in those days – no computers or huge filing systems,' she recalls. 'A small group of people were able to get out there on the streets and get a fundraising base going to support *Fri*. We used the addresses on the peace cards to compile our first mailing list – 3,000 names at first, which was quite a lot in those days. Those people felt they belonged to Greenpeace. Naomi's reports from *Fri* were inspiring. The group put out a regular newsletter and slogged away at it. They kept going not only out of their own concern, but because people kept coming back to Greenpeace and asking them to do things.'

Bette's time in Fiji was spent working alongside the local ATOM (Against Tests on Moruroa) group, New Zealand CND and the Australian trade unions on the first Nuclear Free and Independent Pacific conference in April 1975, which Kay Couper attended as Greenpeace's delegate. Elaine quickly picked up Bette's enthusiasm for the Pacific. She went to the NFIP conference in Hawai'i in 1980, by which time she'd made such progress networking in the Pacific that she knew almost everyone who was involved in the region. Though not an analytical person, she was doggedly persistent, self-motivated and very hardworking. Above all, says Bette, 'Elaine had integrity, which meant people in the Pacific had confidence in her.'

The Peace Odyssey itself lasted three and a half years, technically ending in Madras, India, in March 1977. (India had joined the nuclear club in 1974.) The Odyssey played a very important role in building up Pacific networks and promoting the concept of a nuclear-free Pacific. Japanese anti-nuclear groups, with whom Barry Mitcalfe had first established contact, wrote to invite *Fri* to their 1975 Bikini Day observance. New Zealand's Owen Wilkes travelled to Japan to make advance arrangements for *Fri*'s visit. Bette Johnson's links with ATOM in Fiji and the Micronesia Support Committee were also invaluable. The project had always been envisaged as a media-oriented action. However, media interest in New Zealand waned with distance, as the lines of communication were stretched. From New Zealand to Saipan in northern Micronesia the ship had no experienced photographer on board, and communications with New Zealand were erratic. It soon became apparent that *Fri* could generate at least some of her working funds at each port of call, which gave an indication of the level of support Greenpeace already had in the Pacific.

Naomi Petersen kept up a vivid correspondence with her family and brought the Peace Odyssey to life in the pages of the small Greenpeace newsletter. Oddly, local media coverage improved as the ship travelled north through the Pacific, where the stories of Greenpeace protests at Moruroa were a passport for *Fri*'s peacenik diplomacy. Some of these occasions were formal. There was a moving ceremony in Tahiti, attended by Francis Sanford and Pouvanaa a Oopa, where the peace cards addressed to France were handed over. At Saipan another formal ceremony saw the delivery of many of the American-addressed cards to Senator Olympia Borja, local representative of the US territory, which were later delivered personally to President Ford. There were also civic receptions with the mayors of Hiroshima and of Nahodka in the Soviet Union. But *Fri*'s crew functioned best on a personal level, and the most important exchanges occurred on the streets, at public meetings, in schools, or when hosting visitors on board the ship.

The Odyssey began with *Fri*'s return to Tahiti's turquoise lagoons on 7 September 1974 to a welcome from local Tahitian anti-testing and independence activists, including old friends the Danielssons and Francis Sanford. During their week-long visit 6,000 peace cards were handed over to Sanford at the Faa'a Town Hall and a breadfruit tree was ceremonially planted in the mayor's garden. Orietta Sloth recorded the occasion: 'After the ceremony we drove back to John Teariki's house, passing by military camps... The palms got thicker and higher, the sea bluer and the flowers along the road redder and redder. We were getting high on the waterfalls and clear streams, but were then brought down by the stories of French nuclear power plants planned for those beautiful green valleys.'

Tree planting ceremony at Faa'a, Tahiti, September 1974. Pouvanaa with white hair, Francis Sanford on his left.

Now with an extra crew member, Tahitian Emile Gfeller, *Fri* sailed on via Raiatea and Tahaa in the Society Islands to Suva in Fiji. The Fijian Government supported *Fri*'s goodwill voyage, and more cards were gathered for delivery. ATOM acted as their local contact, and a benefit concert by folksinger Julie Felix raised funds for *Fri* and for the NFIP conference planned for the following year.

After Suva *Fri* followed the trade winds north to Port Vila in the New Hebrides (then a joint French/British-ruled colony, now Vanuatu), a chain of emerald islands north-west of Fiji, arriving on 5 November 1974. There, boxes of postcards were collected while assorted French and British gendarmes wearing absurd colonial-style helmets and knee-length socks looked on. Because of the tension surrounding land ownership and coconut plantations at the time, the crew decided to plant a wild mountain apple tree. A young Walter Lini spoke enthusiastically in Bislama (pidgin) to the assembled group. This was Greenpeace's first encounter with Lini.

After short visits to Tarawa and Arorae in the Gilbert Islands the ship made for the Marshall Islands. On 10 January 1975 *Fri* arrived at Majuro, the capital of the Marshalls, a region of low-lying, palm-fringed atolls. Later Greenpeace would maintain a close relationship with the cruelly abused peoples of these islands. The United Nations-mandated trust territories of Micronesia (comprising the Marshalls, the Marianas, the Carolines – now the Federated States of Micronesia – and Belau) were the product of a unique post-Second World War arrangement that allowed the US military 'unham-

'Event Baker', Operation Crossroads – US underwater nuclear test at Bikini Atoll, July 1946.

pered' access to and use of the island groups thus artificially grouped together, while aiming to avoid conferring on the US the stigma of colonialism. In return, the United States was legally committed to programmes that would 'promote the economic advancement and self-sufficiency of the inhabitants' and 'protect [them] against the loss of their lands and resources.'

The post-war US establishment interpreted their responsibilities towards the Marshall Islanders in a rather one-sided manner. In 1946 the US Navy began a twelve-year atmospheric testing programme on the Marshallese atolls of Bikini and Enewetak that involved sixty-six nuclear explosions through to 1958. After the devastating impact of the nuclear tests and the mass resettlements and related economic and cultural alienation, many Marshallese found the benevolent promises of their 'protectors' less than convincing. Policies towards the trust territories proved to be consistently determined by the requirements of the US military rather than the health and welfare of the islanders, who were subjected to a long-term policy of neglect and cynical exploitation. It has long been a bitter joke in the trust territories that, finally, the post-war deal meant 'the Micronesians had the trust while the United States got the territory'.

During many of the tests the local people were summarily evacuated. The most notorious bomb test, however, codenamed 'Bravo', took place on Bikini Atoll on 1 March 1954 without any warning to the local population. Bravo, the first test of a deliverable hydrogen bomb, involved the detonation of a 14-megaton thermonuclear device, 1,300 times more destructive than the

'During the course of a routine atomic test in the Marshall Islands, 28 United States personnel and 236 residents were transported from neighbouring atolls to Kwajalein Island according to plan as a precautionary measure. These individuals were unexpectedly exposed to some radioactivity. There were no burns. All were reported well. After the completion of the atomic tests, the natives will be returned to their homes.' *US Atomic Energy Commission press release following 'Bravo'*

'There are only 90,000 people out there. Who gives a damn?'
Henry Kissinger

bomb dropped on Hiroshima. The US Atomic Energy Commission, which conducted the tests, deliberately chose not to warn the people of the neighbouring islands – that morning the wind was blowing in the direction of the two nearby inhabited atolls of Rongelap and Utirik – in order that they could study the test's effects on an unprotected population. As a result these involuntary guinea pigs provided what the US Brookhaven National Laboratory scientists called 'most valuable ecological radiation data on human beings' – data that in human terms translated into the horrors of radiation sickness and a legacy of miscarriages, birth deformities, thyroid tumours and other cancers that persists today. Amongst Rongelap's population under twelve years old in 1954, 90 percent now have thyroid tumours. A survey conducted by the US Government in 1978 found Rongelap and Bikini still heavily radioactive.

Following the Bravo test, the off-limits zone around Bikini was enlarged no fewer than eight times. Finally the area included the inhabited islands of Rongelap, Utirik, Ujelang and Likiep, yet no islands were ever evacuated before subsequent tests. On the day of the Bravo test one of the islanders, John Anjain, woke to what he thought must be the sunrise. Then he noticed it was in the west, not the east. A little while later the sun began to rise in the east, then the sky began to fill with smoke and a strong, warm wind swept Rongelap like a typhoon. The sound of the blast was terrifying. By the time the sun reached its peak a few hours later, a fine white powder began to fall like snow. Some of the children had seen photographs of snow, so naturally they started to play in it. Lemoyo Abon, now a teacher and mother, describes her experiences on that fateful day, now referred to by the islanders as 'the day of two suns': 'I was fourteen at the time and my sister Roko was twelve. With Roko and several cousins, I went to our village on the end of Rongelap Island to gather some sprouted coconuts. One cousin climbed the coconut tree and got something in her eyes, so we sent another one up. The same thing happened to her. When we went home it was raining. We saw something on the leaves, something yellow. Our parents asked, "What's happened to your hair?" It looked like we'd rubbed soap powder into it. That night we couldn't sleep, our skin itched so much. On our feet were burns, as if from hot water. Our hair fell out. We'd look at each other and laugh, "You're bald! You look like an old man." But really we were frightened.'
From Jane Dibblin, Day of Two Suns.

Former Mayor of Rongelap John Anjain and a nephew – among the first islanders to be evacuated by the *Rainbow Warrior* in 1985.

The Rongelap Islanders were not the only ones to witness the infernal sun that day. On the *Fukuryu Maru (Fifth Lucky Dragon)*, a Japanese trawler outside the officially declared danger zone, 100 miles off Bikini, Shinzo Suzuki saw the night sky catch fire in a flare of whitish yellow light that quickly changed to orange, then red. After a few minutes, darkness descended again, to be followed by the tremble of the sound wave, which seemed to come at once from above and below. Frightened by the explosion (the crew remembered how another fishing boat had been lost mysteriously off the Marshall Islands in 1952), they immediately headed homewards, away from the area.

As the trawler voyaged north it, too, was caught in the fallout. In Japan two weeks later all of the crew of twenty-three were suffering from radiation sickness. The ship's radio operator Aikichi Kuboyama died from his injuries late in the afternoon of 23 September. That year some 683 Japanese fishing boats were found to have 457 tonnes of contaminated fish in their holds.

From the top: Bikini Atoll – Orietta and Tobias with audience; Rongelap kids; Nelson Anjain and David Moodie.

Fri arrived in the Marshall Islands on 10 January 1975. After visa problems a sympathetic local senator, Ataji Balos, contacted the crew and arranged for *Fri* to visit Rongelap and Bikini. 'Ataji knew of *Fri* from the Moruroa protest,' recalls Rien Achterberg, who had joined the ship in the Gilbert and Ellice Islands. 'When we contacted the people on Rongelap they were keen to meet us and show us how the testing had affected them.'

Fri sailed to Rongelap, uncertain what to expect. 'Of course we were concerned about radiation, but we felt it was important to go as a sign of solidarity. We arrived to an amazing welcome, everyone singing and clapping. It was very moving.'

The ship stayed for three days and members of the crew heard about the islanders' bitter complaints. It was agreed that Nelson (brother of John) Anjain would travel with *Fri* to Japan to seek independent medical advice from hospitals in Hiroshima with experience of radiation-induced illness.

Fri also made herself practically useful by transporting pandanus and coconut seedlings from Rongelap to Bikini, thereby setting up links that would be renewed with the *Rainbow Warrior*'s work in 1985. 'Bikini was a sad sight,' Rien recalls, 'even worse than Rongelap. There were only a handful of older people there, who were hoping to start life again on their beloved home island. Killi, where some of the Bikinians had been relocated, was also barren. The Bikinians were a forgotten people.'

The Odyssey reached Bikini Atoll one blisteringly hot morning in late January, finding it eerie, unnatural and bare, with no mature trees, and scattered concrete block houses. A 1969 US Atomic Energy Commission report had declared the island safe again, and a few Bikinians began returning to the island the following year. They started replanting coconut trees and rebuilding. However, a 1975 radiation assessment showed ground contamination levels were still so high they were instructed not to try to grow any food. In 1977 monitoring showed a marked increase in radionuclides in the people's bodies – all drinking water and food had to be imported. In spite of this, it was not until 1978 that the people were finally evacuated again and relocated to Killi Island.

The islands to which the Marshallese were evacuated were poor and lacking in natural resources, and illness and malnutrition has been their lot ever since. Naturally they were worried about their health. With little reason to trust the official advice they were receiving from the US authorities, they sought independent medical help. Nelson Anjain later wrote: 'When I was elected magistrate of Rongelap in 1975 I decided to begin the journey to seek assistance for my people, for I began to realise that the living conditions on Rongelap had become disastrous… Therefore in the same year, without any travelling documents, I left Rongelap and my family behind and went to Japan on the yacht [*Fri*] to begin seeking that assistance… I knew then, and I know now, that my destiny was and is not an easy one, and truthfully I don't know when it will be ended.'

Under Mt Fuji – *Fri* at Shimizu, Japan.

The pressure of the Odyssey schedule to reach Japan by 1 March, Bikini Day, ruled out an intended visit to Enewetak, so from Bikini they headed north, into a storm. As Naomi puts it, 'Fri was tossed onto the doorstep of the Japanese coast by the breath of a typhoon.' With torn sails and a broken jib boom, Fri pulled in to the port of Shimizu, beneath Mount Fuji, to a welcome from Japanese peace groups. There they secured special permission to enter the port of Yaizu to participate in the Bikini Day commemoration.

Yaizu, where the fisherman Aikichi Kuboyama was buried, was also the Lucky Dragon's home port. Nelson Anjain, himself a victim of Bravo, laid a wreath on Kuboyama's grave and as a gesture of solidarity presented his widow with a traditional Marshallese navigation stick chart from Rongelap. The Lucky Dragon was then being restored in preparation for its transformation into a peace museum, and Fri crew joined local peace activists in a working day on the boat.

Nelson Anjain's visit to Japan established contacts between the Marshall Islanders and Japan's hibakusha – victims of the Hiroshima and Nagasaki atomic bombs – and other concerned Japanese as well as procuring Japanese medical aid for his people. A further 20,000 peace cards were printed in Japan as Fri sailed from Osaka towards Hiroshima through the inland sea, Seto Naikai – like a vast Bay of Islands, according to Fri's crew.

On 6 August 1975 crew members attended the annual Hiroshima Day memorial service in Hiroshima Peace Park. At 8.15 am, the moment of the bombing, while they stood in front of the park's famous ruined dome, the heavy bronze Buddhist bell struck six times. Just thirty years before, on a hot summer day, this great city had in an instant been transformed into a nuclear wasteland of fire and death, the city centre and tens of thousands of its people turned into ash. Fri's crew collaborated with local peace groups to organise an all-night mini-festival, with theatre, films and music lifting spirits after the Hiroshima proceedings.

Naomi Petersen works on the restoration of the Lucky Dragon.

Fri's next destination was Nahodka, close to Vladivostok, the Soviet Union's main Pacific port and nuclear naval base. One day, after a difficult crossing of the Sea of Japan, out of nowhere a massive Soviet submarine suddenly surfaced beside them – Fri had evidently intruded in the middle of a naval exercise! 'We were soon boarded by an official from a fisheries patrol vessel, who asked us how much fish we had on board,' recalls Martini. 'We replied, "Oh, a couple of tins of sardines." "Why are you in Soviet waters?" We showed him the messages in Russian on our peace cards. "Romantics!" he said, but he seemed to like the idea.'

As Fri approached the Soviet coast in darkness, a searchlight caught the ship in its beam – this time the crew found they had blundered into the huge Soviet nuclear submarine base in the next inlet to Nahodka. In Nahodka at last their reception was friendly and unthreatening. The authorities would allow them to stay and promised to carry out repairs free of charge.

Their first plan was to visit schools, factories and farms to distribute peace cards. Access to schools proved no problem, but getting into the workplaces was another matter. Martini: 'The officials were not too keen for us to go into the factories, so after they'd stonewalled us we just went ahead and set up a street stall with our exhibition on nuclear testing, all translated into Russian – we had a good contact at the Seamen's Mission who did the translations for us. So we put up the exhibition in the middle of the town and started to hand out the messages to passers-by. We collected a fair number of cards and – though these were the repressive Brezhnev years of the Cold War – we found they expressed much the same sort of concerns as those we collected elsewhere on our voyage.'

Before *Fri* left, the crew had planted an avenue of peace trees, which would be visited fifteen years later by the crew of *Vega* on Greenpeace's first return visit to the city.

The Odyssey left Nahodka on 9 November 1975, destination Shanghai, first making a brief detour to Pusan, in the police state of South Korea. Then across the Yellow Sea to Shanghai and the People's Republic of China during

Schoolchildren look over *Fri*'s Rongelap exhibition, Nahodka, Soviet Union.

the final stages of the repressive Cultural Revolution. China, at that time almost entirely cut off from Western contacts, had been seen from the outset as a touchstone for the success of the Odyssey. In the Yangtze River delta, these hopes were dashed when officials discovered the crew had no visas and sent the ship back out to sea. Disappointed, they headed for Hong Kong to try to get visas and to deliver the postcards addressed to Britain. Finally, when all hope of entering China had gone, the crew inadvertently caught a glimpse behind the Bamboo Curtain. *Fri* was seized off the South China coast for sailing into territorial waters and her crew were held for three days in the small city of Chu Hoi Yuen. Soldiers of the People's Liberation Army, sporting green Mao caps with red stars, treated them hospitably. Below the balconies of the building in which they were held, townspeople gathered for hours to catch glimpses of these strange visitors.

A rare sight for Westerners: a sky-blue Chinese submarine and a sailing junk pass by *Fri* at the mouth of the Yangtze Kiang.

Only India remained. With her arrival in Madras in March 1977 *Fri* brought the commitments of the voyage to a close. During an on-board press conference curious wharf labourers gazed down on the ship. When they too added their rupees for peace, the crew were left hoping fervently that the Odyssey had given value for all the generosity they had experienced along the way.

For Naomi Petersen the Pacific Peace Odyssey was a vivid education, both political and nautical, but her abiding memories are of the quieter moments: 'Seeing the great tail of Scorpio like a question mark, punctuated by an old gold waxing moon, set over Moruroa, the wind sighing over the dark

Naomi Petersen talks with students, Cheungchau, Hong Kong, February 1976.

'Sunset 100 miles off Vietnam's coast.'

ocean. Experiencing the Siberian winter high forming off the Tartary Coast as the ship approached Nahodka, lips cracked and pages curled as the parched air lifted the moisture out of the ocean into fine suspension that lay all round our horizon so that it seemed as if we were sailing in the depths of a huge bowl. The magical sense of being suspended in the centre of a vast sphere of space while crossing the Bay of Bengal, the sparkle of phosphorescence over the extraordinarily calm ocean. Sunset 100 miles off Vietnam's coast – spectacular bright green, blue and orange sunbeams flashing across the horizon and distant anvil clouds raising their heads over the land – the start of a wild, clear fullmoon night, racing before a boisterous force seven monsoon.'

What really sets the Pacific Peace Odyssey apart in Naomi's memory was the sense among those involved of being pioneers. 'We were already familiar with the nuclear South Pacific, but beyond lay the unknown, epitomised by the Soviet Union and China. Permission for *Fri* to enter Nahodka came from Moscow, whose official peace policy was well served by a qualified generosity towards us. The xenophobia of the Cultural Revolution defined our reception in China, yet for the brief three days *Fri* was held in the Yangtzhe Kiang we were treated as warmly and courteously as anywhere in our travels.'

Despite the crew's universal identification with the privileged West, there were times when the basic living conditions on board *Fri* permitted an avenue of communication to the Third World people with whom they mixed. In Hong Kong, on the day Martini spoke at the august Hong Kong Jockey Club, Naomi noted in her diary: 'Our wood-gathering forays allow us a way into the local community. A nearby shantytown is a warren of child-sized streets and sheds. I go there to collect water each morning in the dinghy, often being given preferential treatment in the lines of water-sampans, as the women wash under the tap on the shore.' Some of the shanty-dwellers would later visit *Fri* in their sampans, receiving and writing messages on the postcards.

Alexander Shageyev, who helped *Fri* during their Nahodka visit, later wrote to *Fri* crew member Alistair Reese: 'Once, on a sunny October day, I was strolling with a girl in a small square from where Lenin Street starts uphill to the International Seamen's Club. There we saw a big crowd and came nearer to see what it was all about. I was handed a typewritten sheet, which set out the aims of your peace voyage. I interpreted to the people around; then I filled in a peace card and you gave me another card, with a message from Hamilton. A few days later your ship sailed off, but afterwards there were plenty of talks about *Fri*. They remember your ship and your messages.'

'We Sow the Seeds of Peace' was the motto on the peace cards, and in unexpected ways this is what happened.

PART TWO

Sea Changes

CHAPTER FOUR

Whale Soundings

THE WHALES WERE first sighted, stranded on Seagrove Flats, on Thursday by a Maori elder from the Whatapaka Marae while he was out fishing in the Manukau Harbour. It was the first time in his seventy years he had seen whales on the Waiau Pa side of Hikihiki Bank.

Michael Taylor was among the first of the Auckland contingent to arrive the following day. 'When Greenpeace members begin arriving at the beach in the early afternoon, local people from Waiau Pa are already trying to herd a large group into deeper water. Further up the beach other locals, including schoolchildren, are pouring water over the whales in an effort to minimise sunburn and dehydration.

'As the tide rises and the stranded whales begin to float, the volunteers work to steer them towards deeper water. By 4 pm, 160 whales are afloat, though badly disoriented. Some of the whales are already badly sunburnt, large areas of blistered skin peeled off to expose raw red patches. This first attempt to guide them out to deep water proves futile, and as the tide drops, the whales quickly restrand. At this stage 170 distressed whales are counted.

'About 7.30 pm two Fisheries officers arrive. They're sure it's already too late for some of the whales – they try cutting the main arteries, located in their tails, of two whales; with others, they shoot into their blowholes with a .303 rifle. After general discussion we decide on a further rescue attempt during the night to take advantage of the 4.11 am tide. The Fisheries people agree to have one of their officers on the beach to assist.

'We have identified them as false killer whales, *Pseudorca crassidens*, a deep-sea mammal with a tendency, on the rare occasions they approach the shore, to become stranded on shallow, gently sloping beaches. We manage to restore the breathing and balance of most of the whales. Many are on their sides, struggling to breathe, gasping as they heave their blowholes out of the water. If held upright for a time, however, most seem to regain their balance, and their breathing eases. Talking to them seems to help calm them. We are all impressed by their lack of aggression in the face of our clumsy efforts to help, for with their size, strength and large teeth they could easily injure us.

'Contrary to the argument that whale strandings are a form of group suicide, these whales seem to have a strong will to survive and to co-operate with our efforts, even though our touching their sunburnt flanks must cause them pain.

Opposite: Greenpeace confronts Russian whalers, North Pacific, 1976.

'Friends of the Earth are also now on the spot. A radio call by Greenpeace for further assistance brings several offers of boats and over 200 volunteers armed with buckets, sacks, ropes, spades, lights and determination. But the farmer whose land gives access to the beach has the police close his gates to keep people off his drought-stricken pastures, and those arriving are surprised by the lack of knowledge among the officials present.

'Volunteers set out from Waiau Pa wharf after midnight to catch the 4 am tide. In addition to local boaties and fishermen, Greenpeace has organised three boats carrying about fifteen people. Some distance from the beach we come upon a group of over sixty *Pseudorcas*. We drop amongst them in the cold chest-deep water, working in pairs as we try to steer them into the channel. We spend four to five hours in the water with this group until the tide drops around dawn.

'Our whales lie in pairs or small groups. Efforts to split up these groups are resisted, but the rows of whales can be turned by redirecting the whales at either end. The groups are a mixture of strong, healthy whales and weaker, burnt ones supported by their neighbours in the lines. There are obviously strong bonds between them, and when they are brought together there is much whistling and nudging. When the tide begins to drop again, they thrash about in panic, and begin to restrand. Eventually, cold and exhausted, we are forced to wade ashore, the boats retreating with the tide.

The strong, healthy whales support their weaker neighbours in the lines. Waiau Pa, 1978.

'All the whales are shot. Altogether the rescuers have been able to guide between twenty and thirty whales back into deeper water. As we pass by the scene of whales strewn across the mudflats officials wave us away for fear of ricochets as the dull thud of .303 shots ends the whales' ordeal. Even more distressing is the sight of whales whose arteries were slashed the previous evening still thrashing in the mud. On Saturday and Sunday 163 whales are brought ashore by helicopter. Their carcasses are processed into twenty barrels of oil and twenty-two tonnes of whalemeat.'

More than 250 whales died at Waiau Pa during those couple of days in March 1978, and dead whales continued to wash up on Manukau and west coast beaches for weeks afterwards. It was then New Zealand's largest recorded whale stranding. Whales stranded on beaches were at that time still routinely killed. Strandings were a problem environmentalists had long been researching, but at that stage there was little agreement on the cause of this phenomenon, let alone the solution.

It was a traumatic experience for all concerned. Michael Taylor was disappointed by the inability of Ministry of Agriculture and Fisheries (MAF) officials to deal effectively with the stranding. As an active environmentalist he found he knew more about what to do than the officials, and he was convinced that most of the Waiau Pa whales could have been saved had the correct measures been taken.

At dawn, as the tide drops, the whales begin to restrand.

Greenpeace New Zealand was now looking towards new areas of campaigning, and the whaling issue was to be the first of these. Taking up this issue began a new process of education that was to affect everyone's perceptions of the organisation. Some felt that nothing should divert energy from the all-important nuclear issue; others saw it as a natural extension of their nuclear concerns, embracing a concern to protect human health, the environment and the world's natural resources.

It was an expatriate New Zealander who was responsible for first drawing Greenpeace into working for the whales. Paul Spong, a marine biologist researching *Orcinus orca* (commonly known as killer whales) at the Vancouver Public Aquarium, had embarrassed his employers, and lost his job, by publicly claiming that Skana, the orca he was working with, 'wanted to be free'. Spong moved to Hanson Island, close to the Kwakiutl Indian village of Alert Bay, to pursue his work with orcas in the wild. He would swim among them for hours and was astounded by their response to his efforts to communicate. A series of experiments involving music deepened his conviction that these marine mammals were highly intelligent creatures – a view then generally considered absurd. When Spong set about convincing Greenpeace Vancouver in 1973 to establish a campaign to end the mass slaughter of whales for meat and oil, he set in motion a process that would transform Greenpeace from a single-issue protest group into a broader peace and environmental organisation positively celebrating and respecting all life.

The 'Save the Whales' campaign, first launched in 1975, brought in new techniques to Greenpeace Vancouver's direct actions. While poring over photographs of French Navy inflatables during the boarding of *Vega* at Moruroa, Robert Hunter and Paul Spong recalled how Jacques Cousteau had successfully used these versatile craft to get close enough to study and film whales. Very light, and easily and quickly launched from a yacht or ship, the outboard-powered inflatable is above all fast and highly manoeuverable. It was then that they hit upon an audacious plan of action for the new campaign: once the protesters had tracked down a whaling ship they would drive the inflatables between the whale and the whaler's harpoon to deny the harpooner a clear shot. They would act as human shields. This approach seemed to them likely to create real problems for the whale hunters, while remaining entirely consistent with Greenpeace's principles of non-violent direct action.

In April 1975 *Vega* and *Phyllis Cormack,* both freshly painted and displaying the Kwakiutl orca crest formally presented to them by Spong's friends at Alert Bay, were farewelled from Jericho Beach, Vancouver, by more than 20,000 supporters as they headed out into the North Pacific in search of Soviet or Japanese whalers. They caught up with a Soviet factory whaling fleet only fifty miles off the California coast, just in time to witness the slaughter of several adult sperm whales and at least one undersized calf. Their first protests against nuclear testing at Amchitka and Moruroa had taught Greenpeace the importance of good media coverage, that indeed the main purpose of a protest action is its impact as part of the process of public education. So this time they made sure they caught the whole episode on film. By the time the *Cormack* motored into San Francisco Bay, media attention was at fever pitch.

The first Greenpeace protesters were inspired by a 200-year-old Native American myth attributed to a Cree woman named Eyes of Fire, who prophesied that a time would come when the earth would be ravaged of its resources. The sea would be blackened, the streams poisoned, and the deer would begin to die. Before it was too late, the Cree would regain their spirit and teach their colonisers reverence for the earth, banding together with them to become the Warriors of the Rainbow. *(Willoya and Brown*, Warriors of the Rainbow *(1962))*

The *New York Times* eulogised, 'For the first time in the history of whaling, human beings have put their lives on the line for whales.' Greenpeace's eye-witness accounts and photographs were snapped up, and the mission was judged a great success.

Later that year *Phyllis Cormack* confronted Soviet and Japanese whalers off Hawai'i, again using the new direct-action tactics. Paul Spong believed that these two Greenpeace expeditions had directly saved the lives of some 100 whales, while saving an estimated 1,300 indirectly by luring the fleets away from their hunting grounds. They also thrust Greenpeace into the forefront of the burgeoning anti-whaling movement.

Encouraged by their success in the new campaign, the following year Greenpeace extended its marine mammals operations and launched an expedition to Newfoundland to disrupt the annual harp seal cull. Traditionally the indigenous people of northern Canada had taken adult seals for meat, skin and oil. By the mid-1970s, however, commercial sealers were targeting the young pups, whose snow-white pelts were turned into luxury fur coats. Greenpeace Vancouver actions included spraying the pups with a non-toxic green dye, thus ruining their 'value' to the sealers. The Canadian Government's response to this tactic was to draft new laws forbidding the practice. In their next mission Greenpeace hired helicopters to drop activists onto the shifting ice floes off the sealing zone. Here they attempted to shield the defenceless pups from the sealers' picks with their bodies, while all around them they could hear the wails of the mother seals, helpless as their offspring were brutally clubbed to death and skinned.

The *Ohana Kai*, contracted by Greenpeace in Hawai'i, sets out after Japanese whalers in the North Pacific, 1976.

Mike Taylor, Opua 1973.

Internationally, Greenpeace was now primarily associated with the highly emotive issues of whaling and sealing. These campaigns swept up those involved in work whose successes could be recorded in real lives saved. Many people were more comfortable giving their support to protecting endangered species than to the problematically 'political' issues surrounding nuclear weapons. Certainly children, always an important part of Greenpeace's constituency, found these activities easier to relate to. In Auckland Michael Taylor and Patti Kearney took up the whaling issue for GPNZ.

One of those who had helped work on *Fri* in Opua in 1973, Michael hadn't made a conscious decision to work for Greenpeace but found himself drawn in by shared sympathies and ideas. During 1975 he had travelled first to Fiji to meet *Fri*, then on to Vancouver, where he met up with David McTaggart and arranged to send on spare parts to *Fri*. A move to Auckland in 1978 allowed him to get more directly involved in the organisation.

Greenpeace New Zealand joined with others, like Ross Guy from Project Jonah and Michael Bland from Friends of the Earth, who were already campaigning to change the New Zealand Government's pro-whaling policy in time for the upcoming International Whaling Commission (IWC) meeting. In 1978 most people involved in GPNZ were still primarily concerned with the nuclear issue. As Michael Taylor says, 'Whales were very much a fringe thing in those days.' A change of focus would require the New Zealand group to rethink their priorities. Some felt that taking on a completely new issue would spread them too thinly, that it would be better to stick to what they knew rather than take on more than they could cover effectively. But change in Greenpeace is not always by design.

Most New Zealand-based Greenpeace activities in defence of whales and other marine mammals, notably dolphins and seals, were limited to symbolic protests. Greenpeace held embassy vigils and demonstrations, such as the banner protests that met visiting Japanese and Soviet Fisheries Ministers Nakagawa and Ishkov in 1978, and organised petitions like those presented to the Canadian Ambassador opposing the harp seal cull in Canada. Project Jonah and Friends of the Earth had also been organising submissions, petitions and other local educational efforts.

For thirty years the International Whaling Commission, the regulatory body that set the annual kill quotas in the industry, had presided over the commercial extinction of many of the world's great whale species, earning itself a reputation as one of the world's most disastrous management conventions. In that time the Japanese, Soviet, South Korean and Icelandic whaling fleets had wreaked havoc on the oceans' whale populations. New Zealand's pro-whaling stance at the IWC's meetings was a cause for shame, and Michael Taylor was determined to put sufficient pressure on the New Zealand Government to change the way the delegation voted.

At the 1978 IWC meeting, a ten-year moratorium proposed by Panama was dropped without discussion, and the New Zealand delegation was suspected of sharing the US delegation's relief at the move. In the meantime some 23,500 whales were still being killed legally each year. Michael had joined the process of public education and debate to encourage pressure on the Government to take a more positive line at the IWC. Then an unforeseen local event, the great 1978 whale stranding at Waiau Pa, at a stroke did much of the work for him.

In the aftermath of this tragedy, Michael successfully applied on Greenpeace's behalf for a grant to organise a seminar about whale strandings. The aim was to convince MAF officials that in most cases, and with the right approach, stranded whales could be rescued. Greenpeace member, MAF consultant and veterinary scientist Dr Marjorie Orr enlisted the help of the Veterinary Association in organising the seminar, which resulted in MAF's drafting detailed guidelines on rescuing stranded whales, later outlined in a widely distributed booklet.

Greenpeace and others were invited to comment on the Marine Protection Bill that became part of the 1978 Marine Mammals Protection Act, which authorised members of the public to give humane assistance to stranded whales and gave protection to whales and dolphins inside New Zealand's 200-mile economic zone. In fact, there is now a wide public understanding of how to deal with strandings, thanks to the work of Frank Robson, Project Jonah and, more recently, Mike Donoghue with the Department of Conservation.

During this period, events across the Tasman also had a major impact on whaling policies. Since the IWC meeting in Canberra in 1977 whaling had become a national issue in Australia, and popular pressure had led to a commission of inquiry into the industry. The ensuing report was the most significant development in whale protection since 1972, when the United Nations Conference on the Human Environment voted unanimously for a ten-year moratorium on all commercial whaling. The Australian Frost report set a precedent by recommending that Australia prohibit all whaling within 200 miles of its coastline, end imports of whale products and work for a worldwide ban on whaling.

Greenpeace New Zealand continued to publicly challenge visiting Japanese and Soviet ministers on the issue. A 'whale embassy' was established in Wellington to represent the 'whale nation' during IWC meetings. Greenpeace carried a giant model sperm whale in a mock funeral procession through the streets of Wellington to draw attention to New Zealand's poor voting record, and in particular its vote during the November 1978 special IWC meeting in Tokyo, which supported a legal kill quota for 1979 of 3,800 male sperm whales.

Feedback from the IWC conferences remained disappointing; it was difficult to get the information from the meetings needed to bring immediate pressure on the New Zealand Government as the decisions were being made. GPNZ decided to send Michael Taylor to the 1979 IWC meeting in London to keep them informed of developments. Public awareness on the whaling issue had reached a new high internationally. Before the 1979 meeting 15,000 people attended a Friends of the Earth 'Save the Whales' rally in Trafalgar Square, where Michael, kitted out in an orca suit, rubbed flippers with Spike Milligan, Bob Geldof and other star supporters.

Environmental pressure groups were now beginning to play an important role at the meetings. By the time the meeting was opened the ecologists were well organised, and for the first time individual environmental campaigners

Humpback whales – mother and calf.

were able to relay information between countries' delegations as well as to the media. This was especially important because many of the delegations were poorly briefed and depended on Greenpeace and other environmentalists to provide reliable information and advice. Much of the negotiations required complex compromises, some of which were influenced by the lobbyists, especially where delegates were sensitive to public pressure at home.

The outcome of the 1979 London conference was something of a triumph for GPNZ: the New Zealand Government delegation, responding to public pressure, had reversed its traditional pro-whaling voting position, and in May of that year the Minister of Foreign Affairs, Brian Talboys, publicly announced the change of policy. The delegation had evidently found the presence of New Zealand campaigners at the meeting valuable, as Greenpeace was able to provide a representative on it the following year. For the next four years this role was filled by Michael Donoghue, a marine biologist and longline fisherman from Coromandel, his costs met partly by Greenpeace's fundraising 'Save the Whales' concerts in Auckland and partly by Greenpeace International.

From London Michael Taylor joined Greenpeace's international team of campaigners at the IWC meeting in Brighton. In international terms the 1979 IWC conference had been a partial victory for the environmentalists. Although the pelagic whaling moratorium and the Indian Ocean Sanctuary (which prohibited whaling in that area) were achieved, the commission had actually increased the minke kill quota and maintained other quotas. Overall the 1979 quota total was 15,891 whales – just 400 fewer than the 1978 total.

Quotas for whale kills were reduced for the first time, and the meeting also marked the first serious challenge to 'pirate' whaling. Pirate or outlaw whaling referred to the practice whereby IWC member nations such as Japan and Norway bought whalemeat from non-member countries not constrained by the commission's quota system. Chile, Brazil, South Korea, the Philippines, Spain and Taiwan were all used as proxy whalers by Japanese companies. Since the New Zealand delegation at the IWC had elected to follow up the issue, GPNZ agreed to take on this campaign, and the problem was to tax Michael Taylor over the following year.

The full scale of pirate whaling was first brought to light in 1979, when data on the hunting of undersized and protected species by the pirate ship *Sierra* (owned by Norwegians and operated by South Africans and Japanese), as well as other non-IWC activities, was presented to the commission. All the evidence pointed to the involvement of the largest privately owned fisheries company in the world – Taiyo Fisheries. The Japan-based Taiyo Fishery Company, the world's main whalemeat processor, was suspected of being behind the pirate whalers, but there was insufficient information to prove these suspicions.

Michael Taylor set to work with other groups to compile a list of Taiyo products and all its subsidiary companies – nearly 150 of them – for use by anti-whaling campaigners organising boycotts. More importantly, GPNZ was able to initiate research on outlaw whaling in both Chile and the Azores. Michael took the initiative by asking Naomi Petersen and David Moodie on *Fri* to investigate unregulated open-boat whaling in the Portuguese Azores in the North Atlantic. *Fri* and crew had completed a long and fraught voyage to Namibia – Operation Namibia broke an information embargo on the South African-controlled territory by delivering a cargo of banned books – and in early 1979 they were on their way north to Europe for a much-needed refit. Would they be willing to divert their efforts while in the Azores? Of course!

Traditional whaling in the Azores. The harpooned whale breaches and dives again; the launch sets off in pursuit.

As part of the research for this project David and Naomi went out in a small support vessel on a sperm whale hunt carried out from an open whaleboat. A traditional harpoon cannot kill outright, so the whale must be harried and hacked to death – in this case an unusually long ordeal. Soon after their experience, this form of whaling was finally banned. Small-scale as it was, open-boat whaling nonetheless represented a significant threat to the rapidly dwindling species. David and Naomi's account, probably one of the last descriptions of the custom, now stands as a valuable historical document.

Naomi: 'There are only eight traditional whaleboats active in these Portuguese Islands. They are eleven metres long, extremely narrow, and double-ended, rigged for a gaff sail. There are long sweeps for six oarsmen and a long steering oar for the seventh, the master. Several razor-sharp harpoons, spades for cutting work and a large coil of rope are also carried. Each is therefore a replica of the original nineteenth-century Yankee whaleboats that worked from their square-rigged motherships, as

The double-ended whale-boats carry seven crew – six oarsmen, one of whom doubles as harpooner (seen here standing in the bow) and the master.

related in Melville's *Moby Dick,* for the Azores' long isolation has meant this technique has remained unchanged for a hundred years. The only concession to modern technology is that the boats are towed out to the whale ground by motor launch.

'An old-fashioned factory with Dante-esque boilers dripping with the rendered remains of the whale, surrounded by bleached bones and a foul smell, converts the animal into fertiliser, vitamins from the bones and meat and, if the whale is big, up to forty barrels of oil. The cutting or flensing of the whale is still done by hand. David and I have got to know one of the crews and have been offered the opportunity of observing the next whale hunt. Three rockets fired from the shore signal a whale has been spotted from the land lookout. Within ten minutes the crew, master and harpooner have dropped their shore jobs and have the boat in the water.

'When it comes, the hunt is traumatic. It starts early in the morning. On the water the harpooner, in this case a huge-chested young man, is as important as the master, the success of the hunt depending on his strength, accuracy and nerve. He has to heave a seven-kilo harpoon some twenty metres – the boat must be close enough for him to hit the whale but far enough away that the hunters can stay safely clear of its flukes.'

A whale is harpooned at 10.15 am.

David: 'Our launch takes off as soon as we hear on the radio that a whale has been harpooned. We cross a totally quiet, glassy sea towards them. It's a bull sperm whale fifteen metres long. Usually the whalers harpoon, chase and kill their whales in about an hour and twenty minutes, but this is an unusually wary and resourceful whale who has already managed to evade the follow-up lance for two hours. He doesn't seem to tire as he surfaces, spouting several times, then sounds again when the whale boat tries to draw near, hauling the line attached to the harpoon hand over hand. The sounding whale

The follow-up lance is thrown – the whale is already grievously wounded.

stays below for periods over half an hour, dragging along the whale boat at a steady one to two knots.

'Just after midday the whale surfaces again, and the harpooner transfers to one of the launches racing after the whale in order to stab it with the lance. These whalers are unable to kill the whale outright, as they are unable to penetrate far enough into the body to reach vital organs; they must instead wound the animal as much as possible, chasing it until it is exhausted.

'Three hours pass as the whale sounds eight times, displaying flukes as he dives. By three o'clock in the afternoon the whale has 300 metres of rope out. Twice a pod of dolphins swims by us. In the next three hours the whale shows signs of fading. It sounds twenty-three times and spouts more quickly than before, now every six seconds. The sun sets and within an hour the light is all but gone. Some of the crew want to cut the line and let the whale go, but the master, an old man known for his tenacity, elects to hold on through the night.

'Into darkness the whalers work the harpoon line, trying always to keep the tension on it, paying it out when the whale sounds, hauling it in hand over hand when he surfaces. The whalers' hands are by now chafed and bloody. The master and harpooner get no sleep, the other oarsmen only an hour or two draped over their oars. Two nights after full moon, the sky is lit by its soft hazy glow and the sea remains dead calm. No lancing is attempted during the night.

'As dawn breaks the hunt resumes, the whale sounding ten times an hour and by now swimming slowly. The whale boat creeps up slowly, hand over hand, the men rowing the last fifty metres. The harpooner throws the lance repeatedly, now using it to jab deeply without throwing it. Twenty-one thrusts and the whale begins to

The cutting, or flensing, is still done by hand.

spout fountains of blood. He sounds again, grievously wounded, surfacing, flukes askew, then swimming in a slow circle on the surface. Over the following hour the whale is lanced so many times I lose count. He sounds twice more, surfacing almost immediately, then lies still in the water only just maintaining his balance, the men now taking turns at stabbing.

'When the boat withdraws the whale still takes another two hours to die, wallowing in a widening pool of blood until he rolls on his side. Nearly twenty-four hours after being harpooned the whale finally dies.

'It is a deeply shocking hunt, the whale not so much killed as tortured to death. The only redeeming factor is that the slow death of this one whale will mean safety for others.'

David and Naomi's report of this experience went to the IWC and a ban on this method of whaling was subsequently introduced.

Despite the quota setbacks the 1979 commission meeting marked a turning-point. After years of patient work and active lobbying, and with generous support from sympathisers all over the world, not least in New Zealand, Greenpeace and other environmental groups had helped turn the tide against the whalers, using the mechanisms of the IWC.

Greenpeace New Zealand launched its boycott of Taiyo products in 1981. But what was really needed to stop the pirate whalers was to catch them red-handed and prove to the world what was happening. This was the task GPNZ set itself.

In 1980 New Zealander Paul Bruce was working at Nadi airport in Fiji as a weather forecaster. He was involved with local trade unions and active in anti-nuclear work, often, in the company of fellow activist Lopeti Senituli, sparring publicly with the French Ambassador to Fiji. Fijian anger over the continuing French nuclear tests still ran high. Many of the older villagers had vivid memories of the nuclear aurora in the 1960s following the high-atmosphere US tests in the northern Pacific, but the primary focus of their anger was the French Government, whose persistent high-handed dismissal of the local people's real concerns over the health effects of the Moruroa tests betrayed an imperious arrogance that outraged many Fijians.

Paul decided to write to Greenpeace New Zealand, offering to help in its anti-testing campaign. As a result Michael Taylor began corresponding with him, which led to Michael's raising the subject of pirate whaling in Chile. 'I was very pleased when Michael told me of the pirate whaling operation in Chile, as I was planning to go there to get married at the completion of my contract. Five years before, I had spent two years working in Chile, Bolivia and Peru and had grown to love their spontaneous cultures and to respect the ordinary people in their struggles against militarism and US domination.'

In Chile Paul divided his time between investigating the pirate whalers and probing human rights abuses. Together with his Chilean wife, Catalina, Paul visited Talcahuano. 'I really didn't know where to start investigating the whaling operation, and visited Talcahuano just on spec at first. With hindsight we were exceptionally lucky to catch the pirate whalers in port and get such good photos, but my initial approaches got nowhere once the officials became suspicious of me. Returning to Santiago, I renewed my contacts with various active socialists and Allende supporters who provided me with the names of reliable people and trustworthy trade union officials. Here local trade unionist Juan Sepulveda told me of the disastrous impact of the newly unleashed free-market economy on Chile's marine species and forests.'

On Paul's third trip to Talcahuano a comprehensive itinerary was arranged for Paul by local trade unionists, including visits to the universities and the shore whaling station and interviews with sailors who had worked on the factory ship and in the refrigeration unit. Paul recorded valuable interviews on tape. 'The locals had a great way of talking amiably and inconsequentially to me in initial conversations, and only really speaking out after they were sure I was genuine and trustworthy.' A key contact in Santiago was Godfredo Stutzin, who had worked for environmental causes most of his adult life, adopting Francis of Assisi as a role model. Once Godfredo was convinced of Paul's trustworthiness he found a young university student, Hernan Verscheure, to accompany him on his dangerous journeys investigating the clandestine whaling industry.

By the end of his journey Paul had incontrovertible documentation of Chile's 'free enterprise' pirate whaling operation. What's more, he was able to return to New Zealand just ten days before Mike Donoghue was to leave for England and the 1980 IWC meeting, where the report would be released.

Evidence of pirate whaling was a feature of the 1980 IWC conference in Brighton, where whaling countries were forced to accept further concessions.

Flukes of a humpback whale in Gerlache Strait, Antarctic Peninsula.

Though moves sponsored by environmentalists to impose a moratorium on commercial whaling failed, the 'whale nation' was slowly but surely gaining ground. Quotas were down to 14,000 compared to the mid-1970s figure of 46,000. The New Zealand delegation successfully pushed for further discussions on pirate whaling, an issue on which Greenpeace had been very active during the previous year, including very visible protests during the January visit by Japan's Prime Minister. And the inclusion of Greenpeace expert Michael Donoghue as the nongovernmental organisation (NGO) representative gave GPNZ good access to the proceedings.

The previous year the New Zealand delegation had promised to investigate pirate whaling. Now, without a governmental finger being lifted, Michael Donoghue was able to hand the officials a comprehensive and incontestable Greenpeace report of one such operation, and an embarrassed Chilean delegation immediately undertook to cease all whaling.

Pirate whaling in Chile has remained unviable since 1980 only as a result of the close watch kept by committed local activists over the following years. Michael Taylor sums up the story: 'All our evidence was collected in just a few weeks by a lot of people with a lot of guts. None of the IWC governments made any attempt to find out what was going on in Chile.'

'GPNZ's whaling campaign went from strength to strength after 1980,' recalls Carol Stewart, who had joined the staff the previous year. 'Michael Donoghue was NGO advisor to the New Zealand delegation to the IWC. Tom Donahue took over from Michael Taylor on marine mammals. Patti Kearney took the seals issue under her wing, as well as running the merchandise operation, and the rest of us just helped when and where required.'

The big breakthrough for the anti-whaling groups came in 1982, when the IWC voted twenty-five to seven in favour of a halt to all commercial whaling,

Pirate whalers – Talcahuano 1980.

to be phased in over three years. Although the Japanese were expected to ignore the ban – indeed, Japan, the Soviet Union, Norway and Peru had all lodged objections to the decision – the whaling industry had suffered a major setback, and Greenpeace was justifiably pleased with its lobbying efforts over the years.

While the loophole of 'scientific whaling' (which was justified as valuable scientific study rather than commercial exploitation) would continue to occupy Greenpeace at subsequent IWC meetings, the way was now open to pursue other marine mammal issues. Whaling was the most popular cause in environmental work concerning marine mammals, but there were other scourges with equally drastic consequences for marine life. Driftnet fishing, for example, was responsible for the deaths of thousands of smaller whales, porpoises and dolphins each year; dolphin and seal culling continued in Japan and Canada; and in New Zealand, Hooker's sea lions, fur seals and Hector's dolphins were all in danger from trawlers and set nets. The time was now ripe to tackle these issues. Over the coming decade campaigns encompassing the whole marine environment would take shape.

CHAPTER FIVE

Rocking the Boat

'I BACK-PADDLED to give the sub lots of time to see me. The captain must have, as I could see him clearly on the conning tower, but the sub held its course – straight at me. The bow wave hit me, pushing me off centre then over the side of the bow, slamming me nose first into the side of the sub. He ploughed straight over us and obviously didn't care what happened to those in front of him.'

Terry Bell was hurled aside by the giant nuclear submarine USS *Haddo* as it cut through the blockade of yachts, dinghies, kayaks and surfboards thronging the entrance to Auckland harbour, his kayak wedged between the submarine and Pat MacQuarrie's speedboat. At that moment Stephen Sherie leapt from the speedboat onto the sub and threw his arms in the air running up the

Opposite: Chris Robinson manoeuvres *Vega* ahead of the USS *Phoenix*, 1983.

'Hot welcome' – Stephen Sherie takes to the *Haddo*'s foredeck.

black steel deck, by now spattered with yellow paint-filled eggs. Defiant, but with more than a touch of slapstick, he yelled at the captain to 'turn the bloody thing around!' It was 19 January 1979. 'Hot Welcome for a Yellow Submarine' ran the *Auckland Star*'s headline.

The *Haddo* protest was the climax of the Auckland Peace Squadron's first phase. US Ambassador Anne Martindell would later claim that she advised against further US naval visits during her posting to New Zealand, considering them 'not in the best interests of the United States', though Owen Wilkes believes the eighteen-month lull probably had more to do with the Three Mile Island reactor emergency than developments in New Zealand. There would be no nuclear-powered ship visits to Auckland for five years, until 1983, though nuclear-armed warships continued to call in occasionally, and there was no let-up in either type entering Wellington Harbour.

The Peace Squadron actions, inspired by Gandhi's philosophy of civil disobedience, while in the mould of the non-violent but direct and vigorous tactics that had become Greenpeace's trademark, were nonetheless quite independent of Greenpeace. The blockaders knew they could never completely halt the visits without a sympathetic government. The game (and, despite its deadly serious message, it was fun for many who participated, in a way that the Moruroa voyages rarely were) was to generate headlines, so raising the profile of the debate.

It was the election of Robert Muldoon's National Government in 1975 that thrust the twin issues of nuclear ship visits and nuclear power onto New Zealand's political agenda. Energy issues were already at the forefront of the

Campaign Half Million on the march, Auckland waterfront, 1976.

environmental debate in the 1970s. The fuel price rises that followed the 1973 oil shock prompted investigations into alternative energy sources and other means of protecting the economy from overseas price fluctuations. This was good news for New Zealand environmental groups advocating greater energy efficiency and ways of reducing dependence on imported oil. What they had not bargained for was that the nuclear option might be seriously considered in a country with potential for many green alternatives.

An inquiry into the viability of nuclear-generated electricity for New Zealand was planned for late 1976. In March more than twenty anti-nuclear and environmental groups, and individuals from Greenpeace, met in Wellington to decide on a response. What emerged was the Campaign for Non-Nuclear Futures (CNNF), a loose coalition set up to oppose the introduction of nuclear power in New Zealand and to promote renewable energy alternatives, such as wind, wave, solar and geothermal power. Pressure was on the coalition to mount a massive public education exercise. CNNF produced their own international experts to counter the pro-nuclear arguments of members of the Government and the international nuclear industry. Professor Walter Patterson, brought over by Friends of the Earth, presented a particularly authoritative package of alternative energy arguments during an exhausting national tour.

CNNF's main lobbying tool, launched in June and organised by Raewyn Mackenzie and Birdie Mann, was Campaign Half Million, a petition against nuclear power that aimed to collect half a million signatures.

Campaign Half Million produced the then largest petition in New Zealand's history, with 333,087 citizens signed up by October 1976, drawing together radical and conservative opinion. It was a gruelling campaign with two vital goals: to check the momentum towards nuclear power in New Zealand and to deny nuclear-powered warships access to her harbours.

Irene Petersen was one of those who collected signatures for the petition. 'I tramped many of the streets of Birkenhead and Beachhaven, door-knocking, talking to people and gathering signatures. I put posters and pamphlets in shops and doctors' surgeries, and set up my table in shopping centres during the day – in the evenings too when there were late shopping nights. A great many others across New Zealand were doing the same. It was utterly exhausting but immensely valuable as a public education campaign.'

The Royal Commission on Nuclear Power Generation in New Zealand was set up in September 1976. Irene and Elaine Shaw prepared the Greenpeace submission, one of several presented to the commission at its Auckland sitting on 5 May 1977. The royal commission report, which in general rejected New Zealand's need for nuclear power, was tabled in Parliament in May 1978. The National Government, unable to ignore the strength of feeling against nuclear power, stopped short of rejecting the option altogether, declaring instead that a decision could in the meantime be deferred. It was nonetheless seen as a backdown by the Government and a victory for the soon-to-disbanded CNNF coalition.

The five-month period from June to October 1976 was crucial for the anti-nuclear movement in New Zealand. It saw the first two hectic Peace Squadron actions and the first of the really big anti-nuclear marches. It included

Campaign Half Million and the preparation of public submissions to the royal commission. It was the most concentrated period of public debate and education on the nuclear issue the country had experienced. Inevitably this led to a further hardening of anti-nuclear attitudes, which had been spreading since Peace Media's first sorties into the testing zone, and in which groups such as CND had long played an important part.

But GPNZ had more immediate concerns. When Bette Johnson moved to Fiji in 1975, the group was faced with the need to find a new base. The problem was eventually solved by an arrangement that drew Greenpeace together with other environmental groups around the nuclear energy issue. The Environment and Peace Information Centre – Epicentre for short – was set up in late 1976 in a pleasant, well-lit area on the third floor of the Auckland Town Hall, later moving to a poky little shop in Upper Symonds Street. The centre allowed CND, Ecology Action, Greenpeace and other small voluntary groups to pool their meagre resources and share office and meeting space, an old Gestetner machine for running out leaflets and educational material, and volunteer help to organise school and public seminars. Pitching in together also helped to spread information and stimulate debate.

By the mid-1970s Auckland was alive with pressure groups: Project Jonah was fighting for the whales; Ecology Action was doing its best to address local ecological issues; Friends of the Earth, CND and others had their own niches. In practice, though, the borders between the groups' activities were sometimes hazy. People often belonged to more than one group; different activists would attend one another's meetings, pitching in together when a specific action was called for. From the early days New Zealand's effective pressure groups managed to avoid most of the factionalism that plagued Europe's peace movements.

Between 1977 and 1981 Elaine Shaw took her turn at running the shop, organised demonstrations every Bastille Day, fired off endless letters to friends and allies across the Pacific, to local friends of *Fri*, and of course to nuclear apologists at home and abroad: her persistent acid pen was an irritation to successive French ambassadors. For the meantime at least, the domestic nuclear power debate had been won. The more contentious issue of nuclear ship visits was to embroil the anti-nuclear movement in a much longer and more acrimonious struggle.

US nuclear-powered and -armed ship visits to New Zealand ports increased over the decade to 1985. There had been 120 such visits since 1960. Concern about the dangers of nuclear-powered ships, especially in or near population centres, increased after two US nuclear submarine reactor accidents at sea in the 1960s. A request in December 1971 for visiting rights for an American nuclear submarine was refused by National Prime Minister Keith Holyoake on safety grounds. This informal ban on nuclear propulsion was upheld by the 1972-75 Labour Government, though visits by nuclear-armed vessels were permitted to continue.

Under pressure from the United States, the National Party Opposition and the media, Kirk's successor, Bill Rowling, announced in July 1975 that the Government was 're-examining its policy of not permitting nuclear-powered ships to call at New Zealand ports'. By this time, however, there were plenty

The Auckland Peace Squadron confronts the USS *Long Beach*, Waitemata Harbour, October 1976.

of New Zealanders, following the example set by the Moruroa protest boats, who were prepared, personally and actively, to oppose this particular aspect of the nuclear threat.

Auckland City, blessed with two sheltered harbours and an inviting climate, is probably home to a greater proportion of small-boat owners than any other city in the world, and its traditionally libertarian boatie community provided the core of the distinctive protest movement against the US ship visits. In November 1975 George Armstrong, a lecturer at St John's Theological College, and several others set up the Auckland Peace Squadron as an open group for people with their own boats who wanted to protest actively against the nuclear visits. Over the years St John's has produced many firm friends of the peace movement and other progressive causes, not least among them Walter Lini of Vanuatu.

George had been one of *Fri*'s many supporters at the college. 'The Moruroa protests had captured people's imaginations, and I wanted to organise something equally imaginative that might also be fun. To this end we had picnics and parties after the actions on the harbour, so we were able to relax in a way that stopped us all burning out too quickly.' The Peace Squadrons, which had spread into the provinces by the 1980s, received their prime support from the Anglican Church, combined church peace groups and the Labour Party. They were to prove an influential and enduring vehicle for active peaceful protest, and one that Greenpeacers were quick to involve

The daring surfboard riders – 'the first New Zealand kamikazes'.

themselves in. Bernard Rhodes, recently returned from *Fri*'s Peace Odyssey, became an active member, as did Joan and Ron Cavaney and numerous others who had helped with *Fri* and the other early Moruroa voyages.

In 1975 the new National Government wasted no time in displaying its pro-American colours by abandoning the ban on nuclear propulsion. Soon after the election Muldoon met US Pacific forces commander Admiral Gaylor. After a half-hour chat the Prime Minister emerged to announce that nuclear-powered ship visits would resume immediately. Greenpeace's request that an inquiry into the possible environmental impact of nuclear accidents be set up was brusquely dismissed, as were efforts to persuade the Government to co-sponsor a South Pacific nuclear-free zone treaty through the United Nations.

On 27 August 1976 the nuclear-powered guided-missile cruiser USS *Truxtun* entered Wellington Harbour during a south-westerly storm to a reception by six small craft of the newly formed Wellington Peace Squadron. Not exactly an armada, but with the land-based vigils in Auckland and Wellington that accompanied the action, a good start to the new campaign. The City of Sails could draw on a far larger resource, and a visit to Auckland by the nuclear cruiser USS *Long Beach* in October was met by a blockade of some eighty craft, including several audacious surfboard riders. Determined action succeeded in halting the *Long Beach* several times before it elected to anchor in the stream.

Irene Petersen was on Takapuna Beach the day the *Long Beach* arrived and remembers the scene well: 'People had been preparing for days. Some of us had decided to have hot food and drink ready on the beach for those returning from the foray on the water. The night before, Elaine came over to our house in Birkenhead. We had a big sheet spread across the lounge and paints all over the floor and worked till late that night. The banner, our pride and joy, read "WRONG BEACH, LONG BEACH!"

'Early morning, Friday 1 October. Cold but fine. We were up at 3 am and away by 4.15, picking up people on the way. There was a tremendous air of excitement, with cars already arriving as we drove down to the Takapuna launching area. Through the darkness we could see there was already a lot of activity out on the water. Small lights bobbed up and down, and voices drifted back to us across the water.

'It was a wonderful sight to see those little boats halt the *Long Beach* three times! In the end the ship just kept moving, ignoring all the little boats around it. I just hoped they could read our banner as they passed into the inner harbour. Dishevelled and cold, but still excited, people began to arrive back at the ramp in little boats of all shapes and sizes, as the smell of the barbecue and hot fresh coffee wafted over the beach.'

By the time the nuclear attack submarine USS *Pintado* arrived on 14 January 1978, the Auckland Peace Squadron was able to muster a formidable ninety-three boats and to present both the US Navy and the harbour police, now employing helicopters, with a sizeable challenge. The protest successfully delayed the submarine and produced 'Kiwis Take on Nuclear Sub' headlines around the world.

Marching against the *Long Beach*, Auckland waterfront, 1976. Elaine Shaw, far right.

The 'mutants march' – Greenpeace street theatre, Auckland 1979.

A few weeks later a victorious Muldoon announced that a second nuclear submarine, the USS *Haddo*, would visit Auckland the following January. This time Greenpeace joined with the Peace Squadron, CND and others in taking out an ultimately unsuccessful injunction to stop the visit on the grounds that allowing such a ship to enter the harbour without a towing escort would be a violation of the Government's own Nuclear Shipping Code. Port authorities had sidestepped this regulation for fear that the protesters would exploit it to obstruct the ships' entry.

In New Zealand as elsewhere, growing numbers of people were coming to question their political leaders on a wide range of issues, but especially environmental and nuclear matters. The nuclear ship visits and nuclear power controversies provided Greenpeace and other peace and environmental groups with the opportunity to inform an increasingly receptive public.

Greenpeace picket during French Naval visit to Auckland.

A theatrical anti-testing march, Auckland 1982.

During the 1970s, and especially after 1974, when Britain, still the 'Mother Country' to many New Zealanders, joined the Common Market, sweeping away the economic safety net on which generations of New Zealand producers had relied, there began a process of national re-examination that had implications for New Zealanders' perceptions of themselves in a changing world and their identity as a South Pacific nation. For Greenpeace pioneers like Elaine Shaw and Bette Johnson, a Pacific orientation had always underwritten their anti-nuclear work. Common cause in opposition to nuclear testing had been made with other Pacific nations, with whom we shared an experience, though of vastly different rank, of the imperial arrogance of the nuclear nations. The 'Mother Country', of course, had carried out her own nuclear testing programme in the Pacific during the fifties and sixties. Even at this stage, there was a recognition by many involved that the nuclear issue could not be neatly separated from broader concerns. Perhaps what was required was for small countries such as New Zealand to develop an independent voice, which in itself could be a source of pride.

Looking for a place in the world had made New Zealanders more aware of the nuclear threat, a questioning process that underpinned later change in the 1980s. Already, dissenting Maori and women's voices were being raised over land, language and equality. These voices would soon be joined, in the highly charged aftermath of the 1981 Springbok tour mobilisation, by the mass peace demonstrations of the early 1980s.

For Elaine, one of the frustrations of being based in Auckland was that the main target of the local anti-testing campaign, the French Embassy, was in Wellington. When the Peace Odyssey was being planned in 1974 it had been a toss-up between basing Greenpeace in Auckland or Wellington, but in the end the fact that Irene and Hugh Petersen, Bette Johnson and other strongly committed people were based in Auckland was decisive. 'We had lots of marches in Auckland. In the late 1970s we really got going, with regular Bastille Day marches on 14 July, Hiroshima Day marches on 6 August, Bikini Day demonstrations on 1 March – later that became Nuclear Free and Independent Pacific [NFIP] Day – and then marches or vigils whenever there was a nuclear ship or French naval visit. Hiroshima Day especially was used to promote a nuclear-ships ban, a South Pacific nuclear-free zone treaty and a non-aligned policy for New Zealand. Mostly these marches were still quite small, but we tried to make them visually interesting, with colourful banners and street theatre.'

Four minutes to midnight – Mark Roach (left) and Phil Scotford outside the Soviet Embassy in Wellington.

The Greenpeace group in Wellington, though small, was often energetic and enterprising. 'It seemed to come in waves. Sometimes an enthusiastic bunch of people would come up with really imaginative protests; at other times they were happy just to sell T-shirts,' says Carol Stewart, then a new face at Epicentre. Tensions between the Wellington and Auckland groups arose periodically, some in Wellington feeling marginalised and undervalued, but a second office was rarely economically viable then, and Auckland remained the hub of the organisation. In the early 1980s Mark Roach and

Phil Scotford ran a dynamic and effective Greenpeace operation in Wellington, and for most of 1984 they maintained a full-time Greenpeace office in the capital.

When David Moodie, Martin Gotje and Naomi Petersen attended the newly formed Greenpeace International's council meeting in 1980 as observers for GPNZ, they discerned a shift back to the nuclear priority. Tentative proposals were put forward to set up a 'Nuclear Free Pacific' campaign and to organise a visit by Greenpeace's flagship, the *Rainbow Warrior,* or *Vega* to Moruroa as part of a new international campaign against nuclear testing. McTaggart was keen: 'The Moruroa campaign put Greenpeace on the map and we should finish it.' It was agreed that *Vega* should return in 1981.

The first step was to send someone who would not be linked to Greenpeace to Tahiti to follow up contacts there and try to interview workers from the test site. Roger Wilson, who had visited Tahiti on a separate research trip the previous year and knew the issue quite well, was working for Friends of the Earth in Auckland. He agreed to take on the mission, and in October he flew to Papeete, then visited the islands of Huahine and Moorea. Though he talked to a wide range of people, a conspiracy of silence seemed to surround the subject of the tests. Few Polynesian workers were prepared to speak to him, partly for fear of losing their jobs and partly because he was a European and an outsider. The voyage, however, proceeded on schedule.

Vega left Manzanillo in Mexico on 30 October 1981, on her third voyage to Moruroa, this time a 4,000-mile sail with the prevailing winds. The crew of five comprised American radio operator Lloyd Anderson, Brice Lalonde, South African-born Tony Marriner, David McTaggart and Australian Chris Robinson. Lalonde, of Servan-Schreiber's 1973 Bataillon de la Paix, was now president of the French Ecology Party and had polled one and a half million votes in the recent French Presidential election.

Elaine and Roger worked on the New Zealand end of the expedition, liaising with their Tahitian contacts and producing materials in English and Maohi for distribution in the islands. The Maohi language booklets to be distributed by the Polynesian Evangelical Church were seized for a time by the authorities, increasingly edgy after news of a spate of accidents on Moruroa in 1979 leaked out via workers at the test site.

Vega crew, 1981 (from left): Lloyd Anderson, David McTaggart, Tony Marriner; front: Chris Robinson, Brice Lalonde.

Nineteen eighty-one was an even worse year at Moruroa. A cyclone in March had torn away tarseal covering a plutonium spill on the northern side of the atoll, sweeping 20 kilograms of plutonium debris about the atoll and into the lagoon. A second storm in August scattered more irradiated waste about the atoll. Two and a half thousand civilian technicians on Moruroa threatened to strike if the radioactive waste littering the atoll was not cleaned up. The French trade union representing the CEP workers released a report revealing that loose barrels of radioactive waste had been washed up on beaches around the atoll. The report estimated that the atoll had sunk one and a half metres since the start of underground testing, and that this had caused an underwater crack to appear that could be leaking radioactivity into the ocean.

At least fifty underground tests had been carried out under the atoll's 25-kilometre outer rim by 1981. Because of the cavity formed by each explosion, the bomb shafts had to be drilled 400 to 1,000 metres apart. Official documents confirm that each detonation creates a chimney up to 350 metres high – more than 200 metres of fracturing radiating out from the cavity. In November, in protest at the continuing veil of secrecy, three CEA engineers released a public statement claiming that radioactivity levels had doubled in the previous four months, and that the north beach of the atoll was a vast radioactive rubbish heap measuring 30,000 square metres. They also spoke out about the storms in March and August that had exposed and scattered irradiated debris into the ocean. After fifty tests, the CEA had run out of space under the atoll's rim (technicians jokingly referred to the atoll as 'like Swiss cheese'), so in December 1981 they brought in a huge drilling rig that enabled them to begin sinking new shafts directly under the lagoon.

From the zone *Vega* called on President Mitterrand to agree to a comprehensive ban outlawing all nuclear tests and to allow an independent scientific team to carry out an environmental analysis of Moruroa. Six weeks later, with supplies running low, the protesters received a reply via the Greenpeace office in Paris: The Government of France would not stop the testing, but it would allow an independent scientific survey of Moruroa. Could this be true? *Vega* sailed to Tahiti to await developments. It was to be a very long wait.

Following up on France's promise, in January 1982 Greenpeace New Zealand, in consultation with Les Amis de la Terre in France, submitted a proposal to the French Government for a geological and epidemiological survey of Moruroa. Instead of negotiating on a team of independent scientists both parties could agree on, however, the French hijacked the proposal to organise their own 'independent' mission and reneged on their promise to allow Greenpeace a say in the survey.

Later that year Paris sent a team hand-picked by Defence Minister Charles Hernu and led by vulcanologist Haroun Tazieff. The Tazieff mission, which spent just three days on Moruroa, produced a report that generally downplayed the risks of the tests but was nevertheless highly critical of the safety and environmental monitoring. Tazieff admitted there were still significant amounts of radioactivity in the environment from the atmospheric tests, but said further study was needed to ascertain the risk of radioactive release into the ocean through cracks in the atoll following underground tests.

There was now a steady flow of new blood into GPNZ's Auckland office. One newcomer was Jane Cooper, just home from England, where she had been active in CND. 'I came into the Auckland office and spoke to Elaine, who quickly seized on my ability to speak French, so I started by translating endless French documents. Over the years Elaine had built up extensive files on political struggles in the Pacific, so an apprenticeship under Elaine was an excellent introduction to the world of NFIP activism.'

With no breakthroughs in negotiations with France for an independent survey, it was decided that *Vega* should return to the zone to keep up the pressure. Jane was sent to Tahiti for two months to help support the next voyage and liaise with the media, and here she met with Tahitian activists Tea

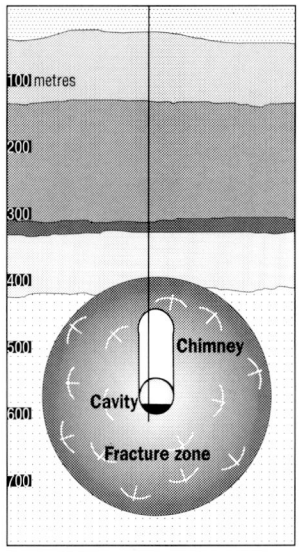

Schematic section of a Moruroa bomb shaft, cavity and fracture zone.

Jane Cooper

Hirshon, Oscar Temaru, Charlie Ching, Henri Hiro and Jacqui Drollet, all leaders of local anti-testing and independence parties. 'In the past Greenpeace had got itself a bit of a reputation as a bunch of great white heroes who would swoop down on the testing site. We were keen to change this perception and work with the local activists.'

Party politics in Tahiti had become more complex since *Fri*'s visits in the 1970s. Some Tahitian political parties chose not to work with Greenpeace because it had no explicit pro-independence policy. There was apprehension, as elsewhere in the Pacific, that outside groups would try to impose their own structures and priorities on indigenous groups striving for self-determination. Jacqui Drollet was not ready to publicly align his party, Ia Mana Te Nunaa, with Greenpeace but, like Charlie Ching's Te Taata Tahiti Tiama party and Oscar Temaru's Tavini Huiraatira (Polynesian Liberation Front), his party was prepared to collaborate in areas of common interest, allowing each group to maintain its own integrity.

Oscar Temaru laying a wreath commemorating Tahitians who died during two world wars.

When Jane sought out workers from Moruroa she again found most were too frightened to speak out. Those who were prepared to speak to her did so in secret, fearing police harassment and the loss of their jobs. But Tahiti came to life for the festival Jane helped organise with Tea Hirshon and the Polynesian Liberation Front. Tea: 'It seemed logical that we work together to organise a peace festival, as that seemed to be what people were into then and I had contacts with a lot of musicians. It was really magical because it happened really quickly and didn't cost us a cent. I suppose we wanted to reach a different and wider audience and raise awareness of the effects of the tests. Political rallies were held every year but they were preaching to the converted. We wanted to reach out.' Called 'Puhi Hau', Maohi for 'Breath of Life', the event drew an enthusiastic crowd and featured traditional Polynesian musicians like Bobby Holcomb, rock groups, political speakers and poets – all openly opposed to testing and French colonialism. Marie-Thérèse and Bengt Danielsson were there too, helping to liaise between Greenpeace and local groups.

Jane's stay in Papeete did much to strengthen Greenpeace's links with the people of Tahiti. It was clear to her that protesting off Moruroa was by itself inadequate. It was still difficult to interest the international media in these remote actions. The 1982 voyage, which received Greenpeace International's approval late, had been arranged hastily, and Jane could find only one Tahitian crew member. 'I had hoped more would be willing to go, but too little notice was given. Tahitians prefer to take their time before jumping into something like this, which is a far more dangerous proposition for them than for us.'

The Danielssons, who brilliantly catalogued the cultural, political and economic effects of French testing in their book *Moruroa, Mon Amour* (later revised and extended as *Poisoned Reign*), had always been among Greenpeace New Zealand's most dedicated correspondents. Having lived and worked in Te Ao Maohi for more than thirty years, they were able to help clarify for Jane the risks Tahitians ran in openly defying French colonial rule. 'The issue for Greenpeace in Tahiti had to be one of finding ways to oppose the nuclear tests that were appropriate in relation to the independence movement. That trip

Henri Hiro, president of Ia Ora te Natura, a Tahitian ecology group, addresses the crowd at the Puhi Hau peace festival, 1982.

proved to me that making personal contacts is a better way to get results than assembling a file of dry facts. Greenpeace needed to be seen in Tahiti not as some impersonal organisation but as individual people. Elaine was doing this before me and the work has since been carried on by others.'

Vega and skipper Chris Robinson had remained in Tahiti all year after the promise of a jointly arranged scientific survey. Finally, in October 1982, with France still stalling, they returned to the zone. This time Chris's crew were Tahitian Guy (Jacky) Taero, of the independence group Te Taata Tahiti Tiama, Lloyd Anderson and Briton Jon Castle. A week after *Vega* arrived off the twelve-mile limit, marines from *La Hippopotame* boarded and arrested the crew and towed the yacht to Moruroa again. Guy Taero was released while the other crew were held for twenty-four hours and were forced to sign a document agreeing never to return to French Polynesia before being deported. *Vega* was held for a year before being returned to New Zealand on board a freighter in 1983.

In 1982 Elaine sent another proposal to Greenpeace International, this time calling for the *Warrior* or *Vega* to be sent to the 1983 NFIP conference being held in Vanuatu. The request was turned down by the international council, whose priority at the time was the campaigns against radioactive and toxic waste dumping in Europe. 'At the 1981 council meeting, Tom Donahue had to deal with a very uptight Remi Parmentier from the French office, who insisted that Greenpeace should widen the nuclear testing campaign to include the other testing nations,' recalls Carol. A tentative agreement was reached on the idea, but such an expensive and logistically complex campaign was unlikely to materialise in the immediate future.

By the end of the decade local Greenpeace groups were springing up all round New Zealand. To some even then, Greenpeace and the peace movement were thought of as

From left, *Vega* skipper Chris Robinson, Charlie Ching and crew member Jacky Taero, Tahiti 1982.

synonymous. It was not always understood that Greenpeace was just one of a profusion of organisations including various local CND groups, the Maori group PPANAC (the Pacific Peoples' Anti-Nuclear Action Committee), umbrella organisations like Peace Movement New Zealand and the Peace Forums, the Christchurch-based Nuclear Free Zone Committee and a kaleidoscope of small local groups. From its traditional base among Christian and left-wing groups, the peace movement was now a wide coalition reflecting its broad popular base.

'One catalyst,' says Nicky Hager, of PMNZ, 'was the women's peace camp at Greenham Common in England. A huge number of women had become active against nuclear war, and it was this that brought about the big expansion. Women began to run most of the groups and that changed it from a fringe lefty thing into a mainstream mass movement. Until that time we didn't really expect to win, but things suddenly started going our way that year.'

'Women had really started taking charge of their own lives,' says Carol, 'speaking out and actively seeking solutions to the many injustices in New Zealand society, including men's attitudes to war, racism, sexual harassment and inequality. It was no coincidence that the then largest peace march in New Zealand, organised by Women Acting for Nuclear Disarmament (WAND), had 20,000 women out on Queen Street – organised by women, for women.'

As a student attending Greenpeace meetings in Wellington, Stephanie Mills, now GPNZ's nuclear test ban campaigner, also speaks of the importance of the Greenham Common phenomenon in motivating women in New Zealand. 'They gave us a sense of being involved in an international movement, very much a women's movement.' But it was the grassroots nature of the movement that made it successful. 'Had the peace movement simply limited itself to big marches as a show of strength, it is arguable whether the nuclear-free legislation would have gone through.'

Wellington anti-nuclear rally, 1983.

Grassroots peace groups campaigned for local nuclear-free zones. Having a realistic local goal was always a factor in their success, and in provincial areas these groups got many local people involved, often for the first time. In the main centres, meanwhile, Greenpeace organised pickets of every visiting French warship and every freighter carrying Australian uranium shipments bound for the United States or France.

After the USS *Haddo* in 1979, Auckland was spared nuclear-powered warship visits until the cruiser USS *Texas* arrived on 2 August 1983, four days before Hiroshima Day. With little more than three weeks to remobilise the Auckland Peace Squadron, more than 100 vessels came out to blockade the harbour entrance, in the largest turnout ever. On the same day, about 30,000 marched against nuclear weapons, followed by a huge Hiroshima Day rally in the Domain. Three months later, a similarly hot welcome was organised in Auckland for the nuclear-armed submarine USS *Phoenix*. At last *Vega* was back on the harbour, now refitted after the cyclone damage sustained while she was held at Moruroa after the 1982 protest. With skipper Chris Robinson for the *Phoenix* protest were Anna Horne, veteran of the 1973 *Vega* voyage to Moruroa, Elaine Shaw, Carol Stewart, Tom Donahue, wildlife campaigner Susan-Jane Owen, Hilari Anderson, a former *Rainbow Warrior* crew member, and Hilda Halkyard-Harawira and Grace Robertson of PPANAC. That evening Susan-Jane wrote to her parents, the day's events vivid in her mind:

'We left Westhaven marina just before dawn to join the other Peace Squadron boats assembling off Devonport wharf. I counted fifty-two boats – yachts of all sizes, launches, cats, trimarans, fishing boats, surfsailers, one Tahitian pirogue and a raft! The atmosphere was festive; everyone seemed to know everyone else and people were calling to one another. Sometime after 8 am (I lost track of time once it all started to happen), things got serious. The *Phoenix* swung into view around North Head amid an armada of about forty police boats and twenty inflatables strung out on either side. The Peace Squadron gathered near the centre of the channel, tacking back and forth.

Greenpeace Bastille Day 'funeral march', Auckland 1982.

'When we met the line of police launches it was chaos, with police and Navy inflatables charging everywhere. Chris started the engine to give us some much-needed manoeuverability. Then the *Phoenix* was sitting dead in the water, everyone in the Peace Squadron cheering and chanting like crazy – "Go home, *Phoenix!*" Things happened very fast, yachts, launches and zodiacs going in all directions in a small area of water.

'One moment we were on the fringe of the protest, the next instant a police launch, some Zodiacs and the huge black submarine were only fifty metres away! We were in the middle of it all, the closest yacht to the *Phoenix* – God knows how we got there. *Vega* ran in front of the submarine, matching its speed. The water was now choppy and whitecapped with all the action. Chris stood at the stern, steering *Vega* through all the chaos with his foot, weaving his body from side to side to see what was happening in front of us.

'A police launch came up astern and called to us to move away. We ignored them. The sub had stopped because of *Vega* in front of it. Then more police launches surrounded us, hitting the sides.

'All the time we managed to keep within about fifty metres of the ship's bow. Suddenly the pack of police boats eased and I noticed they'd managed to attach a tow rope to the bowsprit. The boat the rope was attached to started to move away, pulling *Vega* after it. Quickly Anna grabbed a pocket knife, leant over the bowsprit and cut the line, leaving it dangling in the water behind the police launch…'

Wellington continued to receive US nuclear ships through to 1985. In 1983-84 the Wellington Greenpeace group was one significant player in the diverse and active Wellington peace movement, which held regular demonstrations outside the Wellington Town Hall, where French diplomatic receptions were held each Bastille Day. CND and Greenpeace often collaborated to organise demonstrations, such as the 10,000 who marched against the nuclear-powered cruiser USS *Texas* during Hiroshima Week 1983.

A third nuclear ship visit to Auckland came at the end of November, this time the British nuclear-armed aircraft-carrier HMS *Invincible* fresh from the Falklands War. In March 1984, the nuclear-powered submarine USS *Queenfish* visited Auckland. By now rumours were rife about what was behind the US and New Zealand Governments' persistence.

This time Auckland Mayor Cath Tizard and several Labour MPs joined the Peace Squadron, which numbered some fifty-eight yachts, twelve canoes and thirty assorted small craft, including, according to the *New Zealand Herald*, 'a naked man on a surfboard'. Greenpeace was again involved. Chris Robinson turned out this time in *Vega*'s pirogue. Mike Donoghue had brought up his fishing boat from the Coromandel and a dozen Greenpeacers joined him on board. The much-harassed submarine finally dropped anchor in the stream inside a circle of protesters beating drums, holding flares with arms raised

Bikini Day demonstration, Tahiti 1981. Nelson Anjain and Tea Hirshon lead the march.

in a gesture of peace. The protesters had won: that was to be the last such visit before the Labour Party won the 1984 general election by a landslide with a clear mandate to declare New Zealand nuclear-free and ban the visits.

US nuclear ships were also being blocked from entering other Pacific ports. In 1983 Elaine Shaw attended the NFIP conference at Vanuatu, where she renewed links with Father Walter Lini, now the Prime Minister, and his sister Hilda, the Minister of Education. The determinedly nuclear-free and progressive ni-Vanuatu had already denied port entry to the frigates USS *Marvin Shields* and USS *Robert Peary* in 1982, after the US Navy refused to declare whether or not the vessels were armed with nuclear weapons.

Elaine had long talks with Father Lini while catching up with other activist friends, many for the first time since the Hawai'i conference in 1980. 'Vanuatu was an incredible experience, with both the people and government totally supportive and helpful.' Unsurprisingly, at this conference independence issues were firmly on the agenda, with none of the diplomatic hedging that had characterised earlier meetings.

Elaine had first met Walter Lini in 1978 when he visited New Zealand as a representative of the pro-independence Vanuaaku Party from the then joint Anglo-French colony of the New Hebrides. They met again in 1979, when Elaine accompanied Father Lini to Bastion Point during the occupation by Maori land rights activists. The New Hebrides became the independent nation of Vanuatu in 1980 after the failure of an attempted takeover by pro-French expatriates. The informal links between Elaine and Walter Lini's new Government led to co-operative efforts against French nuclear testing and other environmental problems in the Pacific. These personal links would become the basis for further co-operation when the *Rainbow Warrior* came to the Pacific in 1985.

CHAPTER SIX

Private Bag, Wellesley St

THE 1980S BEGAN for Greenpeace with a new international structure drawing the widely dispersed national offices into a cohesive 'federation'. After financial problems in the Canadian office and a punishing legal battle between the San Francisco and Vancouver groups over copyright of the Greenpeace name, David McTaggart had stepped in on behalf of the European groups with a call for unity. Out of the fracas emerged a new umbrella organisation – Greenpeace International.

The original structure instituted a council of five trustees, comprising representatives from the larger offices, and a chair. In 1983 a two-tier system was established, and this is basically the arrangement that guides the movement today. Now based in Amsterdam, the Greenpeace International Council comprises representatives from each of the member countries, who elect four board members, who in turn elect a chair, a position held by McTaggart since 1980. The council meets once a year to determine overall policy and direction, approve new international campaigns and set the annual budget of the organisation. The board, which meets several times a year, serves as the decision-making body between council meetings.

Each national group, while it is expected to conform to the main international campaign areas, maintains its autonomy, devising its own local campaigns. Greenpeace is not a multinational, in as much as there is no absolute central control, yet it is more than a loose collection of national offices. Each national office draws on an unrivalled global network, focusing on international environmental problems rather than duplicating the work of national organisations.

Greenpeace International's establishment had a mixed reception in the New Zealand office. The local organisation had grown out of small autonomous pockets of activity and information-sharing, and any kind of centralised control tended to be regarded with suspicion. The development of an international structure made sense organisationally, but no one was keen on having campaigns directed from an international office located on the other side of the world. What would happen to local autonomy when it came to New Zealand issues? The Wellington group was suspicious of deals being made between the Auckland office and GPI without its being consulted. There was also concern over the merging of different styles of campaigning, and in many ways this problem is still being resolved with the

Opposite: Human peace sign in Auckland's Domain, Hiroshima Day, 1984.

development of specifically New Zealand-focused campaigns.

While GPNZ was one of the oldest Greenpeace offices, it was also one of the smallest and poorest. Having laid claim to the Greenpeace logo long before copyright became an issue, GPNZ now found itself 'out of the fold' simply because it lacked the funds that could be secured by the bigger, wealthier offices overseas. How could such a small group raise the required revenue to secure a voice and a vote? As an interim measure Greenpeace New Zealand was given observer status at the 1980 council meeting, but it would have no voting rights until it paid its way.

While attending the first international council meeting in November 1979 as observers for Greenpeace New Zealand, Naomi Petersen, Martin Gotje and David Moodie finally met up with David McTaggart, seven years after events around Moruroa had changed all their lives. As chair of the council McTaggart was a powerful ally for New Zealand, and he began by pushing for a return to basics – nuclear testing and other Pacific issues. The possibility of an Antarctica campaign, which became something of a crusade for New Zealand's Roger Wilson, was also brought up. From the predominantly European and North American viewpoint of the meeting these proposals initially seemed far-fetched, but again the seeds were planted.

As the New Zealand peace movement grew, so did Greenpeace, often collaborating with others and working with smaller groups and local communities with less resources to draw on. Local campaigns, however, remained a weak area in GPNZ's work.

Irene Petersen had bowed out in 1977, when she left, with her husband Hugh, for a year away from New Zealand. Hugh's subsequent illness ended her close involvement with the organisation. Elaine Shaw and Michael Taylor took over as co-ordinators, and were joined by three new campaigners: Tom Donahue (whales), Paul Jackman (nuclear) and Patti Kearney (seals).

GPNZ staff Bev Cormack, Jude Seaboyer and Pip Burch.

Carol Stewart was a single parent working as an insurance clerk when she first walked into the Symonds Street office in March 1980. She had been impressed by film of one of the early whaling actions on television, so when she discovered Greenpeace had an office in Auckland she called them up, and within a few days she was helping out at Epicentre. After a few months she was working full time for GPNZ. Four years later she was voted co-ordinator, then in March 1990 she took up the new post of campaigns co-ordinator. Like Elaine, she has watched the organisation grow and, ultimately, prosper after investing years of sustained voluntary work. Through its four changes of street address, GPNZ maintained Private Bag, Wellesley St as its Auckland mailing address – Elaine was once asked by a non-English-speaking visitor whether *she* was the Private Bag!

When Carol first saw the Epicentre, it was still located in the rundown little shop in Symonds Street, with a tiny backroom, kitchen and bathroom and a meeting room up a rickety flight of stairs. Staffed solely by volunteers, the centre put out an informative monthly newsletter. 'It was a relatively primitive operation. Lack of storage space meant there were boxes stacked up in every available space. The hall and upstairs room were a mass of banners, placards and fancy-dress costumes for demonstrations. Efforts to tidy up lasted only until the next newsletter mail-out or demonstration, when chaos would be restored.'

Opposite the upstairs meeting room was another small office, which Greenpeace rented. Apart from doing shifts in the shop when it was short of volunteers, Greenpeace people worked independently, though all 'facilities' were shared. Operating the antique and temperamental Gestetner duplicator, even for the simplest, short-run flyer, was a dirty, inky and frustrating experience. Photocopying was done at a print shop a few doors up the road and telexes were sent via a nearby recording studio.

Auckland street theatre by SPANA, Bastille Day 1983.

The most frustrating aspect of those years for Carol was the difficulty in recruiting volunteers who would commit themselves to regular hours. 'Rosters were drawn up, but often people just didn't show up. Others came a few times, then drifted away. Luckily there was a small core of dedicated volunteers who came in regularly to do specific jobs. I remember being totally amazed by the stamina of people like Patti Kearney, who worked night shifts as a psychiatric nurse at Carrington, then came into the office to handle the merchandise operation (T-shirts, posters and badges in those days), write articles for the newsletter and contribute wherever needed.

'Elaine and I took to each other straight away, mainly because we were older than most of the others in the office and were both bringing up kids. Elaine also felt isolated by some of the men. Her skills were certainly undervalued. Having another woman around was probably good for Elaine, though it took me a while to appreciate her need for support. That grew as she showed me the enormity of the problems facing the Pacific.'

Elaine's personal experience of travelling in the Pacific and talking to people wherever she went led her to develop her own sense of 'Pacific' ways of doing things. But her constant questioning sometimes irritated her co-workers, according to Carol. 'She had an endless curiosity for everything to do with life in the Pacific, and soaked up information, filing it away in her head to be retrieved at the appropriate moment. Her commitment was felt rather than thought, and though she could absorb complicated political and scientific material, her strength lay in showing people she cared about them and their situation. Ironically she didn't always show the same concern for those around her. Sometimes her patience ran out and she would explode with frustration. She particularly disliked being "directed", especially by someone she considered did not have the necessary knowledge, which was often the case with the single-minded men around.'

Trying to juggle her responsibilities to her family and to Greenpeace was difficult and exhausting for Elaine, and Carol sympathised with her dilemma. 'Elaine was aware she would not always be able to sustain the balance, and was very concerned that her marriage and children might suffer because of her work. She always liked taking the kids out but really resented household chores. In the end her marriage could no longer take the strain. That her husband Keith had little interest in her work must have been hard for her. On the other hand, living with Elaine must have been tough on him too. Still, their three children have grown to be strong, well-balanced adults – her second daughter Giselle is now a staunch Greenpeace worker.'

Tension between Elaine and Mike Taylor revolved around conflicting personalities and priorities. For Elaine, the only area that counted was the nuclear issue and its various aspects as played out in the Pacific – 'the whales and seals stuff's just a bloody nuisance,' she once told Carol. 'She had no time for bureaucracy and soon tired of long debates,' Carol recalls. 'At long meetings she was famous for eventually stretching out in a clear space on the floor and going to sleep!' Nor was she keen on the administration other than that directly related to her nuclear work. Consequently the burden of day-to-day administration fell on Michael and Carol in 1980.

By the time *Fri* reached Falmouth, England, in 1979, Naomi Petersen was thoroughly run down. She desperately needed peace and privacy, and to see her family again, so after almost seven years on *Fri* she left the ship in England and returned to New Zealand. Greenpeace New Zealand had continued to send funds to *Fri*, even after, once she had reached Hong Kong in December 1975, *Fri*'s crew had absolved them of this responsibility. Through *Greenpeace News* and Elaine's and Irene's long letters, Naomi had kept in touch with the growth of the small Greenpeace group she had left behind in 1974.

Inevitably things had changed enormously in Greenpeace New Zealand while she was away. 'I could sense the change, a kind of depoliticisation away from nuclear issues to the preservation of whales and seals, but those were concerns we could strongly identify with from our long sea passages. This change of emphasis seemed to occur as Michael Taylor and later Tom Donahue, started to play leading roles in Greenpeace.'

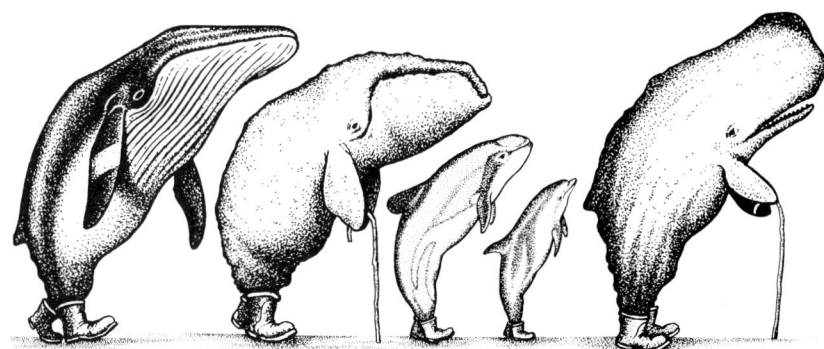

A popular graphic for the 1984 Auckland Whale Walk.

With change in the air it was relatively easy for Naomi, on her return to New Zealand in February 1980, to see how the two distinct directions had developed. Anti-nuclear and wildlife campaigns had not co-existed entirely harmoniously in the New Zealand office. Elaine felt under siege from what she saw as Mike Taylor's inflexible aims and methods; she in turn caused irritation to some by being obsessed with the nuclear-free Pacific issue.

'At the 1981 annual general meeting Tom Donahue was voted in as co-ordinator, with Wayne Hennessey as assistant co-ordinator,' recalls Carol. 'It was a surprise for many of us, and I think it hurt Michael, who with Elaine had been co-ordinator for several years. Michael continued to work in the office, but after one godalmighty blowup with Elaine, both of them ended up storming out, vowing never to return. Michael went back to university to do his masters degree in archaeology and Elaine worked briefly for Corso.' It wasn't long, however, before Elaine was drawn back in to help Roger Wilson prepare for *Vega*'s next trip to the zone.

In 1981 GPNZ moved from the Symonds Street Epicentre to the relative luxury of new premises in Nagel House in the city, with a main communal room and two small offices overlooking the old District Court. Here they shared a floor rather incongruously with the Society for the Protection of the Unborn Child (SPUC) and a seedy, all-but-invisible outfit that apparently trafficked in Philippine brides.

The move into the city reflected a gradual growth in income. Greenpeace New Zealand now had a fairly large mailing list, a few hundred paid-up supporters and a fragile bank balance of a few thousand dollars. Still totally dependent upon its dedicated core of volunteers, the notion of buying a boat – even an inflatable – to help with local work was as unthinkable as securing such basic office equipment as an electric typewriter or a second telephone. After a long week in the office a couple of staffers or volunteers would lug a trestle table and a suitcase full of T-shirts, badges and posters down to Queen Street on Friday night. They would feel well satisfied if, by nine o'clock, they had sold a couple of $10 T-shirts and talked about the issues with a few shoppers. The small profits made from merchandise in the late 1970s and early 1980s often meant the difference between being able to pay the rent and not.

Occasional benefit concerts involved campaigners in an enormous amount of extra work, and their unpredictable profits hardly allowed for financial forward planning. A successful 'Save the Whales' concert in the Auckland Town Hall in late 1981 raised the then princely sum of $3,300. At the end of the year GPNZ's income stood at $4,000, of which $1,000 went as GPNZ's contribution to international campaigns.

By late 1982 Greenpeace had a membership list of 953. For a subscription of $8, members received a quarterly newsletter. Net income now stood at $13,000, of which $1,700 went to Greenpeace International while the remainder paid for two small salaries of $100 a week (to Pip Burch as office manager, then later to Tom Donahue as co-ordinator), office overheads and campaign work – which at this time meant mostly the nuclear campaign. The early

The 1984 Auckland Whale Walk.

Antarctica, wildlife and toxic waste campaigns were each expected to operate on a few hundred dollars for the year, though GPI sometimes contributed extra funds for a specific project.

Clearly, something had to be done. As campaign proposals continued to remain pipe dreams because of the lack of money, GPNZ rather reluctantly decided to follow GPI's persistent advice and try a new approach to fundraising. Direct-mail fundraising was used very successfully by the North American offices, but the approach that worked there wasn't right for New Zealanders. American mail-outs tended to be low on information and high on emotional content, and it was agreed that any package produced here should aim at raising awareness as well as money. International provided a substantial grant to set the programme up, and GPNZ hired a professional to put together the first trial package.

Whale Walk entertainment

Like everything Greenpeace undertook in those days, everyone had a say, and no one agreed with anyone else. After months of writing and rewriting, the final artwork was agreed and 3,000 envelopes, packed with information about the pollution of the Tarawera River, the plight of the Hooker's sea lion and French nuclear testing, were delivered to mail boxes around the country. The response was unexpectedly good, and allowed the introduction of another small wage – $100 a week to wildlife campaigner Susan-Jane Owen.

When Pip Burch left in November 1983 to have her first baby, Jude Seaboyer came in as office manager. As the staff's workload increased, so did the stresses of keeping a sane and viable family life. Elaine and Carol, putting in very long days and working through many weekends, were still unpaid. Jude was an effective organiser and office manager but loathed book-keeping, so she put forward a proposal that she take on the job of full-time fundraiser.

'None of us who worked in the office were self-supporting,' says Jude. 'Pip and I were fortunate in having husbands who were willing to support us because they believed in the importance of the work, but the financial stress was considerable. Everyone who was working full time needed a living wage, and I wanted there to be enough money in the bank for campaigns to be properly funded. We were all sick of calling meetings to discuss new plans and ideas, only to have to set them aside because we couldn't afford the canvas and paint to make a new banner, let alone pay researchers and campaigners. I felt sure we could change this.

'The next package was to be devoted to the nuclear issue. Again we started with professional help, but it quickly became apparent that we wouldn't be able to afford it. Anyway, we now knew how to go about producing a package, so we took over and did it ourselves – later we would find that every time we brought in professionals things would go wrong. The antinuclear "Enough!" package was very successful, and I enjoyed the creative aspect of the whole thing. It had been a big risk, since aside from considerable production costs it also meant finding another salary, but it paid off.'

Now the membership was growing fast. In 1984 Jane Pullen was employed to run the office, with Pip later returning part time to do the books, her baby son taking up residence in the corner of the marine mammals office.

SPANA street theatre, 1983.

It was an important turning point for GPNZ, for within six months all GPNZ's full-time staff were receiving a living wage.

Jude felt strongly that the mail-out packages had to inform as well as raise money, and she also knew people had to be given the opportunity to do something more than give financial support. 'The peace movement in the early 1980s talked a lot about people taking personal responsibility for bringing about change – not leaving it to the politicians. The mail-outs offered people the opportunity to do something themselves to turn things around.

'The first sponsored 'Whale Walk' was really an extension of this idea. All over the city kids jumped at the idea of raising money to help save the whales. As we talked at schools about the walk, teachers confirmed to us the feelings of despair children felt at the prospect of nuclear war and the destruction of the environment. They agreed that a sense of helplessness could perhaps be turned around if children were given the opportunity not only to show their concern but to do something practical to help. Saving the whales seemed a good place to start.

'Auckland children worked hard to collect impressive lists of sponsors for this first 'Whale Walk', and the results were astonishing. Pip, Carol and I took the money home late on Sunday night. We'd hoped for $20,000, and by midday on Monday we were pinching ourselves to check we weren't dreaming – more than $60,000 had been raised!' There had been walks for the whales before – Greenpeace Hawai'i and Washington had provided us with advice on how to do it – but Auckland's kids broke all the records. It was enough to cover the campaign costs for a marine mammals co-ordinator, to help fund

Mike Donoghue's trips to the International Whaling Commission meetings, to give money towards a whale-stranding pontoon for Project Jonah, and to buy new educational materials for use in schools.

'I think it's important to remember such fundraising successes, if only to correct a later false impression, because contrary to popular belief, we were not totally poverty-stricken before the bombing in 1985,' says Jude. 'We didn't achieve financial independence just because of the *Rainbow Warrior* bombing, but through years of hard and careful work. The turnaround from a small-budget outfit to an organisation approaching financial independence happened between 1982 and 1984.'

The early 1980s saw an extraordinary expansion in the peace movement internationally. It was the height of the Second Cold War. The greatest military and political power in the world was led by a president who, if not unhinged, was at best simple-minded. Ronald Reagan symbolised the resurgent militarism that had taken over American society. There was much loose talk about moving beyond the stalemate of deterrence to pre-emptive nuclear-war-fighting strategies, of which Reagan's trillion-dollar 'Star Wars' programme and a raft of exotic new-generation weaponry were a part. The Soviet Communist state, in the last throes of its own doctrinal delusions, could come up with no more creative response than to embrace the same pernicious nuclear brinkmanship as its opponent. The deployment of the new weapon systems in Europe triggered a mobilisation of anti-war fervour without precedent.

Around the world, burgeoning peace movements were crying out for sanity, and New Zealand was very much a part of this reawakening of anti-nuclear activism. Between 1982 and 1984 a profusion of new peace groups were set up, ranging from the hundreds of neighbourhood peace groups up and down the country to the big umbrella organisations like Peace Movement New Zealand and the Auckland Peace Forum, and professional groups like SANA (Scientists Against Nuclear War) and IPPNW (International Physicians for the Prevention of Nuclear War). By this time the New Zealand peace movement had escaped from the 'left wing' to become a truly broad-based movement, and people were well-informed and mobilised. The anti-nuclear stand taken by Lange's Labour Government came about as a response to grassroots pressure and a broad-based mood for change, from which long-established groups like CND and Greenpeace also benefited. Greenpeace was at last drawing in new volunteers interested in a long-term commitment. It was a period when women in particular were openly rejecting the traditional roles ascribed to them, and in Greenpeace the staff gender balance now tipped decisively in favour of women. A loose group of women would be the backbone of the office for the next five years.

Pip Burch: 'The 1981 Springbok rugby tour had been my political awakening. After that I got involved with Greenpeace because I wanted to do something socially useful, and since I was most concerned about French nuclear testing and the nuclear issue, it seemed like the right thing to do. A friend of mine knew Elaine, so I called her up for a chat and she invited me into the office. 'They were looking for someone to manage the office, and I started almost straight away. After a week I was asked to organise a demo and help produce the newsletter, neither of which I had done before. I was elected onto the Greenpeace committee because there simply weren't enough people to do everything!'

Jude Seaboyer had also been drafted in after the Springbok tour. 'It was a small thing when I first looked a policeman in the eye and refused to move during a tour protest, but it went against everything that had made me the nice middle-class woman I was, and there was no going back! It's a bit of a cliché, but the tour radicalised me. Later I was involved in organising the women's peace march, and I met the women in the Greenpeace office through that, and through my partner's involvement as a volunteer. Apart from a couple of years teaching, I'd been a typist since I'd left school. As a Greenpeace worker I found myself for the first time in a position where I was responsible for initiating and organising substantial projects. For a lot of women like me, volunteers and paid workers, Greenpeace provided the opportunity to work for something we really cared about and to develop self-confidence and a range of skills we might not otherwise have gained.'

Anneke Ursem, one of a small core of committed volunteers of the 1980s, was a member of Greenpeace in the Netherlands before she emigrated to New Zealand in 1981. 'For twenty-five years I'd worked hard as a hairdresser and bringing up a family in the suburbs of Amsterdam, where I had seen the Vietnam demos and thought how I would have liked to join in if I'd had the time. How many times have I heard that excuse since! When I came to New Zealand, with my family mostly grown up, I got involved as a volunteer at Greenpeace. Everyone started as a volunteer. Some of the women lacked self-

After the Auckland Women's Peace March, the rally in Aotea Square, 1983.

confidence, being used to seeing men do things without consultation. That soon changed though!'

Bev Cormack, who would become GPNZ co-ordinator in 1987, was another of this core group. 'My first local environmental work had been with Project Jonah in 1978. In 1984 I worked for the Auckland Peace Forum, then helped Elaine prepare for the *Rainbow Warrior* tour. We put together a Pacific slide show, which I took around schools and community groups to interest as many as possible in the background issues.'

Graham Gulbransen, an Auckland GP, had been an active volunteer since 1977, when he met Elaine at Epicentre at the first meeting of the Campaign for an Independent East Timor. A leading activist with the New Zealand branch of IPPNW, Graham worked on many different peace projects through the 1980s. In 1985 he joined Elaine and Greenpeace USA's Steve Sawyer at the South Pacific Forum in the Cook Islands to lobby on the South Pacific Nuclear Free Zone Treaty. Elaine also encouraged him to take on a research project on the medical consequences of the British hydrogen bomb tests at Kirimati (Christmas) Island in the 1950s, which had involved many New Zealand servicemen. The results of this study were published in mid-1991. Over the years, Graham has remained a valued friend of GPNZ, and now acts as medical consultant to the Greenpeace Antarctica base teams.

Auckland's 1984 Hiroshima Day peace march.

Elaine had always been drawn to visitors at Epicentre from the Japanese peace movement. In 1984 she had received an invitation to the Hiroshima Day commemoration in Japan, but just before she left, several Japanese peace movement representatives came over to participate in the big Auckland Hiroshima Day march, which was led by Naomi Iwai, a councillor from the nuclear-free city of Kobe. Another long-time office volunteer, Didi Swete, was a survivor of a Japanese prisoner-of-war camp in Indonesia. At first Didi shrank from meeting the Japanese delegates, because her memories were still too painful. 'For a long time I had fooled myself into believing that dropping the atom bombs on Japan had actually saved lives. When I came back from

Children light candles for peace, Hiroshima Day, Auckland 1984.

the kitchen Elaine stopped me and introduced me to the Japanese delegates, explaining to them why the situation was difficult for me. They all stood up, the women hugging me and the men shaking my hand. Silently we stood together for a moment, then they expressed their sorrow for what had happened. I realised the war had also left them with deep wounds. It was an important moment for me.'

The women's movement was a vital force for change during the early 1980s and a strong influence on peace politics. People were beginning to make connections – between military and political developments, between the personal and the political. Groups seeking to bring about social change were painfully formulating new ways of working together, and the issue of hierarchical versus co-operative structures came to the fore. GPNZ had originally been set up along non-hierarchical lines, and now the influence of the women's movement in particular reasserted this tradition.

Carol Stewart: 'I can say with all honesty that until the bombing of the *Rainbow Warrior*, working in the GPNZ office was generally fulfilling, a pleasure, and an example of trust and co-operation. Everyone helped out when needed and no job was too lowly for anyone to perform, no matter what their position. Of course there were problems, but most of them were solved by talking them out. The steady growth of GPNZ during that period is proof that a non-hierarchical structure is workable.'

Once Roger Wilson moved to the Greenpeace International office in England to work on the emergent Antarctica campaign in 1982, the only man left in the small Auckland office on a daily basis was Tom Donahue. 'After his exposure to Greenpeace International, Tom tried to change Greenpeace New Zealand along the more corporate lines being adopted in European offices,' says Carol. 'The problem was that GPNZ had solidly grassroots origins in New Zealand, while many of the new Greenpeace offices opening in Europe in the 1980s were set up as functioning bureaucracies – offering a model many in New Zealand had no wish to emulate.'

Tom Donahue was less than enthusiastic with the way things were going, and was determined to change the organisation into a more 'efficient, businesslike' outfit. Tom saw shared decision-making as a time-consuming luxury Greenpeace could ill afford and favoured delegating responsibility to individuals for each aspect of their work.

Lines of disagreement were drawn between those in favour of a tightly defined, albeit more slick and efficient operation, and those advocating a broader vision, encompassing a more collaborative approach to uniquely Pacific problems. Jane Cooper: 'When issues like New Zealand's membership of ANZUS or changing our name to Greenpeace Aotearoa came up, Tom used to send Elaine or me off to write position papers as a way of placating us!' Issues of control and authority emerged, often along gender lines, to parallel the tensions between Greenpeace International and GPNZ.

The difference between Tom Donahue's vision of GPNZ and the rest of the staff's wishes was continuing to widen. Just before the 1984 annual general meeting the growing unrest in the office came to a head. In desperation they called in Helen Yensen, a trained counsellor who worked for a number of groups for social change. Helen, however, felt too close to the people involved, so she recommended a Lifeline councillor. But it was already far too late.

Carol: 'Three days before the AGM, Tom contacted GPI, claiming the Auckland staff were attempting to subvert the organisation by taking on board Maori land rights issues. We had been talking about the idea of a name change to Greenpeace Aotearoa, mainly because of a petition then being circulated by Maori activists calling on the country's name to be changed to Aotearoa. We had agreed that a discussion paper would be presented at the meeting to determine the feelings of supporters – nothing more than that.' Ultimately the proposal was not taken up. There was no great flood of opinion from supporters, and GPI was against it. Greenpeace New Zealand remained, like it or not, a solidly Pakeha organisation, and recognised that changing its name in sympathy with Maori aspirations was not appropriate until deeper structural issues within the organisation had been tackled.

'At that time we were still collecting our telexes from a bureau. I picked them up on my morning walk to the office, so I was the first to see the reply from International the next day. Talk about a knee-jerk reaction! The then executive director, John Frizell, instructed Tom to close down the office, fire everyone and hire himself a secretary till he could get things up and running again. There was also a long separate message addressed to the rest of us, informing us just what GPNZ could and could not do about land rights and name changes. Well, that was the last straw! Tom was voted out of office two days later and I was very reluctantly persuaded to become co-ordinator and trustee.

'All sorts of crazy stories filtered through to us later from other offices about our "feminist coup". It seemed to us then that the idea of people working co-operatively and with genuine concern for each other was still not generally acceptable for Greenpeace elsewhere. With the exception of Tom and Lyn Donahue, we had all decided that a hierarchical structure was not what Greenpeace was about, that imitating the structural organisation of a multinational corporation was disempowering and did not fit with Pacific ways of doing things.'

After this incident relations between GPNZ and some at GPI were strained, yet in terms of productivity things were never busier for New Zealand. Carol attended the GPI council meeting shortly after the 'coup' in Auckland; that meeting decided to fund a Greenpeace expedition and base on Antarctica and to promote the idea of a World Park on the southern continent.

Jude's fundraising continued to bring in a healthy income. By early 1985 a few thousand dollars was available for each campaign; the largest, the Antarctica campaign, had a budget of $8,500. The nuclear campaign had most of its funds diverted to the *Rainbow Warrior*'s forthcoming Pacific Peace Voyage, leaving a small float, $1,000 or so, for overheads in New Zealand. There was a lot of preparation work and enormous excitement as the *Warrior*'s visit approached. All this changed on 10 July 1985, the night the *Warrior* was bombed.

Carol: 'Nineteen eighty-five was emotionally and physically draining. None of us really had time to come to terms with the trauma of the whole *Rainbow Warrior* affair. The bombing changed the face of the office: Susan-Jane and Jude left to go to university and Pip left to have her second child in 1986, though both she and Jude were to remain on the board for some years. Renate Kroesa, our fill-in toxics campaigner, left in late 1985, and her job was taken over by Peter Whitehouse, a volunteer who had been one of the firefighters at the ICI warehouse fire.'

On the eve of *Vega*'s 1986 Pacific tour Elaine wrote to friends in the Pacific: 'Carol departed for a well-earned three-week holiday yesterday, and she's going to think about her future while away – she's making noises of departure from Greenpeace altogether. So am I. I think we're just burned out. There has got to be more to life than Greenpeace! So I've decided to leave when I return home in October.'

Carol Stewart

In 1987 Carol resigned as GPNZ trustee; in December she became Antarctic campaigner for a year, then moved to Amsterdam to continue work on Antarctica with Kelly Rigg and others. Peter Whitehouse took over as trustee until 1989.

In the years following the bombing, Bev Cormack progressed as a volunteer from producing the newsletter and acting as an all-round helper to being a member of the GPNZ board, keeping an overview of everything.

'The board had evolved out of an executive committee, which consisted of the national co-ordinator, associate co-ordinator, secretary and treasurer, and others who were elected or co-opted as they expressed willingness. For the most part, the committee was the office staff, but as the organisation grew, it became apparent that the committee needed to be redefined. In 1987 the executive became a governing board, whose members were no longer employed as staff but were drawn from experienced and qualified outsiders, who could

approve campaigns and budgets and employ the executive management of the office. I became co-ordinator, and when I resigned two years later Yoshimi Brett and Carol Stewart came in to co-ordinate the office and the campaigns, respectively.

Greenpeace action against Japanese Antarctic survey ship, Lyttelton 1983.

'By 1987 the paid staff had grown to thirteen. Our growing merchandise department, managed by Eve Manning, had moved downstairs. Over the next three years Eve and a dedicated team of volunteers turned the merchandise arm into a profitable operation that put out one of the largest summer catalogues in the country, with a popular range of specialised clothing, posters, cards and other campaign-oriented products. For the years 1989 and 1990 we were proud to report that merchandise profits fully covered GPNZ's administration costs, which meant every cent of every donation went towards funding campaign and education activities.

'The Nagel House office was already too small when I started in 1984,' says Bev, 'and the overcrowding added to our stress levels. By 1987 the Antarctic campaign's MV *Greenpeace* was permanently based at Auckland's Western Viaduct, and while the team worked mostly from the ship, crew and campaigners also sometimes added to the space problems at the office. A new and much larger space simply had to be found. At last we could afford an office that would accommodate us all as well as an increasing amount of electronic equipment, and it was my brief to find it.

Antarctic minerals negotiations demo, Wellington 1988.

'After months of searching I found one floor of a modern office block in Hobson Street – about five minutes' walk from Queen Street. For the first time each campaigner had such essentials as a space in which to work and a telephone, and it was possible for meetings to be held without disrupting the whole office. Within a year we had taken over a second floor, and we now occupy three. At the end of 1990 GPNZ had fifty-nine full-time paid staff, more than 100,000 paying supporters and a total income of close to $2.3 million.'

GPNZ was struggling to cope with its extraordinary growth. In 1988 Tony Lindsay, who had experience in management was brought in to offer advice. 'As a volunteer in 1986, I had been struck by the open and co-operative nature of decision-making in the office. No obvious hierarchy existed. Coming from the strongly hierarchical corporate world, I found it fascinating that such a dynamic and successful organisation could function in this way. When Bev asked me to help, we were determined to retain these essential strengths. Rather than simply copying overseas or corporate models, our approach was to take the best from both worlds and apply it selectively and flexibly, always ensuring that GPNZ's structure continued to reflect our commitment to personal empowerment and action.'

Greenpeace USA's Steve Sawyer, who made frequent visits to the Auckland office from 1985 onwards, was impressed by the changes he had seen during these years. 'GPNZ has undergone an incredible transformation from my initial impressions in 1985 into what is now a major campaigning office, becoming more politically active and playing an ever-larger role in our international campaigns. The change was very marked between June 1985 and my next visit in the spring of 1987, after the second Antarctic expedition and the establishment of the World Park base, and even more by the end of 1987, when I returned again for the ceremonies for the *Warrior* at Matauri Bay. The move to Hobson Street had been completed and the transformation of the office into a "professional" outfit was achieved.'

For most of GPNZ's staff of 1985, their 'professionalism' was never at issue. Rather, there were two crucial changes in the years following the bombing. First, GPNZ's resource base increased enormously: access to adequate funds, to the necessary office space and equipment, and to vastly greater human resources, certainly made it easier to work efficiently and project a professional image. Secondly, Greenpeace's public profile changed radically. In a dizzying reversal from their longstanding indifference to Greenpeace's work, the media were suddenly taking the organisation seriously and actively seeking out Greenpeace news and views. This was crucially important for an organisation that relied heavily on media publicity about its activities to help bring about change.

CHAPTER SEVEN

Exodus – the Final Voyage

NINETEEN EIGHTY-FIVE, the fateful year that would see the Greenpeace name hold the front pages of newspapers all over the world, started optimistically for GPNZ. Local campaigns were up and running, and fundraising was now successful enough to finance several new campaigns. The long years of work were at last yielding dividends. But the real prize was that after years of lobbying GPI had at last agreed to a Pacific tour by Greenpeace's famous flagship, the *Rainbow Warrior*.

'In 1984, Elaine had submitted yet another proposal for a *Warrior* tour – one that took in all the so-called "nuclear victim states",' explains Carol Stewart. 'In June Elaine and I went to Hawai'i to attend the first-ever meeting of Greenpeace's Australia, New Zealand, United States and Canada (ANZUSCA) region. That's when the idea came up for a visit to the Marshall Islands. The original intention had been to link up victims of nuclear testing in the Pacific and the states supporting a nuclear-free Pacific, but we were insistent that any activity in the Marshall Islands should be decided in consultation with the local people. Steve Sawyer, then director of Greenpeace USA and a GPI board member, was the only one who seemed to see merit in the idea at the time.

'Elaine and I were also adamant that we did not want the whole campaign to be run from the Northern Hemisphere. We also persuaded Steve to meet with Giff Johnson. Not only was Giff very familiar with the Marshall Islands, but we knew he would share our view of the importance of working with the local people. This led to a later meeting in the Marshalls with Nelson Anjain, and eventually his people's idea of the evacuation from Rongelap to Mejato was agreed to.

'We still agonised over who would be given the job of campaigner and were terrified that one of International's gung-ho types would get it and spoil the whole project as we envisioned it. But Steve himself was so fascinated and enthusiastic that he took it on, and we were more than happy with the way things turned out.' Steve later got together with GPNZ to prepare a statement for independence groups and the media, which stated that 'Nuclearisation is a means of colonisation in the Pacific today. Greenpeace opposes the nuclearisation of the Pacific, and by so doing is in fact opposing colonialism.'

'In 1984 the Pacific work of GPNZ, GPI and Greenpeace USA wasn't co-ordinated,' says Carol. 'Certainly the New Zealand office didn't have much

Opposite: Missile tracks light the night sky over Kwajalein.

say over *Rainbow Warrior* crew selection. The only person Elaine knew was Martin Gotje, but his inclusion was encouraging because of his knowledge of the Pacific. We had never heard of Bunny McDiarmid, but agreed that a New Zealand woman on board could only be an asset.'

The final itinerary was much as GPNZ had hoped, with the addition of a Peace Media-style flotilla to accompany the *Warrior* from New Zealand to Moruroa. In the end it was decided against including Tahiti in the itinerary because of the risk that the French authorities might try to confiscate the ship. Elaine and Carol returned home to co-ordinate the New Zealand end, working with other groups to organise the peace flotilla and liaising with Greenpeace's friends in Tahiti. *Vega* would join the flotilla in Auckland in April after her Australian tour.

But first the *Warrior*, laid up at Jacksonville, Florida, had to be fitted with sails for the Pacific voyage. Bunny McDiarmid and Henk Haazen had been based at Jacksonville for two years on board *Fri*. Bunny had left Canterbury University and New Zealand behind her in 1979 to travel. She and Henk, a ship's engineer, had met in the United States and had travelled through Latin America together, where the poverty and political repression they witnessed had sharpened their political views. Returning to Henk's native Holland, they were living on a barge in Amsterdam when they made contact with *Fri* and her crew.

Greenpeace was then a rapidly growing organisation in the Netherlands, and Henk, motivated by his travel experiences, decided to see if he could

Rainbow Warrior crew, 1985.

help. In the Amsterdam office he met David Moodie and Martin Gotje, and he and Bunny were soon helping with *Fri*'s refit for her long Atlantic crossing to the Caribbean. That summer, as they helped replace the ship's rotting deck, they were regaled with stories of the 1975 Pacific Peace Odyssey by old *Fri* hands Martini and Rien Achterberg, another native of Holland who had settled in New Zealand, and they became close friends. The passage to the Caribbean was another epic voyage for *Fri* – at fifty-seven days, taking longer than it took Columbus. For the next two years *Fri* worked as a transport ship for a grassroots US development group, visiting Haiti, Nicaragua, St Lucia and other neighbouring countries from her Jacksonville base.

In early 1984 Martini returned to Europe to help with preparations for the *Rainbow Warrior*'s Pacific Peace Voyage. When he told Bunny and Henk about the plan, they immediately applied and were accepted as crew, so in October 1984 they, too, moved from *Fri* to a new home on the *Warrior*.

Shortly afterwards, Steve Sawyer visited the crew in Jacksonville to teach them a little of the Marshallese language and to discuss cultural aspects of the voyage, as only Bunny and Martini had any real experience of life in the Pacific. GPNZ had lobbied hard for a careful, culturally sensitive approach to the campaign, and Steve was also determined to avoid the kind of well-meaning but ill-considered intrusion that Greenpeace had sometimes been guilty of in the past. There would be no barging in, flags flying, with ready-made solutions. This time they would be there to listen and learn, to find out the real needs and concerns of the people, and to help if and when they could.

After her two new masts were fitted in March, the *Rainbow Warrior* left Jacksonville en route, through the Panama Canal, to Hawai'i. There they were joined by Jeton Anjain and three other Marshall Islands representatives, ship's photographer Fernando Pereira, Steve Sawyer, and New Zealand journalist David Robie. The ship's Swiss doctor, Andy Biedermann, had arranged with the Greenpeace USA office for the *Warrior* to carry medical supplies to the Majuro and Ebeye hospitals in the Marshall Islands. By now, after many months of preparations, plans for the first assignment in the peace voyage, dubbed Operation Exodus, had been finalised.

This expedition marked a significant departure for Greenpeace International and was controversial within the organisation, not least because it involved making a long-term commitment to the people of Rongelap. 'The Rongelapese had asked us for help, and Steve Sawyer had already spent time in the Marshalls with Jeton Anjain, so we were well prepared,' Henk recalls. Sawyer, whose task it was to co-ordinate the 20,000-mile tour, had become interested in Pacific issues through his anti-nuclear work with Greenpeace in the United States, where he had focused particularly on Belau and the Marshall Islands and had worked with nuclear test veterans in the United States – service personnel deliberately exposed to nuclear blasts in the Pacific and Nevada during the 1950s.

In October 1984 he had a meeting with Giff Johnson to discuss the Pacific voyage and the potential of a visit to Rongelap as a sign of support to the ill-used Marshallese. Giff, who with his Marshallese wife Darlene Keju-Johnson had long been active in the struggle to free the islands from US dominance, followed this up with a call to Jeton Anjain, Rongelap's senator in the Marshallese Nitijela (Parliament) and brother of Nelson Anjain, who had

Rainbow Warrior en route to Majuro.

sailed to Japan on board *Fri* in 1975. According to Giff, Senator Anjain literally leapt up and down with excitement at the idea of the *Rainbow Warrior* visiting Rongelap. Old ties between *Fri* and Rongelap would be renewed with the *Warrior*.

Steve had talked of the *Warrior*'s performing some sort of symbolic evacuation from a contaminated island, but when the senator flew to Honolulu he told them: 'To hell with this symbolic business! I have to move my people, and if you can help us, please do!' So came about the agreement that the *Warrior* would evacuate the entire population of Rongelap to uninhabited Mejato, fifty miles south of their poisoned homeland.

In January 1985 Steve flew to Majuro, the Marshallese capital, to meet Jeton and Nelson Anjain, also visiting Kwajalein. Some 100 Rongelapese were then living on the neighbouring island of Ebeye because they believed that by staying on Rongelap they risked almost certain death through radiation-related illness. During the 1950s and 1960s the Kwajalein Islanders had themselves been forcibly relocated to the tiny island of Ebeye, where 10,000 people still live in appalling conditions in overcrowded shanty houses on the thirty-hectare site. Ebeye was used by the US military as a dormitory island, providing a handy but heavily controlled cheap labour force for the neighbouring base. Kwajalein Atoll has the world's largest lagoon, covering more than 1,000 square miles, a necklace of tiny islands rimming the crescent-shaped coral reef. Since the 1950s Kwajalein's lagoon has been used by the US Air Force as a target range for testing ballistic missiles launched thousands of miles away, in Hawai'i and Vandenberg and Point Mugu in California. In recent years Kwajalein has played a vital part in the development of Reagan's 'Star Wars' weapon and sensing systems.

Ebeye, the 'slum of the Pacific'.

Around the same time, in early 1985, as the *Rainbow Warrior* sailed across the Pacific to Hawai'i, Elaine Shaw had made her own journey to Tahiti and Rarotonga to meet activists, publicise the impending voyage and make the many necessary practical arrangements. 'Considering the scale of the peace voyage and the possible repercussions for those involved in the Marshalls and French Polynesia,' wrote Elaine on her return, 'it seemed essential that Greenpeace have close liaison with people in both regions.'

Elaine was again keen to collaborate closely with local people, or at the very least to ensure that activists in Tahiti were fully informed about the voyage, about which they were sure to get a twisted picture through the French-controlled media. 'In late 1984 I had written to various activists about the peace voyage, but had received a reply only from Charlie Ching, of the small pro-independence group Te Taata Tahiti Tiama, in which he gave his support for the venture.

'In my first week in Tahiti I stayed near Bengt and Marie-Thérèse Danielsson, where I met representatives from all from the main anti-testing groups, including Jacqui Drollet from Ia Mana te Nunaa, John Doom from the Polynesian Evangelical Church, Tea Hirshon from Tavini Huiraatira and Charlie Ching.'

Charlie Ching burns the tricolour at an Auckland demonstration, 1983.

From Tahiti Elaine travelled to Huahine, an island eighty miles northwest of Papeete, though it might have been a world away. 'Huahine has a strong history of independence; the people here resisted the French military takeover of Tahiti in 1842. It is also the birthplace of Pouvanaa a Oopa, who started the original independence movement in French Polynesia.'

On Huahine Elaine was looked after by Dorothy Levy, who had helped *Fri* in Tahiti and New Zealand during the return leg of the 1973 Moruroa voyage. Dorothy and Guy Taero, a young Tahitian who had crewed on *Vega* during her 1982 Moruroa trip, saw to it that Elaine met many Tahitian activists. 'They took me to see Georgina Oopa, a teacher married to one of Pouvanaa's relatives and a dedicated peace worker. I was impressed by all the women I met on this trip; they seemed strong and steady, though I couldn't find many who had taken a leading role in politics there, which seemed a great loss.

'When I got back to Papeete I was instantly struck by the French influence, the bustle, the political intrigue, and the pollution. Here I caught up with Oscar Temaru and Jacqui Drollet. Jacqui was fully behind the voyage and promised to provide Maohi crew if Greenpeace needed them. Oscar's first question was, "Why just go to Moruroa? Papeete is where the people are. Moruroa is a symptom of the wider problems facing us, so why not bring the *Rainbow Warrior* here first."'

Thinking it through on her way back to Auckland, Elaine came to support Oscar's view, and she now recommended that the *Warrior* first visit Tahiti and that Greenpeace set about inviting local anti-testing leaders to join the protest. Later these events would be deliberately distorted by certain French journalists and by Paris in an attempt to justify the bombing of the ship. But meanwhile Greenpeace's attention returned to the Marshall Islands, where the *Rainbow Warrior* was beginning her Pacific Peace Voyage.

The definitive chronicle of Operation Exodus can be found in David Robie's Eyes of Fire *(see Further Reading), from which the following account is partly drawn.*

Leaving Hawai'i at the end of April, the *Warrior* arrived at Majuro on 12 May to the news that France had just carried out two nuclear tests at Moruroa.

> 'When we decided to leave Rongelap Atoll, the old people cried to leave their homeland. But I said, "What about your grandchildren? Do you want them to die?"'
> *Senator Jeton Anjain*

Martini greeted the information with a characteristic expletive, and the crew sent a caustic telex to President Mitterrand informing him of the *Rainbow Warrior*'s humanitarian mission to Rongelap and their intention to subsequently sail to Moruroa as the mother ship of a peace flotilla from New Zealand.

At Majuro a US official informed Greenpeace that there was no medical reason to move people from Rongelap – in spite of his own admission that Rongelap's coconuts were too contaminated to eat. Even on this picturesque island the crew were reminded of the dangers of radiation. A poster outside the post office headed 'Listen to Your Bodies' listed the warning signs of cancer. Little wonder that a local shopkeeper told David Robie, 'Greenpeace and New Zealand are doing good things – standing up to the Americans. We want to be nuclear-free.'

The *Warrior* arrived at the seemingly idyllic tropical paradise of Rongelap on 17 May. As they entered the lagoon, Bunny saw a group of women heading

Rongelap women welcome the *Warrior*'s crew.

towards them in one of the small motor launches the locals affectionately call bumbums, for the sound they make. 'The women came out to greet us singing Marshallese songs – one of them, Mengerick, holding up a banner that read "We Love the Future of Our Kids". We could only watch in silence. With all we had heard and read about the story of Rongelap, it was overwhelming. Leaving their land was like giving up their names; it was everything to them. Losing their land was like losing their spirit.' 'The atoll provides food, fish, everything,' Henk adds. 'On Rongelap everyone is born with land rights, with

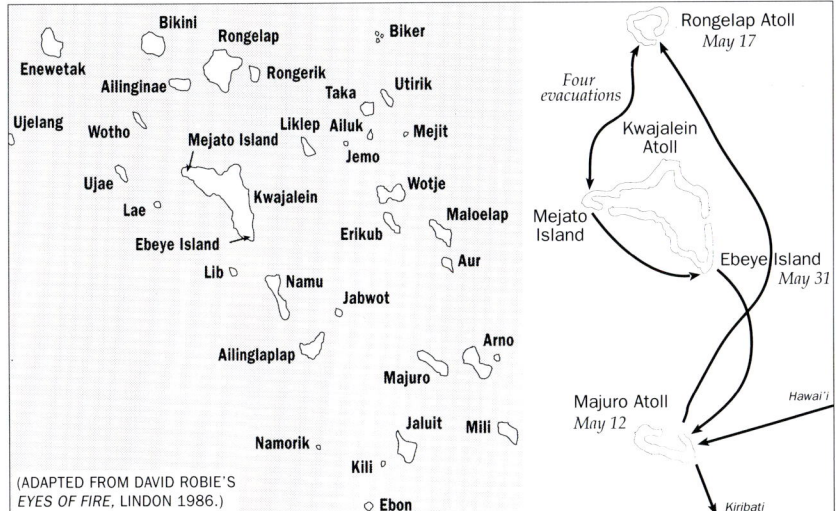

The Marshall Islands – Operation Exodus.

(ADAPTED FROM DAVID ROBIE'S *EYES OF FIRE*, LINDON 1986.)

Leaving home. 'The people looked to me to find a way to save them, but they didn't really believe a ship would come all the way from Britain. It wasn't until they saw the *Rainbow Warrior* in their lagoon that they really believed me.'
Senator Jeton Anjain

Fernando's photograph of these Rongelap children was among many damaged as a result of the bombing in Auckland Harbour two months later.

A makeshift shelter on Mejato. 'We know it's going to be tough, trying to make a new life, to be alienated from our land and our spiritual roots. But we have no choice. The future of our children is most important – by staying here they have no hope. They are bound to die from cancer.' *Julian Riklon*

Rongelap families arrive on Mejato.

a place to live and gather food. No one is landless, so giving up the atoll was in one sense like giving up their kids' future. Each piece of land had its own story.'

On the beach an archway of coconut timber and plaited pandanus leaves covered in hibiscus flowers stood as the focal point for their welcome. Bunny noticed how the younger men sat silently behind the gathering on the beach. 'Nobody really wanted to leave and I think our arrival brought a final realisation that they were going away, perhaps for ever.' As they wandered around the island the crew found houses whose roofs and walls had already been

'American scientists have been lying to us for thirty years about the radiation on our islands. The poison from the Bravo monster bomb is still being felt today. Our people suffered then, and we are still suffering from radiation diseases such as thyroid tumours, cancer, leukaemia, birth defects, stillbirths and miscarriages. Now, as we all decided last year, the time has come for us to leave for Mejato Island. For the sake of our children and our grandchildren.'
Senator Jeton Anjain

stripped down, corrugated aluminium sheeting and plywood stacked in neat, labelled piles.

That afternoon everyone converged on the shadehouse next to the village church for a last community meeting. There was much sadness, even despair, in the eyes of the mostly silent gathering. Senator Anjain and other leaders reminded them of the reasons why, in order to spare their children the legacy of illness and early death that faced them should they remain on their contaminated island, they had made the hard decision to leave their ancestral home.

For the next few days the Greenpeace crew and the islanders worked together, dismantling the houses and using the bumbums and two Greenpeace inflatables to ferry load after load of building materials, furniture and other possessions out to the ship. Martini and second mate Benne Hoffmann slung a tarpaulin over the boat deck to provide shade for the passengers, which made using the sails impossible as there was no deck room.

The ten-day evacuation to Mejato required four trips by the *Warrior* between the islands, during which more than 300 islanders, all their possessions and 100 tonnes of building materials were relocated. Bunny and Henk presented their new friends with a hardwood dugout canoe they had brought with them all the way from Nicaragua – 'from a small people struggling for their sovereignty against the United States to another small people doing the same'. Before they left they were given in return a Marshallese outrigger canoe, which has since become a familiar sight on Auckland Harbour.

Most of the crew were desolated when it was time to leave Mejato. The experience of the past two weeks had stirred up powerful emotions, and they hated the idea of abandoning the people of Rongelap before they had at least helped them rebuild their homes. But they could not afford to delay the rest of their voyage, so they sadly said their goodbyes and headed for Ebeye, where they were again feasted by their generous Rongelapese hosts.

Kwajalein: 'We Cannot Relocate the World'.

The *Rainbow Warrior*'s crew could not leave the Marshall Islands, however, without registering a visible, dramatic, Greenpeace-style protest against the US military activities on the atoll believed by Owen Wilkes to have 'contributed more to the nuclear arms race than any other spot on earth.' At dawn on 6 June Bunny, Andy Biedermann and Irish crew member Grace O'Sullivan set off in a Zodiac driven by Benne Hoffmann for the heavily guarded military base on nearby Kwajalein Island. After climbing the tall security fence around a massive radar dome they unfurled a banner reading 'Kemij Jab Maron Lomoren Aolep Ri Lol' (We Cannot Relocate the World – Stop Star Wars). By the time the military police caught on, the group had made their escape, the action safely captured on film.

The ship's next port of call was Tarawa in Kiribati. Martini had last visited these islands in 1975 on board *Fri*, when Tarawa was still part of the British colony of the Gilbert and Ellice Islands. Kiribati had already played a crucial role in opposing the dumping of radioactive waste at sea. Together with neighbouring Nauru, the tiny island nation had in 1983 joined the London Dumping Convention, a treaty restricting waste dumping at sea, in order to combat plans by the Japanese Government and the US Navy to dump low-level nuclear waste and obsolete nuclear submarines in the Pacific. These plans met with strenuous opposition from Pacific nations, whose protests eventually ensured the indefinite extension of a Pacific nuclear-dumping moratorium.

The *Warrior*'s crew were accorded an official welcome by the Kiribati Government, which encouraged them to hold several public meetings and an open-air video session on ocean dumping, and they were swamped with invitations and kindness from this enthusiastic and generous people.

'We got an even more amazing reception in Vanuatu,' recalls Bunny of their next port of call. At the entrance to Port Vila they were welcomed by a flotilla of boats, including government launches, flying peace and nuclear-free flags. 'There were big groups with banners, one welcoming the *Rainbow Warrior* to nuclear-free Port Vila, another from the ni-Vanuatu Women's Group. The Lini Government gave us a great official reception, where Martini was to make a speech. It was late in the evening and he was already pretty well oiled and relaxed, so he just got up and told everyone how he really felt about Moruroa. He was "really pissed off about the continuing focking nuclear tests there"… We were all shocked for a moment, thinking his language might have really offended the people. But the government guys all told us later he was great and they were really into what he said!'

With a good party behind them, the crew went on to more formal talks with Prime Minister Lini about nuclear testing and radioactive waste dumping. Walter Lini, a former Anglican priest, led his people to independence in 1980 and two years later introduced a nuclear-free resolution, barring port visits by all nuclear ships. Since then Vanuatu has been an enthusiastic advocate of a nuclear-free Pacific and a strong

'The farewell on Ebeye really got me. We ate, we drank, we sang, we danced; they shook our hands, they gave money; I cried. How could anyone do to these shy, gentle people what has been done?' Davey Edward, *first engineer*, Rainbow Warrior

'The world is too precious to be ruled and ruined by rich white men with clean hands and sick minds.' Hanne Sorensen, *second engineer*, Rainbow Warrior

Prime Minister Walter Lini on board the *Warrior*.

Arriving at Port Vila, Vanuatu.

'Colonialism and nuclearism in the Pacific are part of the same evil. To eradicate this evil from our region we have to deal with it from its root – colonialism. Nuclear testing will continue for as long as colonialism remains and nuclear powers exploit Pacific people to play with their deadly weapons.'
Prime Minister Walter Lini

supporter of independence for Pacific nations, and Walter Lini has consistently pointed out the links between the two. Lini had first heard of the plan to bring the *Warrior* to the Pacific when he had visited Elaine Shaw at the Greenpeace New Zealand office in December 1984, after attending a South Pacific Forum meeting in Wellington. Elaine had asked her old friend if he would approve a visit by the ship after her mission in the Marshall Islands. The Government and people of Vanuatu would be honoured, he had replied. In Vanuatu the *Warrior*'s crew were left in no doubt that they were among friends.

From Port Vila, now with ni-Vanuatu representative Charles Rara on board, the *Rainbow Warrior* made straight for Auckland, arriving on 7 July 1985 to a Peace Squadron welcome from some thirty boats, including Chris Robinson, Steve Sawyer and some of the GPNZ staff on *Vega*. Catching the first glimpse of the *Warrior* was an exhilarating experience for many that morning – and for no one more than Elaine, on board the scow *Te Aroha* with her family, for whom it marked the realisation of a long-held dream and the culmination of years of planning and lobbying.

It was also Bunny's homecoming after seven years of extraordinary overseas experience. 'Auckland had changed so much since I left – all high-rises flashing with glass, and after the Marshall Islands just like any other rich Western city. We were welcomed mainly by peace movement people. I met Elaine and Carol for the first time on Marsden Wharf. Titewhai Harawira also came on board and gave a really impressive, fiery speech.'

Other Greenpeace activists from around the Pacific and North America were also converging on Auckland. An ANZUSCA (Greenpeace Australia, New Zealand, USA and Canada) regional meeting had been planned to coincide with the *Warrior*'s visit. Kelly Rigg, from the US wildlife campaign, had arrived in June. She was immediately struck by the contrast between the Washington and Auckland offices. 'I'd left a bustling office of some 30 people structured in departments, each with their own computers, assistants and telephones. Arriving at GPNZ, I felt as if I'd stumbled into a time warp. There were seven staff members, one computer and a couple of telephones. Driving in to the office with Carol, we picked up the mail at the post office, and on our arrival proceeded to open it as a group. The entire office sat together in the front room, opening the mail, reading interesting bits aloud, and chatting over tea. The phone would ring periodically, and whoever was closest would answer it. It all seemed so civilised.

Elaine Shaw, on the scow *Te Aroha*, welcomes the *Warrior* to Auckland.

'I couldn't recall ever receiving such a warm and friendly welcome from a Greenpeace office. Everyone, regardless of function, was preparing for the imminent arrival of the *Rainbow Warrior* and the voyage to Moruroa. People were busy, although the whole concept of "busy" was entirely different somehow from what I was used to.

'What struck me most about the GPNZ office was that it seemed to be more of a gathering place than a place to conduct business, and the people were not merely co-workers but a community. This community encompassed not only the office staff, which happens in many offices, but a larger activist and volunteer network too. I was constantly amazed that whenever someone got up to make a hot drink, the whole office was canvassed and drinks were made for all.

'When the *Warrior* finally arrived the level of activity increased by an order of magnitude. After more than a year of planning, it was all finally happening, and everyone was excited. There were parties, welcoming ceremonies and planning meetings. This was, after all, the first time a large Greenpeace ship had come to the Southern Hemisphere.'

Steve Sawyer, still recovering from injuries he had sustained as a result of a fall in the Marshall Islands, also arrived in June. 'As was usually the case with visiting Greenpeacers in those days, I was picked up from the airport early in the morning and taken directly to the office. Whether or not you are picked up at the airport on your first visit to a Greenpeace office anywhere usually says something about the character and friendliness of that office, and I was not disappointed.

'The old office at Nagel House was fairly typical of the generally funky Greenpeace accommodation of those days, so I felt reasonably at home; also, the people I met there and the old acquaintances renewed – it seems that GPNZ has been a haven for all sorts of old Greenpeacers going back to the very early days of the organisation – were extremely friendly, accommodating and generally excited about the impending arrival of the *Warrior*.

'What I wasn't fully prepared for was the clash between the operating style I had become used to in working at the international office in the UK and the Washington office, and that in GPNZ. The Auckland office seemed years behind to me; which is to say that everything was done on a very low-key, collective basis, with no clear lines of authority and responsibility, very little division of labour, and very little sign of what we in Greenpeace generally pride ourselves on as "efficiency". These were, I hasten to add, initial impressions, which I believe were accurate but missed some essential elements.

'I remember my first clash on this sort of issue was over the fact that my telexes and mail, along with everyone else's, were opened first thing in the morning with everyone sitting round drinking tea or coffee, and passed around for everyone to read. I instinctively rebelled against this way of doing things, more out of habit than because of any great secrets contained in the messages. It was my first experience of what was "special" about the New Zealand way of doing things. But despite such little things, I thoroughly enjoyed working with the people in the office. It was the first time I'd seen *Vega*, and I began to understand why the little boat elicited such affection from everyone who'd ever been involved with her.'

Jude Seaboyer: 'In the weeks before the *Warrior* arrived the office, which had long since ceased to accommodate all of us, was bursting at the seams. Rien and his Peace Flotilla people, Bev, who was getting her school talks together, and Annie Maignot's Le Groupe, who were organising a boycott of French products – all had to be accommodated from time to time. I guess Steve coped remarkably well with what must have seemed utter chaos! I have vivid memories of him, Walkman in place to drown out the racket the rest of

On hearing news of the bombing, Senator Jeton Anjain said, 'What have they done to our boat?'

us were used to living with, perched either in front of his computer or on top of our inefficient secondhand heater. I think he probably saw the primitive nature of our heating arrangements as symptomatic of the Auckland office, if not all New Zealand! Certainly he found our ways of operating odd, but mostly he kept his feelings to himself, and we accommodated what we could and ignored what we couldn't. I suppose we all thought that once the Moruroa action was over, Steve and the other visitors would go home and we would continue as we had before he arrived. What he didn't, I think, recognise was that while we worked differently, our methods were in fact considered, not random, and every bit as "efficient" as his.

'After the so-called "feminist coup" in 1984 we had decided it wasn't enough simply to pay lip-service to non-hierarchical structures. Helen Yensen gave weeks of her precious time to organising workshops to help us develop new ways of working together and new methods of conflict resolution, so that no one was disenfranchised and turned into an outsider by decisions they couldn't support, as had happened in the past.

'Workers in any political organisation suffer from high levels of stress, and we worked hard to find ways of supporting each other that would reduce the risk of burnout and enhance the work we did. It wasn't an easy process and we weren't always very good at it – we didn't stop being opinionated and bossy just because we were reading books on conflict resolution – but we learned to trust one another and to truly work together.'

The days before the *Warrior* arrived were feverish with activity and endless meetings with the crews of the flotilla boats and other peace groups supporting the venture. One thing that puzzled Carol Stewart was that Steve had advised the office that it was usual for Greenpeace crew and office staff to maintain a distance. '"They just didn't mix," he'd said. This seemed a very peculiar attitude to us. Luckily it was another of Steve's observations we chose to ignore. The night of the *Warrior*'s arrival, despite the warning, almost the entire crew and most of the office staff had dinner together followed by a raging party on board, which certainly broke down the barriers!

'The next couple of days were a flurry of last-minute meetings and work. On Wednesday night, three days after the ship had arrived, a group of us had dinner with Steve to celebrate his birthday, returned to the *Warrior* to drink his health, then I took some of the overseas visitors out to Piha, where the regional planning meeting was due to start the next day. Some time later the phone rang. It was Elaine...'

On board the *Rainbow Warrior* that night were several of the crew and a number of local Greenpeacers. Martini, skipper Pete Willcox, engineer Davey Edward, Benne Hoffmann, radio operator Lloyd Anderson, Rien Achterberg and Fernando Pereira were all having a drink in the ship's mess. Bunny was visiting relatives and Henk was at a meeting in the ship's theatre. All the skippers of the peace flotilla were there. Relief cook and Peace Squadroneer Margaret Mills had baked a chocolate cake for Steve's birthday. After the birthday celebration the assembled skippers met in the ship's theatre to discuss schedules and routes. Around 11 pm Kelly Rigg urged the skippers' meeting to adjourn so Steve could drive out to Piha for the next day's regional meeting. Margaret, Pete and Lloyd were asleep in their cabins by 11.30, all the others either departed or up in the mess talking. Elaine had driven the remaining international visitors out to Piha then returned to her mother's house.

At 11.49 an electric blue flash was seen in the water beside the *Warrior*, quickly followed by a huge explosion. 'Bloody hell... It's from the engine-room,' shouted Davey Edward after he was thrown off his chair against the wall. As everyone raced from the mess, Davey ran to the engine room. He was hardly able to open the door. It was like a huge steam bath, with water hissing in through the gaping hole torn in the ship's side.

Pete Willcox, jolted awake, stumbled down to the engine room. One look was enough. 'Abandon ship, everyone get the hell out of here!' The others were scrambling up to the deck and onto the wharf. It was chaos in the darkness. Someone shouted, 'Look out, the masts are coming down!' as the ship keeled over towards the wharf.

Fernando Pereira was worried about his cameras. He called out that he was going below to get them. He was quickly followed by Martini, who couldn't find his partner Hanne Sorensen and was worried she might still be in their cabin. The two men skidded down the stairs together. Martini checked out the cabin in scant seconds and made for the deck again, then the wharf. Fernando was in his cabin when the second blast went off, barely two minutes after the first.

There was panic on the wharf. No one had seen Fernando come back up. Martini was still asking, 'Where's Hanne?' Someone said they thought she'd gone for a walk earlier.

Elaine had just returned home from Piha when the telephone rang. It was a *New Zealand Herald* reporter, who wanted to talk to her about the *Rainbow Warrior*. 'At one o'clock in the morning!' she snapped. 'Oh, I'm sorry. Didn't you know? Your ship's been sunk.' Elaine slammed the phone down in shocked disbelief. Then it rang again – a local radio station this time. 'No, I don't know anything about it,' she said firmly, heart pounding, and hung up. She rang Steve and the Piha contingent immediately set off for the city.

When they arrived the wharf area was already cordoned off and they were directed to the Wharf Police Station, where the crew, some wrapped in blankets, sat pale-faced and in shock. It was 2 am. The only good news was that Hanne had turned up safe after a walk into the city.

By 4 am divers had recovered Fernando's body. He had drowned, trapped in his cabin, the straps of his camera bag tangled round one leg.

Fernando Pereira

In the mid-1970s Fernando Pereira left his home in Portugal to avoid being conscripted into the armed forces, then embroiled in colonial wars in Africa and Asia. Fernando travelled to the Netherlands, where he eventually joined Greenpeace to turn his photographic skills to what he saw as a politically positive use. After fleeing war to work for peace, Fernando's death was a tragic and cruel irony.

Fernando Pereira and Bonemej Namwe in the Rongelap bumbum.

Margaret Mills wrote a poem for Fernando from which these lines are drawn:

No martyr he,
seeking death between the narrow walls
of man-made faith,
He gave his work and enjoyed the giving.
He should be famed not for dying
but for living.
For how he used his life
and for caring.
He did not give his life,
they took it.

CHAPTER EIGHT

L'Affaire Greenpeace

'ON THE MORNING of 11 July, everything changed,' remembers Kelly Rigg. 'We had sat up all night in the police station, waiting for word of Fernando. It was close to dawn before we received the news. As Auckland started to wake up, the ship's crew went to the home of a friend while the rest of us went directly to the office.

'The phone started ringing. The press wanted interviews. People wanted to know what they could do to help, where they should send food, clothing and money. Then visitors and volunteers started arriving. Most didn't know what to say or do; the entire city seemed to be in shock. Here we were, exhausted, grief-stricken and angry, yet somehow expected to be composed, well co-ordinated and well spoken. Needless to say, it was pandemonium.

'Overnight, GPNZ had become the centre of the world. There weren't the phone lines, people or computers to handle the work that now needed to be done. The office space was too small to accommodate staff, crew (who no longer had their own place to work), visitors, and the provisions that had been accumulating for the peace voyage. On top of that, donations for the crew, who had lost all their possessions on the *Warrior*, were beginning to arrive by the car-load, and the office took on the look of a secondhand clothing store!'

Elaine was in the office early. 'The phone started ringing as soon as we got in the door at seven. A stream of people began to arrive, asking what they could do, so we passed out donation boxes for them to take downtown. The slogan, dreamt up by David Buller of Wellington and passed on in a phone call from Owen Wilkes that morning, was "You Can't Sink a Rainbow".'

'The immediate aftermath of the bombing was pure hell,' says Steve Sawyer, 'but everyone responded selflessly. There were the crew to take care of, funeral arrangements for Fernando, then getting the gear off the ship. The small office with just two telephones seemed to become the primary focus for the world's media, which rapidly became the dominant feature of our lives.

'I'll never forget the overwhelming public support we received from all over the country. People arrived with food, clothing, offers of every kind of help. It was an incredible experience. Also, because my face often ended up on TV, for about ten days my money was no good in shops, restaurants, airline ticket counters, even in pubs in Auckland. I didn't then and I don't now have adequate words of appreciation for all those New Zealanders who

Opposite: A diver inspects the scuttled *Rainbow Warrior*, December 1987.

pitched in to make our work and our lives a bit less traumatic at that time.

'However, after a couple of weeks, when a vague semblance of reality returned, tensions began to rise between me and some of the office staff. There was a feeling that I had "taken over" and was trying personally to orchestrate our responses to events. I'll admit I was probably getting into a very "efficient" mode, running around giving orders, barking at people and that sort of thing – which they didn't take very kindly to. Not that I blame them. I'm sure I can be an overbearing bastard, especially in a situation like that, but I can't figure a better way to proceed under such circumstances.

Elaine at a post-bombing press conference.

'After a blowout or two, though, a generally positive feeling of solidarity was re-established, and I think we all learned from our different ways of approaching things. I learned a lot about the spirit of New Zealand, if that doesn't sound too corny, and felt like I had a glimpse of the essence of what is different about the Pacific in general – which I'd been hearing about non-stop from Elaine for the previous year or so – and New Zealand in particular. It was an education I won't forget, and in turn I hope I was able to pass on some of the useful bits of "northern" organisational ways.

'The major recollection I have of that traumatic time is the enormous respect and affection I developed for all the people of Greenpeace New Zealand. I'll always feel like we share something very special, almost a family feeling. Then there were the *Warrior* crew, who were simply the best Greenpeace crew I have ever had the privilege to work with; and, interestingly, at least half of them have since chosen to settle in New Zealand.'

Kelly Rigg: 'Within a day or two, the mail started arriving by the sackload. There was no longer time to open it all together, let alone read aloud the interesting bits. Cheerful chatter was replaced with the grim exchange of information about the police investigation. We anxiously awaited the newspapers each morning and afternoon, and the relevant articles were clipped and put into a scrapbook that was read and re-read constantly.

'As we tried to get organised, traditional roles within the office were set aside. Since the bombing coincided with a planning meeting of the international Greenpeace trustees, there were a number of extra hands on deck. People were designated to speak with the press, answer the phones, keep other Greenpeace offices updated, handle mail, organise volunteers and so on. Although there was no spoken agreement, it seemed natural for Steve to take charge, and he did, exuding authority and making decisions quickly as was demanded of him.

'A palpable air of tension in the office developed. While the staff had always made decisions by consensus, Steve consulted a minimum of people, usually on a "need to know" basis. No one really argued with the decisions he made, nor did they deny that he was doing a good job in a difficult situation. There was certainly no one clamouring to take his place. Steve did the job in the only way he knew how. People in the office, however, felt disempowered.

'The problem was discussed into the small hours of the morning, with no obvious solution. I believe the issue was not about power but about process. People were waking up to the fact that Greenpeace New Zealand would never be the same, and it was painful. These days, with two Greenpeace ships regularly based in Auckland and a large, dynamic campaigning office, it's hard to remember the quiet little office I first encountered in 1985. But somehow, inside GPNZ today, it still exists.'

Jude: 'How was it that we accepted the "International takeover" of the office, which I think is what happened? The situation was complicated. Steve had been in the office for some weeks. He got on with his business, we with ours, with few problems. We were all far too busy to worry about anything else. I felt International business was not my concern. Elaine, however, was already feeling pushed aside in her campaign. I knew Elaine could be difficult to work with, but I'd seen her cope with trickier situations and I thought she and Steve, who had a great deal of respect for each other, would sort things out. I felt, if Elaine could cope with Titewhai Harawira, she could certainly deal with Steve! He really wasn't an "ugly American" – a bit tetchy and self-centred at times, but we were all fond of him.

'Of course, the "takeover" didn't occur until after the bombing. Suddenly the crowded office was full of Americans and Europeans, and suddenly it was no longer ours – we were reduced to a supporting role. But there was no question of staking claims. In fact, I think it was less a problem for us than Steve perceived it to be. We still thought that eventually the "colonisers" would go home, and we would go back to being Greenpeace New Zealand, a thorn in the side of GPI, but a valued sort of a thorn! As an example of Steve's paranoia, one day the office staff were having a meeting in my office and a volunteer discovered Steve with his ear pressed to the keyhole. He thought we must be talking about him! But no doubt there was projection on both sides.

Police inspect the *Warrior*'s torn hull in the Devonport Naval Base dry dock.

'However, the behaviour of some of the Americans was ugly and objectionable, and we weren't the only ones aware of it. On one occasion a group of us went to see lawyer Rodney Harrison, who had offered to act for us in matters relating to the bombing, but the meeting was quickly taken over by the visitors, to the extent that Rodney later phoned us to suggest he'd like a little less of their input and more of ours next time. It was sometimes as if we were invisible. They just knew they were the best people to handle everything to do with the boat. Ironically, this sort of thing reminded me of France's arrogant, condescending attitude towards New Zealand – a distant sleepy hollow where they could do whatever they liked.

'Eventually Steve worked closely and well with Carol. But I still feel sad that the methods we'd worked so hard to put into practice were largely shelved. In the end we all had to share responsibility for not fighting hard enough to hold on to what we had.

'Three months after the bombing we were told by GPI fundraiser Doug Falkner that a big US concert promoter by the name of Tom Campbell was willing to stage a fundraising concert in Auckland to which he could attract names like Neil Young, Jackson Browne and Graham Nash. The concert was held at Mt Smart Stadium on 15 April 1986. It was a seven-hour musical feast attracting an enthusiastic crowd of 20,000, only marred for us by Campbell himself, who turned out to be an impossibly arrogant bastard, and the small nett take of around $8,000. Fortunately Pip and Bev and I had the foresight to keep the merchandise sales ($36,000) separate from the concert takings. At the end of the day Tom Campbell was insisting that he should look after *all* the money – his hotel, he said, had kindly offered the use of their safe. And disappear with it the next morning, we thought. No way! So while he raged at our obstinacy, we were sneaking bags of money out the back way into a waiting car. We weren't very popular with that American either!'

As it emerged that the bombing was a deliberate act of sabotage, there was little doubt in Greenpeace minds who was responsible. Two days after the bombing the French Embassy in Wellington issued a statement echoing the flat denials emanating from Paris. 'In no way is France involved,' it declared. 'The French Government doesn't deal with its opponents in such ways.' But within a few days police had arrested French secret service agents Alain Mafart and Dominique Prieur as they tried to return their van to an Auckland hire company. While they were held in custody, the charter yacht *Ouvéa*, carrying another team of agents implicated in the bombing, sailed to Norfolk Island and then disappeared a few days out to sea headed north for Tahiti. Her crew was reportedly picked up by the French nuclear submarine *Rubis*, which turned up in Tahiti on 22 July – the first time a French nuclear submarine had been known to enter the South Pacific.

The international outcry pressured the French Government into setting up its own inquiry. After less than three weeks the head of the inquiry, Bernard Tricot, a former Director-General of the Elysée Palace, announced, 'On the basis of the information available to me at this time, I do not believe there was any French responsibility.' The French agents caught in New Zealand were merely there to spy on Greenpeace, Tricot implied, not to bomb them.

Bev Cormack recalls just one example of the French media manipulation that followed: 'In Tahiti the French TV station used film footage, taken by two French journalists on board the *Warrior*, of the Rongelap relocation to back their contention that Greenpeace had been recruiting Pacific Islanders from atolls around Moruroa to carry out an invasion of Moruroa, and that the *Rainbow Warrior* was therefore a legitimate target.' *Paris-Match* also claimed that 'Greenpeace planned to invade Moruroa, with ecologists and Polynesians trying to recapture the atoll.' *Le Point* magazine further elaborated this romance with a story claiming that Bengt Danielsson 'had organised an invasion of Moruroa, to be carried out by the inhabitants of neighbouring atolls with the help of pirogues and dinghies.' Evidence for this assertion was

Greenpeace vigil in Paris. Flowers are laid beneath a photograph of Fernando Pereira.

supposedly gleaned from Bengt's mail, which, it was admitted, had been regularly opened by the French secret service.

Most of the world's media reported on the affair rather more judiciously and were soon roundly condemning the French Government. The New Zealand media, reflecting the mood of the country, reacted with a sense of outrage and growing scepticism of the crude and contradictory French denials. The day of the bombing the *Auckland Star* wrote: 'With an irrationality that is impossible to fathom, bombers have struck at crusaders whose tactics have always been non-violent, whose aims have always been to preserve and enhance life on our planet, in campaigns ranging from saving endangered whales to opposing nuclear weapons testing.

'The Greenpeace organisation has always found a soft spot in our national heart, pursuing, as it has, the campaign against French testing in the Pacific, which we as a nation led a decade ago with the dispatch of a frigate to the testing grounds. But even as terrorist acts go, this must count as one of the most pointless. To blow up a boat dedicated to putting the peace back into the Pacific is not going to win any friends for the perpetrators. Just the opposite.'

Hostility towards the French Government grew after President Mitterrand threatened that any protesters at Moruroa that year would be arrested, and refused to meet with Greenpeace International director David McTaggart. Rather than cool the growing international controversy, the transparently inadequate Tricot report served only to fuel the fires of indignation and further undermine the French Government's credibility, so that a second inquiry was ordered on 5 September, but it was already too late.

Following claims in the London *Sunday Times* that President Mitterrand had known of the bombing plan, and implicitly, therefore, had authorised it, French Defence Minister Charles Hernu resigned and Admiral Pierre Lacoste, the director of the DGSE, France's intelligence and covert action bureau, was sacked. Within days Prime Minister Fabius admitted that French secret service agents had bombed the *Rainbow Warrior* under orders. It was, said New Zealand Prime Minister David Lange, nothing more than 'a sordid act of international state-backed terrorism'.

Before the final journey to Matauri Bay.

Charged with murder and arson, on 4 November Mafart and Prieur, just two of a much larger team of saboteurs, pleaded guilty in the High Court at Auckland to lesser charges of manslaughter and wilful damage and were each sentenced to ten years' jail. Their guilty plea ensured that the facts of the police investigation would never be made public. In June 1986, in a political deal presided over by the United Nations Secretary-General, Javier Perez de Cuellar, France agreed to pay compensation of $13 million to New Zealand and 'apologise', in return for which Mafart and Prieur would be detained at the French military base on Hao Atoll for three years. David Lange's recent book confirms that the result of the 'mediation' was predetermined, with de Cuellar accepting the role of mediator only on the condition that the terms between France and New Zealand be settled in advance. Lange had been persuaded to go along with the charade by

France's crude economic threats. To cap it all, the two spies were both free by May 1988, after less than two years had elapsed, Mafart having been smuggled out of Tahiti under yet another false identity.

'L'Affaire Greenpeace', as it became known, dominated the media and possessed the nation for many months. Perhaps it went some way towards raising the profile of the nuclear test ban campaign and increased New Zealanders' awareness of France's role in the Pacific. Yet the underlying issues were entirely overshadowed by an almost obsessive preoccupation with the military details of the operation and the political fallout between New Zealand and France. As the Danielssons concisely put it in *Poisoned Reign*, 'We cannot find in the metre-high pile of newspaper cuttings that we have collected about the various aspects of this tragicomic affair, one single reference to the problems, sufferings and aspirations of the people most deeply involved, the Polynesians, in whose islands 120 nuclear bombs have been detonated during the short period of twenty years. When reading all these articles, it is almost as if the 118 islands of French Polynesia were uninhabited, except perhaps for the few lovely hula girls who welcome French officials.'

With international espionage, murder, foreign hit squads roaming the country, and a political scandal that threatened to topple the government of a world power, it was certainly the most exciting story the New Zealand media had had in years, and understandably they revelled in it. It seemed as if the whole country relished the gradual collapse of the French Government's efforts to maintain a stance of injured innocence over the affair. Within a few months a rash of hastily compiled books, mostly quick-kill exposés, were published. There was endless debate over the identities, itineraries and missions of the various teams of French agents criss-crossing New Zealand. Then there was Christine Cabon, the spy who 'infiltrated' the Auckland office in order to gain access to Greenpeace's secret plans for the Moruroa action.

For Greenpeace staff, some of these stories bordered on the farcical. Anyone who knew how Greenpeace worked recognised that the notion of an espionage operation to gain access to secret files was absurd. There *were* no secret plans. Actions, where they were premeditated, were usually decided on at open meetings, and there were no locked files in the office. Anyone who wanted to could walk in off the street and gain access to Greenpeace's resources.

For the rest, it made good newspaper copy, and did a fine job of exposing the incurable paranoia among elements of the French Government and military and the bungling of her security forces, but it had precious little to do with Greenpeace New Zealand or its work. Those readers who are especially interested in this episode should turn to David Robie's or Michael King's accounts for the most reliable coverage.

There were of course repercussions in French Polynesia. Local opponents of nuclear testing had over the years faced arbitrary violence, intimidation and imprisonment, while their political representatives had been stymied by the gerrymandering of elections, constant surveillance, media blackouts and every kind of political and economic pressure. Earlier that year in Tahiti the Bikini Day march, to commemorate the day the Rongelap Islanders were poisoned by the 'Bravo' nuclear test, had been declared illegal by the colonial

Charlie Ching arrested in Papeete, March 1985.

authorities under an obscure 1935 Public Order Act. After calling on Tahitians to defy the ban, Charlie Ching and some of his supporters had been arrested and put in 'preventative custody'. This had created an atmosphere of heightened tension in Tahiti between anti-nuclear groups and the French authorities. Now Tahitians took the opportunity to embarrass France by renewing demands for Ching's release. Oscar Temaru was among a dozen Tahitians who staged a hunger strike outside the Territorial Assembly.

Temaru, leader of the independence party Tavini Huiraatira and mayor of Faa'a, Tahiti's largest town, sent a protest letter to the United Nations in which he wrote, 'Ching isn't a criminal; he's just a Tahitian who has tried to protest for independence and against the nuclear tests. How can you liberate criminals [Mafart and Prieur] and keep him in jail?' The question was of course rhetorical, as few Tahitians were more aware of the arbitrary exercise of state coercion to protect what France saw as her 'interests' than Temaru, who had fought for years against colonial repression and its poisonous consort, the nuclear tests.

In New Zealand the impact of the bombing was felt far beyond Greenpeace. Richard Northey, then Labour MP for Eden, maintains the bombing significantly changed perceptions in the country. 'It gave rise to a reappraisal of our national identity and of our place in the Anzus alliance. After a supposed Western ally bombed us, we had to rethink our role as a Western ally. And with the failure of the US and British Governments to condemn the bombing, people felt betrayed. There was already a strong anti-nuclear consensus, but since the bombing, and after the US and French treatment of New Zealand and the people of the Pacific, New Zealanders have become more willing to support independence in the Pacific.'

For Bunny McDiarmid, not only had the French Government failed utterly to understand how Greenpeace worked and why it was effective, but it had totally misread the mood of most people in the Pacific. 'The whole affair was an education for us all,' says Henk Haazen. 'The "justice at the highest level" promised by Mitterrand was really a mockery of justice.' 'To cap it all,' Bunny adds, 'we saw the US Government reveal its double standards when its ambassador to the United Nations, Jeanne Kirkpatrick, declared the bombing of the ship was not an act of terrorism because Fernando had not been *intentionally* murdered!'

'It's hard to remember clearly what I felt then,' says Carol Stewart. 'Everything since has coloured my thinking. I know I felt outraged, for Greenpeace and as a New Zealander – the two are really inextricable for me now. The injustice of Fernando's death – all for want of a warning phone call. The callousness of the attack, timed for when the maximum number of people could be expected to be asleep on board, really astounded me. It was a deliberate attempt to murder as many peaceful opponents as possible.

'Then there was all the media hype. It had been bloody hard trying to interest journalists in the voyage before the boat arrived. Operation Exodus had received little coverage. Even the *Warrior*'s arrival in Auckland didn't rate much interest. Then the bombing, and it became the only thing on the news for weeks. And people ask me why I'm a cynic! I remember being interviewed by a TV crew, and the reporter said off-camera he really identified with what the *Rainbow Warrior* was doing, and I said to him, "That's bullshit! You guys hardly gave us a mention before the bombing." The real issues were avoided by the media even after the bombing. It just became a spy thriller.'

It would also be a mistake to give the impression that Greenpeace today owes its success to the publicity surrounding this event, pivotal though it was for the organisation. As Irene Petersen points out, 'Over the previous ten years Greenpeace had gradually become part of the fabric of New Zealand society. By the time of the bombing there was already widespread public support for us, which had grown rapidly in the early 1980s.' The GPNZ supporters' list, which stood at 16,000 in 1986, dipped to just 10,000 in 1987 before rocketing to 32,000 in 1988, 56,000 in 1989 and over 100,000 by the end of 1990. Clearly there were other factors than the bombing to explain this massive growth.

It was perhaps axiomatic that Greenpeace, now joined by many new supporters, would defy France's heavy-handed message and press ahead with a new peace flotilla to Moruroa that winter. Some of the *Warrior*'s crew, seeking to overcome a sense of helplessness, joined other boats for the action. Henk Haazen opted to stay with the wreck of the *Warrior*. 'In retrospect it was a bad decision. I felt like an undertaker. After all the salvaging and then an awful auction selling off parts to souvenir hunters and scrap dealers, I ended up buying the sails and a load of bits myself.'

The flotilla was sponsored by a number of groups within the wider New Zealand peace movement. Full-page newspaper advertisements elicited supplies, equipment and food for the boats and many willing volunteers to help prepare them. Along with *Vega* were the yachts *Alliance*, sponsored by the Waiheke Peace Group, the *Varangian*, funded by the North Shore Peace Group, and a 24-metre brigantine, the *Breeze*, captained by an old friend of the *Fri*, Jim Cottier. These neighbourhood groups manged to raise $25,000 of the $50,000 needed for the yachts. At the last minute GPNZ was able to announce something of a coup: the *Rainbow Warrior*'s place as mother ship would be taken by a new member of GPI's international fleet. The ocean-going tug MV *Greenpeace* had recently been fitted out for Greenpeace's first Antarctic voyage. After some frantic rescheduling, the ship left Florida earlier than planned, and Bunny flew out to Curacao to meet them on their way through the Caribbean.

Meanwhile the French Navy, unrepentant as ever, deployed three warships, carrying specially trained marines to board the protest ships, with orders to ram the peace boats if necessary. As the flotilla neared Moruroa, the French authorities announced the extension of the internationally accepted twelve-mile territorial limit to thirty miles, a move the flotilla chose to ignore.

It was *Vega*'s fifth voyage to Moruroa. This time she carried a crew of five: skipper Chris Robinson, Pete Willcox, Grace O'Sullivan and Sue Ware were joined by Te Arawa elder Tihema Galvin, who sailed with them to Moruroa, then joined the *Greenpeace* for the trip to Papeete to pass on greetings from the tangata whenua of Aotearoa to the Maohi people of Tahiti.

'After three months' intensive preparation we left Auckland in late August loaded to the gunwales,' recalls Chris. 'But we were spurred on by the radio news of the official French admission of the bombing, Hernu's resignation and Mitterrand's planned visit to Moruroa. We reached the zone in three weeks and began our vigil. At 20.15 on Friday, 20 September, we sighted a vessel, and as they came close during the night, we discovered it was *La Hippopotame*... However, on 4 October the *Greenpeace* joined us, then the *Breeze* and the *Alliance*. It was so good to have friendly company out there at last.'

On board the *Greenpeace*, Franck Charrière, who had joined the organisation in France just before the bombing, was the sole French crew member, but his presence was no accident. Greenpeace had for many years been conscious of the importance of convincing friend and foe alike that their argument was not with the French people but with the French nuclear state, and that it was not only the people of the Pacific who opposed the tests. 'When Moruroa Atoll appeared on our radar screen three warships could be seen on the horizon,' wrote Franck in *Greenpeace News* on his return. 'As we approached, *Vega* came into view, sailing gently just outside the twelve-mile limit. The reunion was full of emotion, and *Vega*'s crew were more than happy to profit from the comforts of the mother ship.'

Among the *Breeze*'s crew of ten was Alice Heather, from Hamilton, who had crewed on *Fri* from 1979. 'On 5 October we rendezvoused with the *Greenpeace*, which had arrived the previous day. What a welcome sight she was, along with her hot showers and cold beers! After transferring water and fuel the *Greenpeace* rejoined *Vega*, and the *Breeze* followed in a more sedate fashion two days later. Under sail we danced and wove our way into the

The peace flotilla off Moruroa (from left): *Alliance, Vega, Breeze* and MV *Greenpeace*.

flotilla amidst the constant click and whir of cameras. With six journalists, a film crew and satellite communications on board the *Greenpeace* (and even more on the French warships), our movements were the focus of world media attention, despite the French Navy's attempts to block radio transmissions from the *Greenpeace*.'

While off Moruroa the *Greenpeace* had received a message from Mayor Lucas Paeamara of Mangareva, the principal island of the Gambier group, sixty miles south-west of Moruroa. During a conference of experts on fish poisoning held in Papeete the previous month, the mayor had tried without success to interest the Tahitian media and the conference experts in the experience of his own people. Several lagoons, including Mangareva's, had been used to clean out contaminated French warships and as a waste dump, and since then ciguatera had poisoned the fish in Mangareva's lagoon. The incidence of ciguatera, a disease in tropical reef fish which can cause serious illness or death in people who eat the affected fish, has been found to be many times higher in areas where nuclear tests have taken place, notably the Marshall and the Tuamotu and Gambier Islands. Now babies were born with eye problems and defective kidneys, and cancer rates were high on Mangareva. Although the population had repeatedly asked for medical help they had received none.

'A meeting was held on board the *Greenpeace* to see if there was any way we could respond to the telex, which, though not specifically addressed to us, was clearly a plea for help,' recalls New Zealand doctor Tony Atkinson. 'The story of nuclear fallout and radiation disease amongst the people of the Gambier Islands had still not been told. When the telex arrived a plan of action was quickly agreed on. The *Greenpeace* would go to Mangareva and contact the mayor by radio; there were many possibilities as to how we might proceed from this point. All the time the ship was made ready for the trip and plans were discussed, two French warships lay off no more than half a mile away.'

As luck would have it, a generator failure meant the *Greenpeace* was unable to make the trip to Mangereva. But Andy Biedermann was subsequently sent in 1987 to Tahiti and the Gambiers to interview people about their experiences of the health effects of the tests, and these were later published by Greenpeace.

Alliance was now within a few days' sailing of the zone, and the *Greenpeace* decided to await her arrival for one last group demonstration before heading for Papeete for repairs. 'On the way,' wrote Franck Charrière, 'we learned that the French authorities would not allow us to enter Papeete, refusing to believe we had mechanical problems. So Oscar Temaru and a delegation of Tahitians met us at the twelve-mile limit with gifts of shells, leis and fresh fruit. And after releasing all our "Stop Nuclear Testing" balloons on the wind to Tahiti, we set course again for New Zealand.'

Only *Vega* decided to stay on in the zone. 'On *Vega* we were never really sure what our tactics would be,' says Chris Robinson. 'Just being there in the company of the other boats and with the large media contingent embarrassed the French. We'd always considered heading off for the lagoon, but it never made sense unless it was done en masse. On the 21st we headed south to rendezvous with the last of the flotilla to arrive, *Varangian*. That evening we heard from Gerd Leipold, nuclear campaign co-ordinator from Hamburg, on board the *Greenpeace*. Apparently the top military and political brass from Paris were converging on Moruroa to witness a test – evidently a major post-bombing propaganda exercise. It was the first time there'd ever been specific prior notice of a blast. Gerd suggested we might like to consider some direct action.

'One of the hardest things to do out there is to keep a level head and a firm hold on reality. The *Warrior* had been sunk, and going in with *Vega* just so they could arrest her again might just make us look like losers. It would also mean more negative press for Greenpeace in France. On the other hand, if we were ever going to head into Moruroa lagoon, now, with the world's media attention on us, seemed like the time. We called up the other boats on the radio to talk it through and they supported action, so it was on.

'On the night of the 23rd we transferred inessential gear to *Varangian*, and in sloppy seas and high spirits we said our goodbyes and headed straight for the atoll. Peter was on the radio to Lloyd Anderson on board *Varangian*. Grace and Sue took turns at the helm while the French warship *Taape* stayed close by. We were eleven miles off Moruroa when we changed to starboard tack with the sou'easterlies easing, then just before dawn we went about to port tack and headed for the lagoon, and the crew on the warship became very agitated. It was first light when eight commandos came over in a Zodiac. It didn't look like a friendly call. It wasn't.'

Chris and Peter were promptly seized and, wrists bound, delivered to the aft deck of the *Taape*. They were soon followed by Grace and Sue. The *Taape* towed *Vega* into Moruroa lagoon, taking their time. Chris and the crew knew the nuclear test would be that morning and wondered where they would be held. As it turned out, they were hurriedly transferred to another French naval boat and taken to Tahiti, from where they were promptly deported to their countries of origin.

As the furore surrounding the bombing died down, a new controversy began over what to do with the wreck of the *Warrior*. By this time New Zealanders all over the country had come to identify with the ship, and Greenpeace was deluged by letters and phone calls urging (sometimes demanding) that it adopt one course or another. 'The *Warrior* had become every New Zealander's property and everyone wanted a say in her fate,' recalls Henk. For Greenpeace, this was at once both heartwarming and disturbing, for ultimately the ship did not belong to New Zealand, nor even to GPNZ, and the final decision would be taken by the Greenpeace International council.

The sad truth was that the bombing had almost certainly dealt a fatal blow to the ship. Basic repair costs were put at $1 million, and even then there could be no guarantees that she would again perform as she had, so alternatives had to be looked at. Cutting her up for scrap was also quickly rejected, as this would never have been acceptable either to many thousands of New Zealanders or to the many in Greenpeace who had a personal attachment to the old ship. Some proposed that the wreck be established on a land site as a memorial, but this too was impractical – the *Warrior* weighed around 600 tonnes and the costs of transporting her overland and setting up a site would again have been prohibitively high.

All realistic offers were followed up. Finally, a proposal was received from the New Zealand Underwater Association to sink the wreck in an area where she would become a living reef and an attraction for both marine life and recreational divers. Writing in *Greenpeace News*, Carol Stewart explained the reasons for the final decision: 'For many of us in Greenpeace the *Rainbow Warrior* has become part of our lives over the years and holds a special place in our hearts... Our feeling is that she deserves a dignified and peaceful resting-place. Her entire working life was spent at sea, protecting the marine environment.

'We feel that to become a permanent part of that environment, in the form of a living reef, is a fitting end for her... We have now accepted an offer from the people of Matauri Bay, in Northland, to sink the ship in the waters of their beautiful, serene bay. If this means that the *Rainbow Warrior* is forgotten because she is out of sight, then people have not understood anything about her work. We hope that the people of New Zealand who feel strongly about the ship will continue to support Greenpeace and the work that will be done by the *Warrior*'s replacement. We will use the trust funds to replace the ship and we are going to stop nuclear testing. That is the only memorial for Fernando and the *Rainbow Warrior* that is acceptable to us.'

'It's hard to describe that period,' says Carol. 'It was such an emotional see-saw: seeing the heartache the crew were going through and the generosity

The *Warrior* begins to settle in the water, a cluster of friends and admirers around her, the little island of Motutapere in the background.

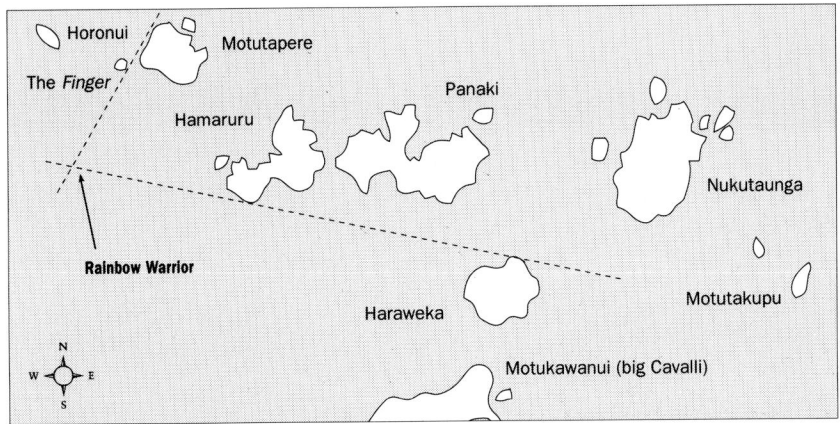

A map of the northern part of the Cavalli Islands pinpointing the *Warrior*'s final resting place.

of the public, but also the opportunism of those who only wanted to exploit the situation. 1985 was so emotionally draining, none of us really had time to come to terms with the trauma. It all had a devastating effect on the office: Elaine went into emotional hibernation after the bombing – I can still see her curled up in the foetal position in the armchair in her office. She only really came alive during the farewells to the flotilla boats, though having the *Greenpeace* on station at Moruroa as the *Warrior*'s replacement just didn't really make it for her. We all knew it was a stop-gap measure, as the ship had to be in New Zealand to prepare for the first Antarctic expedition, so there would be no real push on the Moruroa trip. But the *Greenpeace* did give the French a few headaches, and *Vega* was seized yet again!

'Finally Elaine went off on the *Vega* '86 Pacific tour and never really "came back". She also finally separated from her husband, Keith, that year and began to think about returning to nursing. She began to drift away, in part because of the bombing, but also because she saw how Greenpeace was changing from the close-knit community she had known. Jude and Susan-Jane left to go to university; Pip too had gone… it changed our focus altogether. In a sense, the bombing broke up our lives.'

As one generation began to ease themselves out of Greenpeace, Bunny, Martini and others moved in to help run the office, while Carol remained to guide GPNZ through the changes. Finally, in 1987, the International Arbitration Tribunal ordered France to pay Greenpeace International $8 million compensation, and the hull of the *Rainbow Warrior*, at last released from the courts' jurisdiction, was towed up to Matauri Bay and sunk off Motutapere in the Cavalli Islands. It was 12 December 1987, Carol's birthday.

That same day, with the sort of impeccable timing that had come to be expected from the French Government, Paris informed New Zealand that Alain Mafart was being repatriated to France 'because of illness'. In spite of protests from the New Zealand Government over both cases, Dominique Prieur followed Mafart back to France in May 1988 on the pretext that she was pregnant. Both had been released in flagrant breach of the United Nations agreement and returned home to a hero's welcome.

Above: The *Rainbow Warrior* Memorial at Matauri Bay overlooking the Cavalli Islands, where the ship now rests. The sculpture, incorporating the *Warrior*'s brass propeller, was created by Kerikeri sculptor Chris Booth with the practical and financial support of the local people. The memorial was the result of an initiative by Dover Samuels and the Maori community of Matauri Bay and was unveiled by the Governor-General, Sir Paul Reeves, on 15 July 1990.

Opposite: the *Rainbow Warrior* as seen by divers a year (above) and two years (below and insets) after the scuttling.

PART THREE
Riding the Wave

CHAPTER NINE

Pasifik Talkstory

'A lot of waiting goes on here – the big wait for the illusory independent health survey the Americans promised, waiting for the field trip ship, waiting for the Compact of Free Association with the United States, waiting for other people to make decisions about their lives. There's no need to hurry, and you adjust quickly to the slower pace because of the heat. Time has a different meaning too. Sometimes one event, like the arrival of a boat, can fill up the whole day. Everything moves at a slower pace, and the rest of the world scarcely seems to exist.'

Journal of Bunny McDiarmid, Mejato, Marshall Islands, April 1986

THE PACIFIC BASIN, constituting a third of the globe, holds the earth's largest body of water, washing the edges of three continents. Over the past 200 years colonisers from Europe, America and Asia have brought with them a destructive appetite for the region's resources – land, timber, minerals, copra, fish and whale oil. Rainforests have been consumed, species driven to extinction, and whole communities displaced in the process.

Since the Second World War the strategic interests of two nations in particular, the United States and France, have taken precedence over the interests of the Pacific people and their environment. Following the atomic bombing of the Japanese cities of Hiroshima and Nagasaki, the Pacific region and its people have borne the brunt of the nuclear arms race. While millions around the globe have feared the coming of nuclear war, some Pacific peoples have effectively been living through an insidious and undeclared nuclear war for forty-five years.

For the Micronesian communities of the Marshall Islands it began soon after the war's end, while the islands were administered by a US military governor. In January 1946 US officials selected Bikini Atoll for a series of nuclear bomb experiments. Bikini's population was relocated on the small arid atoll of Rongerik. For the Polynesian people of the South Pacific preparations for the Third World War began in 1963, when France moved its nuclear testing centre to the Tuamotu Archipelago, south of Tahiti.

It was in response to this process of military colonisation and environmental degradation that the Nuclear Free and Independent Pacific movement had been set up in Fiji in 1975. The conference, which drew mainly indigenous non-governmental representatives from Pacific nations, was next held at Ponape, in

'O Ruahatu te Atua o te Moana'. Bobby Holcomb was a popular artist and musician and a long-time opponent of French testing and friend of Greenpeace. Having spent all his adult life in Tahiti, he died there of cancer in 1990. The Greenpeace quotation he set with this painting was: 'Our past, our present, our future. Our planet is two-thirds water – we must protect our bountiful oceans.'

the Federated States of Micronesia, in 1978, then at Hawai'i in May 1980. At Hawai'i a People's Charter was issued by newly independent Vanuatu, which called on Pacific governments to support a ban on all aspects of the nuclear cycle, from uranium mining to nuclear weapons production, testing and deployment. The charter declared: 'Our environment continues to be despoiled by foreign powers developing nuclear weapons for a strategy of warfare that has no winners, no liberators and imperils the survival of all humankind…' The 1980 conference also set up the Pacific Concerns Resource Centre in Hawai'i, to which Greenpeace New Zealand contributed funds.

Through her Pacific networking Elaine Shaw had seen for herself how the wider issues of the region – land, language and colonialism – were related to the nuclear issue. The question of independence also threw up the glaring contradiction between the real history of the Pacific and the more palatable European version Elaine had been taught at school. The history of European settlers bringing 'civilisation, progress, technology and economic growth' had also been a colonial adventure that reshaped the Pacific environment in order to produce the goods required in Europe and the industrialised nations to fuel *their* economic growth.

Recognising the links between the Pacific's environmental problems and the local economies and cultures, Elaine set about trying to convince others in Greenpeace that environmental issues were necessarily also political issues. And while she was aware that Greenpeace's credibility rested on its political nonalignment, she was determined to show that there was a crucial difference between supporting a particular political party and advocating political solutions to environmental problems. As far as Elaine could see, 'Greenpeace has to recognise its own identity as part of a colonising culture. If it is to be genuine in its work in the Pacific, the people who are Greenpeace will have to learn how to listen to the indigenous peoples.'

Long before the *Rainbow Warrior* came to the Pacific, Elaine was convinced Greenpeace should extend its Pacific campaigning beyond Moruroa. GPNZ needed to work with others in the region, as had been proved by the international campaign to stop atmospheric nuclear testing. Elaine's call was now for a Pacific-wide campaign to tackle Pacific-wide problems.

At first it seemed as if the bombing of the *Rainbow Warrior* would set back a Pacific campaign by several years, but ironically it quickly became apparent that, far from hindering Greenpeace, the French saboteurs had massively boosted the organisation's international reputation. In fact, the bombing changed perceptions of Greenpeace faster than years of campaigning could have done, and produced a tide of sympathy that saw Greenpeace's paying supporters swell to the million mark worldwide. Owen Wilkes was moved to observe, 'The New Zealand Government is beginning to treat Greenpeace almost like another government.' Though this wasn't quite the experience of GPNZ staff, they certainly found it encouraging at last to be taken seriously both by government officials and the media.

However, some in the office still thought the whole post-bombing affair a distraction and saw the need to build up awareness of the regional issues through a Pacific Peace Voyage that would highlight the issues that were lost in the 'spy thriller' story the bombing created. The arrival of the *Rainbow Warrior* in the Pacific had been a turning point in the commitment of Greenpeace International to the Pacific and drew together the work of the New Zealand, Australian and US offices and Greenpeace International.

The original proposal had been for the *Warrior* to follow the 1985 Moruroa protest with a low-key educational tour of New Zealand and then to sail back through Polynesia and Melanesia to revisit the Rongelap Islanders on Mejato. The bombing had put an end to this plan, but *Vega* was brought in to fulfil part of the mission until a replacement for the flagship could be found.

On 4 June 1986, decked out in fresh colours, *Vega* sailed out of a rainy Waitemata Harbour, heading northwards. Her crew for the voyage were English skipper Chris Bone, Australian Clare Gerson and New Zealanders

Sue Ware and Owen Wilkes. Leaving Sally Jackman as acting nuclear campaigner in Auckland, Elaine had flown ahead to Rarotonga with Augie Riini, who replaced Owen for the rest of the voyage. A Maori activist and Black Power member, Riini was involved in his (Tuhoe) people's campaign to stop pine forests being planted on their sacred mountain, Taiarahia, in the Bay of Plenty. 'Elaine had recruited Augie through Tame Iti, a Maori activist she knew. He was a good diplomat – always out till late with the locals and more adept at making friends than we Pakeha,' reports Owen.

There would be three other short-term crew members: Cook Islander Papa Teuruaa, Tongan Pio Lautua and Fred Anjain, of the Marshall Islands, Jeton Anjain's nephew. Along the way *Vega* drew hundreds of local people to her wharfside stalls. Many were preoccupied with the continuing health dangers posed by nuclear testing; others simply wanted to express their anger and sympathy for Greenpeace over the *Rainbow Warrior* affair.

The crew for *Vega*'s 1986 Pacific tour (from left): Claire Gerson, Chris Bone, Sue Ware, Augie Riini and Owen Wilkes.

The *Vega*'s tour was an opportunity to meet a wide range of Pacific people, including peace, trade union, women's, church and political groups, and to spread information and promote awareness of nuclear and environmental issues. Rarotonga – Pago Pago – Tonga – Fiji – Vanuatu – Honiara: an exhausting round of meetings, speaking appointments, lobbying, video screenings and low-key actions. Elaine flew from island to island in advance of the yacht, making all the practical and political arrangements, while marine logistics were organised by Martin Gotje, who had settled again in New Zealand after a decade-long absence.

The tour was the crucial seed from which the Pacific campaign grew. Writing later in *Peacelink* magazine, Elaine explained: 'A common denominator in all the groups we met was a feeling of isolation. These mini-states, with their fragile, vulnerable economies and ecosystems, and their unique cultures, are striving to find a way to live side by side with the large, stridently demanding world powers who seek their land, their obeisance, their acquiescence – to control them either overtly or covertly. These are the realities of the Pacific. I don't have the answers. Each island state has its own problems, its own way of doing things… But we should all share our resources, ideas, skills, our triumphs and our failures.'

Since *Vega* was unable to reach the Marshall Islands (the hurricane season was approaching in the northern Pacific), it was decided to send two crew members from the *Rainbow Warrior* on the first planned follow-up visit. In April 1986, before *Vega*'s departure on her Pacific tour, Bunny McDiarmid and Henk Haazen travelled to Mejato to see how the Rongelap people were faring in their new home and find out how Greenpeace could help further. They spent four months in the Marshalls – three on Mejato and one travelling to Ebeye and the western atolls of Lae, Ujae, Wotho and Enewetak. Their home on Mejato was a treehouse, just big enough for a mattress. Out of their trip came a decision to support the building of another boat, which Greenpeace helped fund. The twelve-metre catamaran motor-sailer being built locally, would have room to carry patients to Ebeye hospital, and a refrigerator to take fish to market.

In her journal, Bunny recorded her impressions: 'Mejato has changed a lot in a year. Forty-five plywood houses from Rongelap have been rebuilt. The centre of the island is covered in coconut trees and a few pandanus and is generally jungly. Our first impression is of a small tidy island with too many barren spots. There has been some transplanting of coconuts from the centre of the island to the southern end. The northern end, where most people live, is quite bare. About five breadfruit and ten pandanus trees have been planted. On the lagoon side of Mejato, where the bumbum is anchored, there is about half a mile of shallow water with coral heads. The ocean side also has shallow waters and a reef close to shore.

'Life on Mejato is relaxed, most of the time taken up by food gathering, cooking, eating and "talkstorying". The women spend nearly half their day washing clothes, cooking and taking care of the children! Everyone is taken care of, everybody gets a share. They say, "Kandrikdrik kan yokwe", "Even if it is little, we have, we share".

'The teenagers, especially the boys, seem to have little to do but sleep, talkstory, play guitar or softball and go fishing. They are in between cultures. Outer island life has not prepared them for the imported, materialistic American lifestyle they are exposed to through television, videos and the consumer goods available in Majuro and Ebeye.

Bunny 'at home', working on her journal.

Bunny and Henk's treehouse, Mejato.

A communal meal on Mejato, 1986.

'Food is probably the most critical problem on Mejato; it's often feast or famine, with long periods during which they barely get by. When food is short, people get more homesick for Rongelap. The three-monthly visit of the field trip ship delivers the US Department of Agriculture food that has been coming since 1966. This imported food – canned fish, fruit, juice and the like – is not enough to last the three months and is supplemented by food bought at Ebeye out of the Rongelap Resettlement Fund.

'The staple diet is rice, flour, fish and sugar. Mejato itself offers them very little of their traditional foods like coconut, pandanus and breadfruit. Those they have planted will take five years to bear fruit. The men go spearfishing on the reef, throw nets from the shore, and sometimes go trawling in the bumbum, or use the two well-cared-for outrigger canoes. The mizzen staysail from the wreck of the *Rainbow Warrior*, which we brought with us, will be used for new sails. The men say the fishing is not as good as on Rongelap, and is more difficult because of the shallow waters. There are also sharks.

'We spend a lot of time helping to establish some trial vegetable gardens. There's about sixty square metres of community garden. A group of women also started a garden of their own, and many smaller ones have started up around people's houses. Some things – pumpkin, papaya, banana, cucumber and peppers – are growing well.

'The community is almost totally reliant on the two bumbums for transport. We took a complete mechanic's tool box and some engine spares for them, all from the *Rainbow Warrior*. The big difference from Rongelap is that

The women's garden, Mejato.

here they have no opportunities to make money. Making copra from coconuts was the main source of income on Rongelap and most other islands, along with salting fish and handicrafts. Here there are not enough coconuts, fish or pandanus leaves for a surplus to be sold.

'The US Department of Energy, which administered the nuclear tests, sends over a visiting health team twice a year, but the community has little trust in them. People are still regularly flown as far afield as Cleveland, Ohio, for thyroid operations, after which they receive a statutory $25,000 compensation and are left to take medicine for the rest of their lives. Many of the women are still experiencing birthing problems.

'We decided to visit some of the western atolls to get an idea of what they were like. In ten days we stopped off at five atolls, including what's left of Enewetak, the site of forty-three atmospheric tests. After a 'clean-up', in 1980 the Enewetak people, who had been living on Ujelang about 200 miles away, were returned to their islands. Your first view as you approach Enewetak is of white concrete houses. The place is unbearably hot and has no shade; the coconut trees planted in 1979 haven't grown beyond a metre or two. There's an enormous runway and a cluster of old army buildings and dumped military vehicles at one end of the beach. It's a sad place, everyone driving around in rusty pickup trucks and drinking Coke. The old people wanted to return, but the younger ones were missing Ujelang, where 300 or so stayed.

'On the way back we stopped off at Ebeye. It hadn't changed in the year we had been away. The streets are full of kids with nothing to do and nowhere to go. Half the population is under the age of fifteen, and there's now a second generation growing up on Ebeye who know little of outer island life. Drinking and suicides among the young are big problems, though for the number of people living cramped together there is very little violence. Everybody knows one another here, and we couldn't walk the streets of Ebeye without kids yelling "Greenpeace, Greenpeace".'

During 1986 plans were laid by GPI to bring together the ocean ecology, toxic waste and nuclear campaigns in the region and develop a unique Pacific campaign. Soon after their return to New Zealand, Bunny was asked to take on the new campaign, integrating the Pacific work of several Greenpeace offices. Formally set up in November 1986, the Pacific campaign is co-ordinated jointly by Bunny in Auckland and Sebia Hawkins in Washington, DC.

Sebia Hawkins

Sebia, who had a background in US civil rights issues, had worked for Greenpeace USA as a nuclear campaigner, focusing on nuclear testing. In 1984 she was involved in Belauan efforts to gain greater autonomy from the United States. Working closely with Belauan lawyers Roman Bedor and Roman Tmechtul, Sebia helped to file a successful lawsuit that legitimised the Belauan nuclear-free constitution, which the US Government had vehemently opposed and has continued to block. It was through this work that she got to know Steve Sawyer and began to help with his work in the Marshall Islands, out of which grew the preparatory work in the United States for the 1985 *Rainbow Warrior* voyage and the Rongelap relocation.

'The first thing we had to do was to learn,' Bunny recalls. 'We started by travelling around the region and talking to people, taking our time. We went with open minds, and soon realised that our Western perspective was not always useful in a Pacific context. Environmental problems here do not exist in isolation; they are linked to just about every other aspect of life. So rather than a narrowly defined environmental and peace agenda, a broader, ecosystem approach began to evolve. The Pacific has no homogeneous cultural identity. Campaigning in Kiribati and Western Samoa is as different as if they were on opposite sides of the globe. It is impossible to work effectively with people in the Pacific without understanding that perceptions of nature, kinship and trade are very closely linked.'

Bunny and Henk

Bunny believes strongly that her work will always be defined by the people, politics and cultures of the Pacific. 'There is an obvious coincidence of interest between Greenpeace's work on French testing and other Pacific concerns. But that's not to say we don't recognise both the Maohi and French perspectives. In practice we have to acknowledge that the struggle for Maohi independence is closely linked to ending nuclear testing, and that public opinion within metropolitan France is also important, especially when so little is known there about French Polynesia.'

'Here in the small island states of the Pacific,' says Sebia, 'solutions are often more achievable, and there's a range of potential environmental disasters that can still be prevented. On the other hand, the Pacific ecosystems are that much more fragile and vulnerable to the impact of relatively small-scale tourism, fishing, logging and mining projects. In this sense the next five years will be crucial for the integrity and survival of the Pacific environment.'

One of the key threats to the Pacific today is global warming. The rise in world temperatures, brought about by an increase in 'greenhouse' gases trapped in the atmosphere, will lead to the progressive melting of the icecaps and a steady rise in sea levels. Global warming now threatens the physical survival of some Pacific Island societies, scientific studies suggesting that hundreds of low-lying coral atolls may have to be evacuated within the next few decades. For the most vulnerable Pacific nations, such as Kiribati and the Marshall Islands, the changes are likely to mean further widespread social upheaval. Once the victims of US and British atmospheric nuclear testing, these two island groups are now victims of the developed world's extravagant use of fossil fuels, which over the past 300 years have filled the atmosphere with heat-trapping pollution.

Penehuro Lefale, the Pacific campaign's atmosphere and energy campaigner now working on global warming and climate change issues, is a scientist from Western Samoa. Before moving to New Zealand he helped establish alternative energy projects in several South Pacific countries for the United Nations Pacific Energy Development Programme.

Pene grew up in a small coastal village in Western Samoa. 'That was my whole world then, and we relied on it for all our everyday needs. I was always out fishing, using the traditional methods my father taught me. I used to think of the sea as an endless resource until my father became the matai, or leader, of the village and stopped us using the more damaging fishing practices, like pounding the corals to drive the fish out.'

Seeing Dennis O'Rourke's film *Half Life,* about the treatment of the Marshall Islanders during the US nuclear testing, was a turning point for Pene. 'After that I thought that when I got the chance I'd try to do something to change things in the Pacific. As I grew older, I wandered into the white man's environment to further my education.'

'We have been sustained by the ocean for two million years, and it has been bountiful and continues to yield to us its bounty. We have now learned that this harmony could be interrupted by the actions of nations very distant from our shores... We, the peoples of the South Pacific region, appeal to you in a common voice, the voice of those who may be the first victims of global warming... to ensure the survival of our cultures and our very existence and to prevent us from becoming "endangered species" or the dinosaurs of the next century...'
Ernest Bani, Vanuatu, October 1989

Penehuro Lefale, Pacific atmosphere and energy campaigner, testing a solar-powered battery while working for the United Nations Energy Development Project.

'We do not have the luxury of waiting for proof. The proof, we fear, will kill us.'
Robert Van Leirop, Vanuatu Ambassador to the UN

After studying physics and energy issues at the University of the South Pacific in Fiji, Pene returned to Western Samoa to work on climate issues. He became aware of dramatic changes in his homeland. 'In my early childhood I had lived through a period of cyclones and flooding. These were considered a part of our life; we were used to coping with such things, but all of this has changed in the last decade. Cyclone Ofa, in February 1990, will live in my memory forever. It destroyed everything my parents had worked their whole lives to build, and changed our perspectives on nature. Why are these natural events becoming more frequent and intensified now? Is Mother Nature no longer tolerating our behaviour?

'It made me sad to think that our very survival is threatened as a result of the industrialised world's dependence on fossil fuels to prop up its economic growth. Colonial powers came here to exploit our resources and to use the islands without giving anything back, and even today they still see the Pacific as a place to test nuclear weapons, burn chemicals and dump their waste. We have been the victims of colonisation, world war, superpower confrontation and industrialisation, which now means that Pacific Islands are on the frontline of the global warming problem.

'In my work I have seen how for many people in the Northern Hemisphere and the multinational companies, global warming merely means that a few small unimportant islands will be lost. At an international conference on global warming in Washington in early 1991 an industry lobbyist mistook me for an official Pacific Island delegate. "Climate change isn't *really* a problem," he said. "You guys can always move to the US or Australia." I couldn't believe it! I told him he was talking about my land and my people. He could see I was upset and asked where I was from. When I said Greenpeace he soon disappeared. That's the kind of view we're up against.

'My trip overseas showed me many things. Now I've seen where all the big decisions are made that affect us here in the Pacific, and can work to encourage people in the Pacific to speak up and make their voices heard. Unless this happens, people like that guy at the Washington conference will carry on disregarding us.'

Pene's campaign is closely linked to other Pacific work, particularly the protection of coral reefs. Among the richest environments found anywhere in the world, coral reefs are living underwater reserves of fantastically diverse fish, turtles and other sea creatures, and provide up to 90 percent of protein for many Pacific communities. They are also the first line of defence against sea level change and storm wave damage. Rising sea levels can result in the 'drowning' of reefs and may be linked to the bleaching of coral, in which the living algae is dislodged from the coral, owing to rising temperatures.

In response to these pressures, Greenpeace's Pacific campaign supports exchange projects between the Solomon Islands Development Trust and the Wau Ecology Institute in Papua New Guinea to extend the village-based development awareness work performed so effectively by SIDT. Pacific campaigner Lafcadio Cortesi now works with local NGOs and villagers, travelling and talking to landowners about the local environmental impact of logging, mining and fishing.

Tarawa, Kiribati. Such low-lying island groups are especially vulnerable to the effects of global warming.

With no office in the region, the Pacific campaign uses the *Rainbow Warrior* and *Vega* as mobile campaign bases. Martin Gotje co-ordinates the boats' schedules while also running the campaign against US missile flight testing at Kwajalein, maintaining his own links with the Marshall Islanders. For Martini, the Pacific campaign is now running just the kind of operation the *Fri*'s Pacific Peace Odyssey was aiming towards back in 1974, when Greenpeace New Zealand was first set up, and he derives enormous personal satisfaction from his dual role.

'On the practical side I organise the schedules and logistics; and as a campaigner I work on the missile flight testing issue. My function with the new *Warrior* is to make sure things run smoothly and to plan the itineraries so that the sailing rig is used to maximum effect and optimal energy efficiency, which is why she circulates clockwise round the Pacific with the prevailing winds.'

The *Fri*'s 1975 Peace Odyssey bypassed the US missile-testing base on Kwajalein. 'My first encounter with the Kwajalein base came in 1985 on the *Rainbow Warrior*,' recalls Martini, 'when we hung a banner protesting at the Star Wars tests. As we passed, the first things we saw were the radar domes on Roi Namur, the world's largest and most expensive piece of hi-tech radar hardware. The contrast with the harsh life led by the Marshallese on Ebeye was stark. All that poverty and human suffering next door to a multi-billion-dollar weapons complex developing the means to destroy the earth many times over. I found that obscene.'

Greenpeace missile testing protest, Meck Island, Kwajalein.

In July 1985 Greenpeace pledged to replace the *Rainbow Warrior* with another ship that would take up the peaceful mission for which she became famous around the world. Many thousands of people around New Zealand had contributed generously to the trust fund established for that purpose. Four years after the bombing this long-awaited dream became a reality. The new *Rainbow Warrior* was on her way to the Pacific, and past players were drawn back into the Greenpeace fold.

Naomi Petersen was then living in Auckland. 'I had been continuing my nautical education, as mate on the *Spirit of Adventure* for three years and skippering tourist boats in the Bay of Islands, always with an idea that I might one day return to Greenpeace. Then I heard through the grapevine that Martini, who was by then New Zealand marine division manager, wanted me to join the *Rainbow Warrior* for her voyage back to the Pacific. I really liked the ideas for the new *Warrior's* Pacific voyage. Like *Fri* during the Odyssey, she was not to be a confrontational boat, but rather the sort the Pacific campaign needed – a peacemaking boat.'

The new *Rainbow Warrior,* formerly the *Grampion Fame,* was launched in Hamburg on 10 July 1989, four years to the day after the bombing of her namesake. The two ships had been built in the same Scottish shipyard. Converting the trawler into a Pacific Ocean campaign vessel meant fitting her out with equipment for long-range work, and radically changing the accommodation and engine room. The old fishhold was converted into more cabins, a theatre and exhibition space and a cargo hold. The most important addition was a new sailing rig, designed for maximum fuel economy and energy efficiency. The rig involves three masts with 650 square metres of working sails and 1,710 square metres of light-air sails. The brass ship's bell from the original *Rainbow Warrior* was hung on the new ship to symbolise the continuity of her mission.

Rainbow Warrior on the high seas of the North Pacific.

The ship's crew included the first *Warrior's* skipper, Peter Willcox, Naomi Petersen as first mate, Solomon Islands deckhand Philip Pupuka, on his first trip with Greenpeace, and Sue Ware, veteran of the 1985 and 1986 *Vega* voyages.

In July and August of 1989, the *Rainbow Warrior* made a two-month tour of Europe, during which campaigners and crew promoted Pacific issues in each port of call. The *Warrior's* arrival in the old French port of La Rochelle marked a historic occasion – she was the first Greenpeace ship to visit France since the bombing in 1985, and it seemed auspicious. Over two days more than 3,000 French people visited the ship, some bringing gifts of poems, flowers, fruit and vegetables.

Naomi especially remembers the *Warrior's* passage through the last lock of the Panama Canal and into the Pacific. 'It was a glistening starry night, very beautiful for those of us who stayed up to see the *Warrior* into her new home. But the pace of this voyage was very different from the Odyssey's. *Fri* used to do about four knots; now we were forging along at about ten knots and made the trip from Panama to Pitcairn very quickly.

'I was excited arriving at Pitcairn because it had been such an important landfall for the *Fri* in 1973. We simply wouldn't have got to Moruroa that year without the generous support of the Pitcairners, who looked after us and helped us repair the ship. I was amazed at how well they all remembered me, so it was a real pleasure to be able to at last repay some of their generosity with gifts from the *Warrior's* hold.

Naomi Petersen, first mate, *Rainbow Warrior*, 1989.

Rainbow Warrior arrives in Auckland.

'Then, a hundred miles off New Zealand I got "channel fever", that sense of homecoming. We began to see more birds, then the bright night light of Auckland. A Peace Squadron flotilla came out to welcome us and a big crowd of friends and supporters turned out on the wharf. Ngati Whatua gave us a welcome on board, then we had a party for all the people who had helped in the aftermath of the bombing – divers, the harbour board and all manner of people.'

The Pacific has always had a special place in the work of Greenpeace New Zealand, and the multi-faceted Pacific campaign continues to reflect this. For Sebia, the campaign's success lies in the continuity of the individual people involved, like Elaine Shaw, Bunny McDiarmid and Martin Gotje. 'Inspiration is important too. My inspiration has come from the people of the Pacific whom I have worked with. In many instances these people have lost their sovereignty, yet in spite of the injustices suffered, they have kept their integrity and identity. My work in the Pacific has shown me the underlying message of all Greenpeace's work: that co-operation is the only viable form of survival for us all.'

CHAPTER TEN

Beneath the Surface

'It's 2 am. Heavy clouds mask the full moon; rain restricts our visibility and makes it difficult to steer our small boat along the thin line of plastic floats that stretches for miles into the darkness ahead. Suspended from this seemingly endless thread of plastic to a depth of fifteen metres is the adversary – the net we call the wall of death.'

Mike Hagler on board the Rainbow Warrior, *Tasman Sea, 1990*

JUST WEEKS AFTER the new *Rainbow Warrior* arrived in New Zealand, in December 1989, she set sail for the Tasman Sea, carrying a campaign team of scientists and divers, along with journalists and a film crew. Their task was to monitor the ecological effects of driftnet fishing, the notorious 'wall of death'. Only five days out of Auckland they sighted the first nets, and the *Warrior*'s inflatables were launched to check the damage. The divers used special scissors to free several large striped marlin, a wahoo and a giant sunfish caught in the fine plastic filament.

Greenpeace New Zealand's ocean ecology campaigner, Mike Hagler, was in one of the inflatables. A US-born New Zealander, he had been working as environment reporter for Radio New Zealand before he moved to Greenpeace in 1989. 'I can see the *Rainbow Warrior*'s mast light on the horizon several kilometres away. Our only links with the ship are a small two-way radio and our twenty-five horsepower engine. We're searching for 'hot spots' in the net, where it dips deep below the surface, indicating a trapped dolphin, or a young whale perhaps. The nets are set around dusk, and the driftnetters start hauling them in at about two the following morning. We're all tired, cold and wet. A few hours before, on board the *Warrior,* we saw a small whale just a hundred metres from one of the nets.

'Naoko Kakuta, a Greenpeace Japan campaigner and our interpreter for this trip, has been listening in to radio conversations between the fishing boats in which they talked of the whales and dolphins they'd been catching in their nets. They had even joked about how bad it would be for them if Greenpeace were to get a picture of one.

'The next day the *Meiyso Maru*, a Japanese driftnetter we've been monitoring, slows its hauling winches. A tangle of plastic floats appears by the side of the boat and from the surface rises a large carcass in a shroud of plastic. Skipper Pete Willcox leans on the *Warrior*'s air-horn, sending out four blasts of

Opposite: A dolphin struggles in the driftnet. 'Brian Coffey risked his life to get this photo. The dolphin was close to being hauled in, so Brian zoomed over in an inflatable, dropped into the water and took four shots before being plucked out by the team. Moments later the big driftnetter moved over the spot.' *Mike Hagler*

Naoko Kakuta holding a young casualty of the driftnet.

protest. One of the fishing boat's crew saws frantically at the floatline in a desperate attempt to dispose of the damning evidence. Finally the drowned dolphin falls free and sinks quickly into the Tasman.'

The *Rainbow Warrior* had left Auckland with no reliable information on the location of the driftnetters. They had heard vague reports that six were working in the Tasman, so they set off in search of them. After picking up faint radio signals, the *Meiyso Maru* was intercepted and a small group of other driftnetters was soon sighted.

Throughout the first week, New Zealand photographers Roger Grace and Brian Coffey had painstakingly documented the devastation wrought by the nets, and their photographs were much in demand by newspapers around the world. Peter Scoones' video shots of a huge sunfish being freed by Greenpeace divers armed only with scissors were especially widely used. One of the whales they released turned out to be among the world's rarest. 'We found a southern bottlenose whale, which we managed to disentangle, still alive. Only fifty of these whales have ever been sighted,' says Roger.

'The sea glowed bright blue from the powerful lights we had suspended three metres below the surface. A line of elliptical polystyrene floats stretched off into the night. Away on the horizon we could make out the glow of lights. A Japanese driftnetter was slowly winching in the night's catch; in a few hours it would reach us.

'I slipped into the blue bowl beneath. Ahead of our boat I could see glistening plastic mesh stretched down some fifteen metres. Below was a

Giant sunfish about to be liberated by Greenpeace divers.

seemingly bottomless void, the seabed some 3,000 metres below – not the kind of place to drop a camera. Swimming closer to the mesh, I could see the shining bodies of a dozen skipjack reflected like crumpled tinfoil against the inky blackness.

'Moving back along the plastic wall, I caught a glimpse of something large moving in the half-light near the bottom of the net. Bringing the lights closer I saw it was a shark, three metres long, thrashing about in slow motion, hopelessly tangled in nylon. Just above the shark was the remains of its last meal, the tail of a skipjack tuna still tangled in the net. The shark had been attracted to the skipjack, eaten all but the tail, then itself become caught.

'With dawn approaching we moved a few kilometres east, where the search team had found three striped marlin to photograph before the ships hauled them in.'

On board the *Warrior* there was a stormy debate over what kind of direct action to mount against the driftnetters. A contingency plan had been devised that involved attaching a specially designed piece of equipment to a section of net, which would render it unusable. But Naoko was bitterly opposed to the scheme, insisting it would be seen by the Japanese media as another example of Greenpeace's 'Japan bashing'. Others felt that any damage caused would pale into insignificance beside the carnage wrought by the nets themselves.

The plan was dropped, and another crew meeting was called to canvas new ideas for creative protest. Two attempts to board the driftnetters were aborted after the weather worsened. Finally plywood protest placards, bearing slogans in English and Japanese, were tied to the net, to be hauled up, tangling the net and jamming the hauling gear.

Then Naoko overheard a radio message that the fleet's supply ship, the *We Carrier*, would arrive in Auckland at the end of January to take on fresh food and fuel. Although the driftnetters were banned from New Zealand waters, no law then prevented supply ships picking up stores. It was now a race to get Mike Hagler back to New Zealand to organise a blockade of the ship and put the whole driftnet fleet out of action.

The *Warrior* made for Opua, where Mike left for Auckland to help Rien Achterberg organise the reception for the *We Carrier*. A Greenpeace picket was assembled on the wharf, and a diver chained the ship's rudder to the wharf. After discussions with local unions, the Government and the ship's agents, Greenpeace received written assurance from the agents that the ship would be given enough fuel only to reach Bangkok. The driftnet fleet would be left without the fuel or supplies to continue its Tasman operation.

Below: A shark thrashes in the driftnet. *Bottom:* Driftnetters haul in Greenpeace placard.

The *Rainbow Warrior*'s anti-driftnetting voyage had been Mike's first ship-borne campaign. 'The most powerful image in my mind is of the *Warrior* herself. There she was, an old European diesel trawler transformed into a well-equipped Pacific sailing ship, designed for running with the wind or sailing with the wind abeam. She symbolised for me what we have to do to change our polluting societies, to get back in tune with nature. We need to utilise all that our advanced technology has to offer – but use it in a positive way.

'The other image I have is of the net itself. It had been hard to comprehend what a 60-kilometre driftnet was really like. On a map it's just a short, insignificant line, but out there in the ocean, hundreds of miles from land, the scale becomes apparent: huge grids of netting laid so as to create boxes, moving systematically across the Tasman into the South Pacific, sweeping up vast populations of marine life as they go. In one three-month season Greenpeace estimated that twenty driftnetters killed 6,400 dolphins, 4,000 sharks, 3,000 sunfish, 3,000 billfish and hundreds of small whales.'

While the *Rainbow Warrior* moved to the North Pacific, confronting more of the driftnetters there, Mike shifted his focus to political lobbying to back up the recent South Pacific driftnet ban and the United Nations resolution outlawing specific forms of driftnetting.

In 1989 the South Pacific Forum countries had adopted the Wellington Convention banning driftnet fishing in the region. The United Nations then approved a resolution calling for an immediate ban on large-scale driftnet fishing in areas free from nets, a halt in the South Pacific by 1991 and a provisional moratorium in the rest of the world's oceans by July 1992. Turning its attention to a loophole that would allow driftnet fishing to continue after 1992 if 'conservation and management' programmes are implemented in certain regions, Greenpeace is currently

A diver examines a short-bill spearfish (wahoo) caught in the driftnet.

gathering evidence to show there is simply no programme that would make driftnetting an acceptable fishing method.

Since 1982 Greenpeace had maintained its pressure on the International Whaling Commission because, despite the ban on commercial whaling, Japan, Norway and Iceland still engaged in so-called 'scientific' whaling, which they justified as essential research rather than commercial exploitation. Where the opportunity has arisen, GPNZ has continued to take direct action against the whalers. In early 1986, for instance, two Japanese whale chasers, on their way home from the Southern Ocean whaling grounds, were spotted berthed at Wellington's Kings Wharf. Early on 1 March four Greenpeace Wellington activists boarded the ships, and before they could be stopped, Mark Roach and Phil Scotford had chained themselves to the crow's nests and hung a banner between the two ships, reading 'Stop Japan Killing Whales'.

Mark Roach chained to whale chaser, Wellington 1986.

In 1988 the IWC conference was held in Auckland, and Greenpeace New Zealand seized the opportunity to highlight the fraud of scientific whaling. GPNZ activists gate-crashed the Japanese Festival parade through Auckland and hung a banner outside the Sheraton Hotel, the venue for that year's conference.

'Ninety-four percent of New Zealanders support a ban on

all whaling. Protests like these, as well as those at sea, where our boats continue to confront the whaling fleets, help to spread the message that whaling continues,' says the ocean ecology campaign's Diana Pipke. Japan continues its scientific whaling programme, taking several hundred minkes in Antarctic waters each year. Iceland, responding to international pressure from Greenpeace and other groups, agreed to call a halt in 1989. However, at the 1991 IWC meeting at Reykjavik both Norway and Iceland called for the ban on commercial whaling to be lifted. The IWC also proposes to adopt a management plan for whale stocks that could allow commercial whaling to resume. The international Greenpeace campaign will be following developments closely and is prepared to back its opposition with massive action should the hard-won victories of the early 1980s be reversed.

Since the 1982 ban on commercial whaling, GPNZ's marine mammal work has focused on local issues. Greenpeace's high-profile campaigns against whaling had always grabbed the headlines, but in New Zealand the smaller, low-key fur seal and sea lion campaigns took longer to gain public attention. A protected species, New Zealand's indigenous fur seal was driven close to extinction by the middle of the nineteenth century. Greenpeace strongly opposed the local fishing industry's calls for a cull of New Zealand fur seals.

In 1983 a document leaked to Greenpeace by a government official revealed the poor state of the Hooker's sea lion population, the world's rarest, which lives and breeds around the Auckland Islands. The sea lions were

Gate-crashing the Japanese Parade, Auckland 1988. Henk beats the drum.

threatened by accidental entanglement in fishing nets. Without government action to control squid trawling in the area, sea lions would continue to be killed at a rate of up to 130 a year, which could see the total population halved within forty years or sooner.

Susan-Jane Owen, with a background in zoology, joined Tom Donahue in 1982 to research the Hooker's. 'The office was tiny and everyone was overworked. I was doing sea lion work but was being pulled in all the time to help out in other areas – we all just mucked in then.

'Tom went to see the Ministry of Agriculture and Fisheries (MAF), and petitioned the Government to declare an area with a radius of 100 kilometres around the breeding grounds a marine mammal sanctuary, at least during the mating and pupping season. Our assumption was that the Government would be sure to act once it was briefed by its own researchers, and we were prepared to wait until then. Perhaps we should have pushed them more, but I think we naively believed they would do the right thing if they got the right information. We did get the ball rolling by jolting the Government into doing something, even if it was only research.'

'The campaign of the early 1980s could hardly be called a conspicuous success,' admits Susan-Jane wryly, 'but it did focus us on a local marine issue that wasn't then being covered by any other environmental group. Both the Pacific campaign and the whales were international issues that were a bit removed, so the introduction of a specifically local environmental focus was a real change, and we looked to building on this early work in 1986.'

However, events in 1985 undermined these good intentions. With the changes in personnel and other transformations that followed the bombing of the *Rainbow Warrior,* it wasn't until 1987, when Susan-Jane's wildlife campaign was taken over by Janet Agar, then Tim Gentle, and renamed ocean ecology, that marine mammal issues were picked up again.

In 1988 Greenpeace launched a New Zealand coastal ecology campaign to combat the threat to marine life from plastics – discarded fishing net, plastic bags and other debris. The increase in foreign and local fishing fleets off New Zealand had led to a visible increase in net and strapping scraps, plastic rope and sheet plastic washing up on beaches. Marine casualties included dolphins, young whales, seals and two endangered species unique to New Zealand: the Hooker's sea lion and the yellow-eyed (hoiho) penguin.

The later campaign against driftnetting also linked in with fisheries and the interaction with marine mammals, and has been the main focus of the ocean ecology campaign during 1990 and 1991.

Overfishing of one species can mean the devastation of a whole ecosystem. The commercial extinction of herring and capelin in the North Sea devastated the rest of the food chain, killing seals and seabirds and closing down Norwegian fishing

Below: Distressed fur seal entangled in fishing net.
Bottom: Hooker's sea lion chases penguin, Auckland Islands.

fleets. The Pacific is seen by Greenpeace as a key region where there is still time to stop the same thing happening. 'Modern industrial fishing is doing irreparable damage to Pacific ecosystems,' Mike Hagler says. 'Traditional ways of fishing in New Zealand and the Pacific offer important lessons for the fishing industry. It would be worthwhile to contrast current fishing approaches and the generally sustainable methods and systems used by indigenous people. Modern fishing methods are short-sighted in targeting a single species and failing to take into account the whole ecosystem.

Certainly the way New Zealand fisheries currently operate cannot be maintained. 'As with most modern industries, the fishing industry looks first of all to maximising profits and only afterwards, if at all, to the impact of their methods on the environment. If allowed to continue, this attitude will ensure that one day there simply won't be anything left to fish. For this reason, our whole outlook has to change.'

Fur seals attracted to hoki trawlers.

During 1990 Mike worked closely with Sebia Hawkins on the joint Pacific and ocean ecology 'Freedom for the Seas' project. This was an attempt to redefine the 400-year-old concept of freedom of the seas so that it recognises changing uses of the high seas. As Sebia explains, 'It is clear that nations can no longer be permitted unrestricted freedom to use and abuse the high seas. The international scramble for ocean resources has confirmed the fragility of the marine environment and raised basic ethical questions about the right to exploit the seas, which will not survive an open-market free-for-all.'

While driftnets were destroying South Pacific wildlife, a smaller form of driftnet – the gillnet – was being used by New Zealand fishermen in coastal waters, endangering the Hector's dolphin. Dubbed the 'puffing pig' by the Perano whalers of Cook Strait for its loud surface breathing, Hector's is one of the world's smallest marine mammals and is unique to New Zealand. Found mainly in small groups around the coast of the South Island, little was known about the species until 1984, when two doctoral students, Steve Dawson and Liz Slooten, began to study them in detail. Their research was the first comprehensive work on the distribution of Hector's dolphin and exposed the dual threats to the species' survival of pollution and gillnet fishing. Greenpeace is one of several groups that have supported their work and taken up the dolphin's cause.

After a comprehensive survey of the South Island coastline and targeted North Island locations, Liz and Steve estimated the total population of this species at between 3,000 and 4,000, fewer than a number of marine mammal species already listed as endangered. Next they studied the feeding and breeding behaviour of the dolphin to discover whether they were capable of recovering from such a reduced population. 'Sadly, one of the first findings we made was that the number of dolphins being accidentally caught in gillnets was much higher than we had first thought,' says Steve. 'After four years' study in the Pegasus Bay/Canterbury Bight area, we found 230 Hector's dolphins reported killed in the nets, which represented 30 percent of the population in a key breeding area.

'Compared with other dolphins, Hector's are fairly sedate. They jump only occasionally, sometimes making high leaps and fast passes near the boat. In rough weather we have often seen them catching waves, then peeling off to return – we once saw six dolphins surfing on the same wave. A particularly good ride is sometimes followed by a high, spectacular leap. Our observations suggest that in these conditions they may spend several hours surfing each day.'

After public pressure and extensive lobbying of the Government by Forest and Bird, Greenpeace, Project Jonah and other environmental groups, in 1988 the Minister of Conservation declared the Banks Peninsula a marine mammal sanctuary. Commercial gillnetting is banned from the sanctuary year-round, amateur gillnetting is banned during the summer months, and there are now new, more stringent restrictions on how and where nets may be set. Steve Dawson and Liz Slooten were each awarded PhD degrees for their research on the Hector's dolphin and are now lecturers at the University of Otago. Their continuing research focuses on assessing the effectiveness of the sanctuary in stemming the decline of the local Hector's population. If present measures remain inadequate, the study will help to identify what more can be done to secure the future of one of the world's rarest dolphins.

But marine reserves alone cannot guarantee their safety. Dr Alan Baker's research for the National Museum in Wellington has demonstrated that coastal habitats are susceptible to agricultural chemicals and heavy metals flushed from river mouths. Samples from one dolphin off Banks Peninsula revealed high levels of DDT and other toxic agricultural chemicals in its dorsal blubber.

Hector's dolphin – another victim of the gillnet.

Another fishery problem of concern to the ocean ecology campaign has been the plight of the New Zealand fur seal. An increased quota for the hoki fishery is believed to have produced a rise in the number of seals accidentally trapped in the hoki nets – between 800 and 900 were estimated to have been killed during 1989. 'Two hundred thousand tonnes of hoki have been taken from the West Coast hoki fishery each year since 1988,' says Mike Hagler. 'It is becoming apparent that the fish stock cannot take this rate of harvest. Throwing offal over the sides attracts the fur seals, which are then caught in the nets and drowned. This is the folly of seeing the ocean as a place to plunder and not an interdependent ecosystem from which we can only take limited supplies of food.'

'Most domestic trawlers already have a good fishing ground in the Cook Strait within the twelve-mile limit. The fishing ground is worked co-operatively and seems to be sustainable at present levels,' GPNZ ocean ecology researcher Leith Duncan explains. 'But often the smaller New Zealand trawlers cannot compete with the factory ships and have been squeezed out of the fishery by ships the size of the Cook Strait ferries with nets that have openings the size of a football pitch.'

The big factory ships throw back up to half the weight of their catch in fish offal and by-catch species, which in turn may attract more fur seals, possibly because of the depletion of their traditional food species. 'Again, overfishing one species will have a knock-on effect on the rest of the marine ecosystem around New Zealand. That's why Greenpeace advocates an ecosystem approach to fisheries management, since the only other immediate solution would be a total ban on hoki fishing from the Hokitika fishery, though seasonal closures and more MAF observers on board the trawlers would help. In 1990, with the co-operation of the fishing industry, Greenpeace put three observers on hoki trawlers to see the problem at first hand. That season 138 seals were reported killed, with a true figure for the entire fleet estimated at between 500 and 700.'

The economics of fishing are currently based on the cost of sending out a boat to trawl, and do not take account of the environmental cost of overfishing and the killing of seals. That equation has to change radically. The fishing industry often uses the analogy of seals as the rabbits of the sea, a pest that destroys the ecosystem. Leith Duncan argues that, on the contrary, 'It's the big fishing fleets that are the main predators, that are overfishing irresponsibly and that are ultimately responsible for destroying the marine environment. Fur seals are an indigenous part of the marine environment, and there is no evidence to show that they damage the natural ecosystem.

'Another issue we've pushed forward again is the Hooker's sea lion. Up to 1990 there was still no official movement on the creation of a sanctuary, so at the World Conservation Union (IUCN) meeting in Perth we pushed through a resolution calling on the New Zealand Government to establish a 100-kilometre sanctuary around the Auckland Islands and to enforce a ban on trawling in the area. The resolution was passed and the New Zealand Government subsequently committed itself to a process similar to that which happened to Hector's dolphins. So we now hope to repeat the success of the Banks Peninsula Marine Sanctuary.'

The problem remained that even these local issues did not offer many opportunities for direct public involvement. Aware of this, the ocean ecology team were looking for an activity that would encourage wide public participation while being enjoyable in itself. The 'Adopt-a-Beach' scheme was just such an initiative.

The Department of Conservation, working with Forest and Bird, Greenpeace and other groups, had already identified the seriousness of the marine plastic pollution problem through its short-lived national Marine Debris Network project. Tim Gentle began separate coastal ecology research work for Greenpeace in 1988. Tonnes of plastic was choking New Zealand's beaches and wreaking havoc among seals and seabirds. Plastic marine debris kills in many ways. Birds and marine mammals can die after eating plastic and polystyrene fragments; fish and mammals can become entangled in discarded fishing line and nets and are also often strangled by the plastic six-pack yokes, bottle-top rings and strapping.

Greenpeace set up a network of local groups to monitor selected New Zealand beaches over the spring and summer months and to undertake regular clean-ups. The ultimate aim was to compile a national register on the debris found and the impact on local wildlife. Greenpeace New Zealand had always emphasised the importance of popular involvement to bring about change. The nature of some of the organisation's international actions sometimes conjured up an image of elite shock troops on the environmental frontline who turned to the vast pool of supporters for financial support. This was an image GPNZ was uncomfortable with, since it believes that, above all, environmental change requires that ordinary people take responsibility for changes in their own lives.

'After lobbying so many politicians I had seen the limits of that kind of pressure and knew that only when the public and local groups became active would politicians be persuaded to take notice,' says Mike Hagler. 'Greenpeace is nowhere near as powerful as the public. Our role is more as a whistleblower so that the public know where the problems are; then it's up to ordinary people.'

In 1989 Mike had attended an international conference on marine debris in Hawai'i, where he learned how several of the Aleutian Islands in the North Pacific were being transformed into vast marine rubbish heaps. 'I came back to New Zealand determined to work against the same kind of thing happening here. Everyone has seen the grim image of a dead seabird caught up in a knot of fishing net or discarded plastic six-pack rings on the beach. We decided to put together the two basic ideas of local involvement and the beach plastic problem.'

The ideas were there, but it took two people, Peter Smith and Jess Tooker, to bring this initiative to life. A retired engineering professor from Auckland University, Peter Smith began working voluntarily on the Adopt-a-Beach scheme in July 1989. Peter was joined by Jess, who had just left secondary

Adopt-a-Beach cleanup, Brighton Beach, Christchurch.

Peter Smith presses his point with Environment Minister Peter Dunne.

school teaching with a yen to try something different. She was soon working on the scheme three days a week, also unpaid.

Neither Jess nor Peter had any particular ocean ecology or campaigning expertise, but that did not stop them producing a scientific report on the extent of the problem in New Zealand and liaising with other environmental groups and the Department of Conservation to promote the campaign.

'It has also been a tangible way for local people to see the impact of our lifestyle on our environment,' says Jess. 'The local groups are like local guardians of the environment, an environmental early-warning system linked to Greenpeace, who can provide the resources and informational backing required.

'The response was amazing. The best thing is that this project has been empowering for people. In 1989 people were crying out for things to do. They had given money to Greenpeace for years, usually for international campaigns, but now they wanted to do something for their own environment. I'd always been involved in community work, so it was the sort of thing I liked doing. And Peter and I make a good team. We both like meeting people, and while he's good at the more technical stuff, I'm really an organiser.'

The campaign quickly gathered a momentum of its own, with people phoning and writing in every day to join in and find out more. Within two months some 4,000 people had volunteered to survey and clean beaches all over New Zealand, from Ninety Mile Beach to Stewart Island. Public meetings attracted large audiences, and Greenpeace was receiving over fifty responses a day to its publicity in the first weeks. By the end of 1990 the project had thirty-seven local co-ordinators in coastal centres around the country. It was one of the most successful appeals GPNZ had ever had.

CHAPTER ELEVEN

The Rolling Snowball

'The sun disappeared about two weeks ago, though there is still a distinct daytime, with a few hours of twilight between 1000 and 1500 hours. The last sunset was quite wonderful, even more so as it was our first glimpse of the sun for ten days. I can still see the great golden orb skimming along the top of the Barne Glacier, sinking out of sight, then emerging past the end of it to sink into the sea. The next day was clear but the sun did not quite make it over the horizon.

'In clear weather the sky is a brilliant canopy of stars, some of them friendly and familiar. The Southern Cross is almost directly overhead, with Canopus and Sirius, and sometimes, low on the horizon, you can catch a glimpse of Orion. I've just come back from a walk outside – a brilliant star-lit scene, not a breath of wind, the temperature at minus 30 degrees C, and in the sky for the first time the ghostly transparent streamers of the beautiful aurora australis.'

Cornelius Van Dorp, Greenpeace overwinterer, World Park Antarctica base, 1 May 1987

ANTARCTICA, THE WORLD'S last pristine wilderness, exemplifies the fragility of the earth. This continent and the surrounding Southern Ocean form a unique, irreplaceable ecosystem. Rare plant and animal species thrive along the edges in a fierce icy environment so fragile that even the least intrusive human activity risks upsetting the ecological balance. The 'hole' in the earth's protective ozone layer over the continent signals danger for the entire planet; the fate of the earth is intricately linked with the fate of the southern continent.

Antarctica was once part of the prehistoric supercontinent of Gondwana, a lush tropical forested land inhabited by animals of which we now know little. Around 230 million years ago Gondwana began to break apart to form South America, Africa, India, Australia and New Zealand, with Australasia and Antarctica separating from one another some sixty million years ago. Washed by the cool circumpolar current, Antarctica developed a temperate climate, ice finally covering the continent twenty-five million years ago. Today Antarctica, 98 percent of which is icebound, covers about 10 percent of the world's land area.

A paradox in many ways, Antarctica holds 70 percent of the world's frozen freshwater reserves, yet at the same time it is drier than the Sahara. It is a land of breathtaking, otherworldly beauty. When the air and clouds over the

Opposite: 'The only sound was the occasional creaking of the icefloes.'

polar icecap fill with millions of tiny ice crystals, the sun and moonlight refracts and scatters through the crystals in a surreal geometry of colour and form.

Penguins, seals and seabirds crowd the water's edge; whales and many species of fish live in the surrounding seas. These creatures are all part of the complex ecosystem of the Antarctic, which pivots on the krill, tiny shrimp-like crustaceans that are the main food source for most of Antarctica's marine mammals. Many species were hunted to near-extinction during the nineteenth century – penguins for their oil, seals for their fur and skins and whales for oil, meat and bone.

A succession of expeditions of discovery to Antarctica during the nineteenth and early twentieth centuries left a complex web of overlapping, often disputed territorial claims, the disputes exacerbated by the military rivalry of the Second World War and the Cold War. The United States and the Soviet Union wanted access to the entire continent, uninhibited by national claims. The Antarctic Treaty, signed in 1959, aimed to forestall conflicts arising from sovereignty disputes and promote international scientific co-operation.

The New Zealand Government, at the 1975 treaty meeting, was first to suggest the concept of a world park – environmentalists have since defined this to mean that the continent would be preserved for peaceful and non-commercial scientific purposes. However, narrow national interest gave priority to the negotiations on mineral exploitation and ensured that the prospect of profitable oil, minerals and animal resources kept the world park idea off the agenda.

The year before this photo was taken, thousands of Adélie penguins nested here. During the airstrip construction work the ground was blasted and lowered ten metres, yet still some thirty pairs breached the fenced-off area with an instinctive determination to nest in their traditional sites.

The Antarctic Treaty has in many ways failed to live up to its objectives. Violations of the treaty injunctions have been frequent. Despite its avowed aims of promoting international scientific co-operation, the overall human impact has had direct and destructive environmental consequences. For example, a US military nuclear reactor installed in 1962 leaked repeatedly and had to be shut down in 1972. The reactor was finally removed, via Lyttelton, along with 12,000 tonnes of contaminated soil in the mid-1970s. More recently, the construction of an airstrip at the French Dumont d'Urville base has seen five islands in the Pointe Géologie Archipelago levelled with explosives, killing and displacing penguins and seabirds and destroying their eggs and nesting grounds in the process. The systematic hunting of whales, seals and fish has resulted in the near-extinction of several species – blue whales are now estimated at just 1 percent of their original Antarctic population, the humpback at 3 percent, and fin whales at 20 percent. Overfishing, through its drastic effect on other levels of the interrelated food chain, could now be threatening the recovery of endangered whale and seal populations.

The construction of bases, poor waste disposal, accidental oil spills and tourism have also taken their toll on the fragile fringes of Antarctica. But the potential devastation oil and mineral exploitation would bring to the continent is of another order, for in the extreme temperatures oil takes around 600 years to break down.

Nonetheless, in the 1970s Antarctic Treaty parties were approached by commercial interests for prospecting rights on the continent. By 1981 the stage was set for the commercial exploitation of Antarctica, with scientists already assessing areas of mineral or oil deposits. For ecologists, these moves were clearly at odds with the stated aim of 'preserving the continent' in the original 1958 negotiations for the treaty, and Greenpeace New Zealand joined with other environmental groups to commit itself to protecting Antarctica as an unspoiled place for research and a world reserve. In 1981 special consultative meetings began to discuss mineral activities in Antarctica. The following year Japan began a three-year seismic survey for oil and gas off the Antarctic coast. France soon followed.

As part of an international campaign to create a world park in the southern continent, Greenpeace has maintained a permanent base on Antarctica since February 1987, using New Zealand as the launching site from which to mount its expeditions. Greenpeace believes the entire continent should be preserved as a world park, a totally protected zone of peace and an international research laboratory for future generations. Such a regime, Greenpeace believes, could best be accomplished by negotiating a comprehensive set of rules within the existing framework of the Antarctic Treaty – rules that should accord with a set of guiding, legally binding environmental principles. Mining activities would be strictly prohibited. Every scientific research project would have to provide for stringent protection of the environment. Commercial fishing ventures would need to be evaluated with reference to all species in the food chain, and developed in accordance with an evolving understanding of the marine ecosystem. Finally, the rapidly growing Antarctic tourist trade might continue, but only under strict conditions of minimal impact on the environment.

GPNZ's Michael Taylor first took an Antarctic campaign proposal to the Greenpeace International council meeting in 1980, but at that stage GPI showed little enthusiasm for it. Indeed, the level of ignorance in the Northern Hemisphere was such that when the report was retyped for presentation to council, a confusion between Antarctica and the Arctic had crept in.

GPNZ continued to publish information on the issue, but not much else was done by Greenpeace until June 1982, when the Antarctic Treaty nations met in Wellington to discuss minerals activities. To help fund the lobbying effort at this meeting, Greenpeace International had given a small grant to the Antarctic and Southern Ocean Coalition (ASOC), which drew together all New Zealand's environmental groups with an interest in the issue, including GPNZ, Friends of the Earth, Forest and Bird, Focus on Antarctica and ECO. The mood of the treaty meeting was not auspicious. It seemed inevitable that within two years a regime clearing the way for minerals exploitation would be established, which could have seen oil drilling and mining on the continent by 1985.

Antarctica had also been one of Roger Wilson's main campaigning areas while he was with Friends of the Earth. He had worked with Barney Brewster researching various books on the subject, and was drawn into the small group of Antarctic enthusiasts, including Cath Wallace and Lyn Goldsworthy, who lobbied at the 1982 minerals negotiations. 'There was no way I could avoid getting involved with lobbying at the Antarctic meeting; after all, it was being held only a few miles from my home. But the activists in Wellington worked quite differently from the way I was used to in Auckland. There's a much more political approach to environmental issues in Wellington, which was one of the attractions that had drawn me there in the first place.'

But at the end of the two weeks the activists came to accept that gate-crashing diplomatic receptions and 'doorstepping' delegates was not the most effective way to influence the negotiations. With the vested interests of the world's most powerful nations and oil and mining companies ranged against them, effective organisation on an international scale would be vital if environmentalists were to achieve anything. The task was monumental.

'In 1983 another proposal was sent to Greenpeace International urging that they take up the Antarctic issue, and this time it was positively received,' recalls Roger. 'We started to receive money to set up the campaign on a modest level. Some of this funded more lobbying in Wellington and the first Greenpeace New Zealand direct action on Antarctica, against the French-chartered vessel *Polarbjorn*. This ship was carrying material for the airstrip being built at Dumont d'Urville, the French Antarctic base whose construction was causing substantial environmental damage. We had already had a dummy-run with an action in 1982 against a Japanese seismic survey vessel at Lyttelton, where two activists attached themselves to the mooring lines of the boat. It was a bit amateurish, but it made front-page news in New Zealand and gave us quite a boost.

'Greenpeace International was then preparing to take on a major new campaign. The three main contenders were the Antarctic, tropical rainforests and acid rain. Eventually Antarctica won and we received an initial budget of US$50,000, which seemed like an absolute fortune then.'

MV *Greenpeace*, Cape Evans, Mt Erebus in the background.

At that stage in Greenpeace New Zealand, Antarctica was just part of a broader campaign embracing ocean ecology and wildlife issues overseen by Susan-Jane Owen. 'I worked with Cath Wallace, who had really started the campaign with Roger Wilson in the Wellington ASOC. Antarctica was never solely a Greenpeace project. My role in the New Zealand office was to publicise the issue: we did stunt demos using street theatre. I remember talking with Lyn Goldsworthy, Cath and Roger about the possibility of a Greenpeace Antarctic base, but it was just pie in the sky then.'

Roger returned to the Greenpeace International office, then based in Lewes, Sussex, where in December 1983 it was decided to broaden the appeal of the campaign through more direct actions, as well as to increase political lobbying. The primary aim then was to keep track of the minerals negotiations. It was there that the decisions were made and the most immediate threats to the continent lay. To begin with, pickets were mounted outside the Antarctic Treaty meetings, protesters livening up the meetings.

The world park concept began life as a vague idea. 'We used it in the early days of the campaign without having a real sense of what we meant,' Roger recalls. 'Later we elaborated the idea, but as the prospect of mining and oil exploration loomed we realised that some dramatic direct actions were needed to stress the urgency of the issue. This in turn led us to recognise that our protests would have more impact if Greenpeace could actually bear witness in Antarctica itself. The talk turned to setting up a Greenpeace base to operate as a year-round challenge to the status quo of the treaty.'

The initial expedition was planned for the 1985/86 summer season. 'I was sceptical at first,' says Roger. 'I didn't seriously think Greenpeace had the capacity or resources to mount the expedition and set up a base that soon.' First a design for the base had to be found and adapted to Greenpeace's needs. We got the MV *Greenpeace*, an ocean-going tug and salvage vessel in March 1985. The hull was ice-strengthened, a helicopter pad was built, and satellite communications were fitted.

The Antarctic campaign fund was small compared to some of Greenpeace's national budgets at the time, and the first attempt to establish a base on Ross Island in 1985 was beaten back by the worst sea-ice conditions in the Ross Sea for thirty years. 'Morale on the MV *Greenpeace* was very low,' Roger recalls. 'In retrospect it was probably just as well that we were unable to establish the base. It was a nightmare for me sitting in Lewes, desperately trying to bolster morale on the other end of the satellite link. It was one of the most stressful times of my life.'

What price oil?

The MV *Greenpeace* returned to New Zealand in a bad way. 'After we had to turn back, there were people who questioned the viability of the whole project. There were all sorts of tensions on board, which were inevitably heightened by the isolation. Wellington Greenpeace activists had arranged a big party for the crew the day they returned to Wellington. But by that time the crew were at such odds with each other that only two of them turned up; the rest had scattered all over town, glad to get away from each other.

'This initial failure did influence a lot of people and there were moves to cancel the expedition part of the campaign, or modify it drastically.' Once the expeditions began, however, Greenpeace International decided they needed a full-time Antarctic campaigner in New Zealand because of the importance of a presence at the mineral negotiations. After resigning as Greenpeace New Zealand's trustee and co-ordinator in 1987, Carol Stewart took on the job. A second, better-prepared expedition was mounted in 1986/87.

Greenpeace's World Park Antarctica Base was successfully established on Ross Island during three weeks in February 1987. Near the historic Scott Expedition hut at Cape Evans, the Greenpeace base is within thirty kilometres of New Zealand's Scott and the US McMurdo bases. It consists of three prefabricated, double-walled structures joined by walkways and housing the four Greenpeace staff who spend the winter there, a generator plant and a work room. Power for heat, light, laboratory and satellite communications comes from two diesel generators and a wind and solar energy system. Shipped-in food supplies are supplemented by fresh vegetables grown hydroponically. All wastes are stored for removal during the summer resupply of the base.

The four team members for the first overwinter were: Kevin Conaglen, base camp leader, who had been on a 1984 New Zealand Government expedition; Gudrun Gaudian, a West German marine biologist and an experienced climber and diver; Dr Cornelius Van Dorp, a Dutch-born New Zealander and team medic; and Justin Farrelly, a radio operator with dual English/New Zealand citizenship. All were unpaid volunteers.

First telex message from base camp, Cape Evans, to GPNZ, 26 March 1987:

'It seems a long time since the MV *Greenpeace* left Cape Evans (it's actually about seven weeks). I cried when the boat left, and I'm sure the others had at least a lump in their throats. But the thought of living here at Cape Evans amidst penguins, seals, skuas, icebergs, and next door to an active volcano, soon lifted our spirits and we began the long and arduous task of unpacking, arranging, building shelves, rearranging the layout of bedrooms, building a hydroponics system, and starting beer and wine brews. There's a lot of greenery, future peas, beans, flowers, herbs, cucumbers and tomatoes in the corner opposite the galley, and our walls are covered with shelves brimming with books and videos. Kevin's got a corner for his industrial sewing machine, which he is currently using to improve our winter clothing. Justin has at last got his room into shape, and Cornelius has turned his into an oversized medicine cupboard – he seems prepared for anything, including frontal lobotomies. In his spare time, Cornelius is going through our library at a rate of knots.

'My niche doubles as a laboratory. Presently the desk is covered with sampling bottles waiting to be analysed, publications to be read and plants exposed to the full beam of the desk lamp to encourage faster growth. I am trying to grow some flowers to get some bright colours in here. I go out daily

The *Greenpeace* helicopter was essential for setting up the base.

to collect data on the local wildlife. Counting is getting easier each day, since most animals have left the area as the sea is freezing over. I am also taking hourly readings of wind speed, air and water temperature and barometric pressure and comparing the information obtained with similar data Scott collected some seventy-five years ago. Some very interesting results are showing up already.

Expedition team celebrates successful establishment of the World Park Antarctica base, February 1987.

'Today was such a beautiful day. Erebus was spitting plumes of smoke into an immaculate blue sky. Not a sound, no jennies, no skuas, nothing. Silence. In the distance the trans-Antarctic mountains loomed. Though they are over sixty nautical miles from us, it seems far less because of the incredible clarity of the air. The only sound was the occasional creaking of the icefloes. The ice is becoming quite thick, but with the tidal movements of the water beneath, the ice has broken up into floes of different sizes that gently bump into each other, creating an eerie sound like an old door in a secret castle. A Ross seal lolled about in a tide crack, his head poking through the slushy water.

'Eventually the sun began to set, tinting the snow, the slopes, glaciers and rocks around us the most amazing red hue. I wish I could capture this colour with my watercolours, but whenever I try it comes out too loud.

'It's so easy to let one's thoughts drift here.

'To top the day I went for a run. I just had to let my feelings run wild and run, the sweat freezing instantly, my eyebrows and eyelashes clogging with icicles. I was listening to some wild music until the Walkman batteries seized up in the cold, but the silence that followed had an even stronger impact on my mind while racing along. My lungs hurt like mad after this run and I was coughing for hours afterwards. Still, it was great fun.

'In the evening we listened to Mozart's *Requiem*. I sat knitting, while Justin was meditating and the hydroponics system gurgled away gently in the background, the sickle of the moon shining through the window and the gently moving sea ice creaking and screeching its eerie tunes.

'It's incredibly beautiful here at Cape Evans; the air is pure and the contrasting moods of nature – blizzards, gales and sunny days – follow in rapid succession. A week ago the sun was setting over the mountains of Victoria Land, but now her path is shorter, and she is falling into the Ross Sea earlier and earlier. Soon she will be gone for three months... What a thought! What an amazing place! So full of surprises and beauty that we often stop and wonder at how fortunate we are to be here.

'Greetings from Gudrun and the rest of the crew.'
6 April 1987, *Cornelius Van Dorp*:

'At the moment I'm lying on my bunk thanking my lucky stars, and our good leader Kevin, that we're safely home in our little green box and not out in the blizzard. The wind is howling from the south at up to seventy knots and for the first time large snowdrifts are building up outside, burying our poor little Kobota tractor. The temperature out there is minus 26 degrees C while in here it's jeans and T-shirt weather at 20 degrees C.

'I wish I could convey the supreme sense of comfort I feel just now, with every muscle aching and the blisters on my feet smarting from our seventy-two-kilometre, three-day marathon to Scott Base and back. The plan had been to stay and socialise for a few days, but something made us push our aching

Greenpeace World Park Antarctica base, Cape Evans. Mt Erebus in the background.

Gudrun Gaudian samples an outflow pipe, McMurdo.

bodies back to Cape Evans, despite the wind. Sure enough, just a few hours after our return the black clouds began rolling in and now the wind is howling.

'The walk to Scott Base was our first tentative excursion, and was as much a test of our gear as a mail run. The trip was preceded by five days of brilliantly clear weather, during which time the whole of McMurdo Sound had frozen over with about ten to fifteen centimetres of clear ice. We started out by skirting around the edge of the old ice, which had not broken out this year, but we soon saw that we would save quite a few miles by walking over the new ice. After testing the ice thoroughly with our axes we decided it would support our weight and strapped on our skis.

'We'd only gone several hundred metres, however, when I thought I heard something and motioned for Kevin to stop. We strained our ears. There it was again – a powerful "whoosh" of expelled air under the ice. Kevin's face went white as a few seconds later on our other side and much, much closer came the same noise. "Orcas," he shouted, "and they're hunting. Let's get out of here." We both turned and zig-zagged back towards the thicker ice as fast as our skis would take us. It took ten or fifteen minutes of strenuous effort to reach it, and we were tracked the whole way by the killer whales. Their characteristic sounds only centimetres under our feet lent wings to our skis. We both had the terrifying feeling that we were being hunted. From then on we stuck to the safety of the crumbled old ice.

'When we passed this spot on the way back several Ross seals had made breathing holes in the ice and one of them had a bleeding gash near its right eye. Contrary to the usual placid nature of these animals, this one reared up, snorting and blowing aggressively, as we approached. Nearby, there were several areas of thin ice where it was evident that a massive force had pushed up and broken the surface from below.

'The experience of living here is mind-expanding to say the least. The pristine beauty of the still, clear days is made all the more vivid by the preceding days of furious fifty-knot winds. The vast silence you experience when you get away from the base is purifying to the soul.'

Through the summer of 1987 GPNZ stepped up its campaign against the threat of oil and mineral exploration. After six years of intensive negotiations the Convention on the Regulation of Antarctic Mineral Resource Activities (CRAMRA) was adopted in Wellington on 2 June 1988. Since Greenpeace's campaign for a world park began, Australia and France had moved their positions to oppose CRAMRA, and the New Zealand Government, initially an enthusiastic supporter of CRAMRA, followed suit in 1990.

On 9 November 1987 the Antarctic Treaty nations met in Auckland. At this stage the New Zealand Government was presenting the minerals negotiations, now nearing completion, as essential for preventing a mining free-for-all, and as the only way to control mining and oil exploration. Greenpeace argued that the mining industry had lobbied for the regime as an essential prerequisite to their exploration, and that therefore, far from discouraging mining companies, it would actually create the framework within which exploitation could proceed.

Deputy Foreign Affairs Secretary Chris Beeby, who chaired the minerals negotiations throughout the period, repeatedly refused to receive a Greenpeace plaque representing the one million plus signatures calling for a world park. Greenpeace made its point, therefore, by presenting the plaque instead to a cardboard cut-out of Mr Beeby. A Greenpeace team including Keith Swenson, Antarctic basecamp leader for 1987/88, abseiled from the roof of the hotel meeting hall unfurling a 'Hands Off Antarctica' banner. On the last day of the meeting three tonnes of crushed ice was dumped outside the hotel with a banner reading 'Keep Off the Ice'.

After the *Greenpeace*'s third Antarctic expedition in 1988 she was replaced by another tug, the *Gondwana*, which had served in Finland as an oil-rig supply vessel. With a hull specially strengthened for polar conditions, the *Gondwana* is described by first mate Ken Ballard as a 'maritime bulldozer', built for heavy work in icy water. Special modifications included a helipad and hangar space for two Hughes 500D helicopters. She also carries three inflatables, a small support craft, a satellite communications system, an internal sewage processing and storage system to handle all organic and inorganic waste, including chemicals used in the on-board photo laboratory, and an old cast-iron bathtub mounted on the rear helipad for memorable sunset soaks.

The World Park Antarctica base, tiny in comparison with other bases on the ice, conducts research into local and global pollution and is visited once a year by the *Gondwana* for resupply. In addition to resupplying and relieving the base, the *Gondwana* carries out its own programme of monitoring and direct protest action. In the course of monitoring the Antarctic environment, Greenpeace has documented many violations of the treaty.

During the 1988/89 expedition, for instance, the *Gondwana* visited the French base at Dumont d'Urville to meet French representatives and to mount a protest at the building of an airstrip that had already involved blasting five islands in the Pointe Géologie Archipelago. The construction project breaches several existing agreements on environmental protection in the Antarctic. The breeding sites of over 6,000 Adélie penguins, 500 snow petrels, 500 Wilson storm petrels and 600 Cape pigeons will be wiped out, and it also threatens to cut off access to breeding grounds of the unique emperor penguins.

Carol Stewart, GPNZ's Antarctic campaigner at the time, picks up the story. 'Greenpeace followed the usual procedure, giving prior notice of their intention to visit the base to monitor pollution and protest against the airstrip. The reply from the officer in charge of the French base, M. Houssin, was that Greenpeace could call in at 1000 hours on 6 January, when the "conditions for the visit could be agreed". He saw no problem with a peaceful demonstration, he said. After discussions with Houssin, Greenpeace expedition campaign co-ordinator Pete Wilkinson, a veteran of countless Greenpeace protest actions in Europe, agreed on an acceptable form of peaceful protest.

'Pete's plan involved transporting an igloo-type hut to the southern end of the airstrip construction site. The hut would be occupied continuously by a contingent of five Greenpeace people, who would be chained to a surrounding fence. But at 0700 on the second day, construction site workers arrived with bulldozers and proceeded to move towards the hut, knocking the protesters to the ground and dragging them roughly aside.

'Pete later took a video of the fracas to Houssin, who decided to suspend work on the site until he received orders from Paris. An uneasy truce followed, while Greenpeace continued to occupy the site. Then violence erupted again, a gang of the French workers kicking in one of the hut's panels in order to evict one of the Greenpeacers chained inside. Then the chains were cut and the hut towed fifty metres to the airstrip exit, so allowing the construction work to resume.

Greenpeace holds up work on the French airstrip at Dumont d'Urville.

'Houssin explained that the construction workers had found the peaceful action "provocative". The site manager commented angrily that the work would proceed even if protesters were killed in the process. In an attempt to defuse an explosive situation, Pete offered to restrict Greenpeace activities to the occupation of the southern end of the airstrip in return for a guarantee that there would be no further acts of violence. The officer declared a desire to see an orderly end to the Greenpeace protest and agreed to a day of co-operative work during which a full and comprehensive study of the scientific and other activities being carried out at the base could be undertaken.

'On 13 January the hut was dismantled and the "open day" took place. A group of about twenty people – scientists, administrators, Greenpeace campaigners and media entourage – toured the base, visiting various sites and exchanging views and information. The French admitted to frequently violating the Antarctic Treaty's "agreed measures". They used fireworks to scare seabirds from their nests before blasting, and penguins were removed to pens before their nesting areas were dynamited. The information collected that day highlighted the environmentally destructive nature of these activities at the French base and more than vindicated our protests.'

A few days later, 180 miles north of Cape Adare in the Ross Sea, the *Gondwana* intercepted a Japanese factory whaling ship, the *Nisshin Maru*, with its three attendant catcher vessels. A loophole in the IWC regime allowed for minke whales to be killed for 'scientific purposes'. The whalers now kill several hundred minkes each year in Antarctic and Southern Ocean waters and sell the meat to restaurants in Japan. After a few days of shadowing the factory ship, the crew of *Gondwana* deployed two inflatables and succeeded in obstructing further whaling operations.

An engine fault on one of the Greenpeace inflatables brought the *Gondwana* itself into the action. Positioning the expedition ship at the stern of the factory ship denied the catchers the use of the slipway to unload their kill and thus frustrated further hunting. The *Gondwana* maintained her position for nine days before she was compelled to resume her homeward journey.

The 1989/90 *Gondwana* expedition set out on its first leg from New Zealand with ten different nationalities represented among the twenty-eight crew, including six New Zealanders. The ambitious schedule included two trips to the ice. The first leg would feature inspection visits to several Antarctic bases and a protest against the Soviet fishing fleets in the South Georgia area. Then they would return to New Zealand to pick up supplies and rendezvous with the new *Rainbow Warrior* in Auckland. On the second journey they would return to World Park Base to relieve the overwinterers and resupply the base for the following year.

The reception at most of the bases they visited was more friendly and co-operative than in previous years, the only really hostile reaction coming from one of the Argentine bases, Esperanza. At the British Faraday base scientists even helped to display the Greenpeace banner and took part in protests against mining.

The *Gondwana*, a 'maritime' bulldozer'.

The expedition leader that year was Dr Maj de Poorter, a Belgian zoologist making her fourth journey to Antarctica. Having completed her PhD field research in the Arctic territories of the Yukon in northern Canada, Maj had moved to New Zealand in 1986 to join the Greenpeace Antarctic team.

'The Antarctic is still a paradise,' she reported. 'The wildlife are not afraid of human beings. You can sit on a beach and penguins will come up and start pecking your shoe laces. That's why the contrast between the purity of the place and the human impact there is so frightening.'

On this trip the *Gondwana* had inspected the wreck of the *Bahia Paraiso*, an Argentine resupply ship still carrying diesel on board nearly a year after running aground perilously close to penguin breeding colonies. 'The Antarctic Treaty system has proved unable to cope even with the present level of environmental abuse,' Maj adds. When the *Exxon Valdez* ran aground in Prince William Sound in 1989, 11 million gallons of crude oil flowed into the Gulf of Alaska, contaminating 700 miles of coastline. This was exactly the kind of accident that Greenpeace had warned could happen in Antarctica were it to be opened for oil exploration. Despite a massive multi-million-dollar mobilisation by the US Government, oil companies, thousands of volunteers, and some seventy ships and forty aircraft, not a single mile of Alaskan coast has been adequately cleaned up. The spectre of such a devastating spill in Antarctica has helped block CRAMRA and persuade all the Antarctic Treaty nations, except the United States, to agree to a fifty-year ban on mineral exploration that will be difficult to break.

Antarctic expedition team toast successful Dumont d'Urville blockade.

Already known to thousands of New Zealanders from her nationwide World Park Antarctica speaking tour, and joining her first Greenpeace expedition to the southern continent was American Vicki Getz. Vicki was also no stranger to the Antarctic. 'I'd wanted to go to the Antarctic for years, so when I finished my degree I applied for the only job going on the US base at McMurdo, as a janitor. I got the job and returned after one season to co-ordinate resupplying, gradually building my own little niche at McMurdo.

'McMurdo is basically a frontier town, with a lot of people there just to make a buck and drink beer at one of the five bars on base. In 1986 there was a small core of people who really loved the place for its wild beauty – often the scientists preferred to stay off-base to escape the cowboy atmosphere.

'Greenpeace were seen as intruders when they arrived to set up the base. I first met Cornelius and Justin one day when I was driving my truck along a snow road across the Ross ice shelf. It was minus 40 degrees and there they were. I offered them a lift but they said they could not accept. After that the Greenpeace team would visit me in my office on the base, an island of "normality" in the almost penal atmosphere of McMurdo. I knew I might get into trouble for fraternising – the fear of losing your job keeps a lot of people there in line. The base administration are very sensitive to criticism of the way they treat the environment. But I kept on communicating by radio with Cornelius and the others at the Greenpeace base.

Opposite: Greenpeace pickets mining negotiations, Auckland 1987 (above); French construction workers get rough with airstrip blockaders, Dumont d'Urville 1989 (below).

'When I asked my employers if I could work on the McMurdo overwintering team for 1986/87 I was made to understand they did not want 'any fucking cunts' on the job, so I wrote up my own McMurdo Feminists' manifesto attributed to the 'Committee for Uniform Non-sexist Treatment' and got a bunch of people there to sign it. In 1987 I was dropped from the base – I was simply told one morning to be on the plane that afternoon.

'By then the *Greenpeace* had reached the World Park base for resupply and Pete Wilkinson came over to see me in the helicopter. Apparently the US authorities were worried that I was about to defect to Greenpeace, which I would certainly have been happy to do. But instead I took the plane out the next day, then went to see Kelly Rigg with Greenpeace USA. Later I came to New Zealand, where Henk Haazen took me on as his logistics assistant for the 1988/89 expedition, and the following year I was one of Maj's campaign assistants on the peninsula leg of the expedition.'

A priority for that year's expedition was to monitor the impact on the environment of national scientific bases like McMurdo. On 17 November, en route to South Georgia via Signy Island, Vicki Getz sent this account back to GPNZ:

'Marambio, the Argentine base, is strange. During this trip, we have seen incredible beauty. Snow-covered mountains, islands captured by glaciers flowing to the sea like frozen rivers. The ice sparkling like diamonds in the evening sun. The bases perched on the edge of all this magnificence.

'Marambio is different. Seymour Island rises to 250 metres above sea level, and at the very top, sprawled across the plateau, lies the base. We thought of walking up for the inspection, but the deeply gullied island has virtually no snow cover, and the walk would have been difficult, so we decided to use the helicopter. The flight there gave us a glimpse of what was coming. We flew over gullies strewn with oil drums, and there was a huge rubbish tip off the top of the hill. We could see the gravel strip used by Hercules aircraft from Argentina.

'Seymour Island is like a natural history museum and a reminder of Antarctica's past. A few years ago an entire dinosaur skeleton was found here. As we walked around we found fossilised shells and leaves in abundance.

'Gulls were feeding on food scraps thrown out of the main building. The scraps were scattered amongst broken glass, plastic, cans, scrap metal, bones. We passed huge piles of rubbish showing oil drums, plastic garbage bags, batteries, aerosol spray cans, bits of wire and paper. The melt streams flowing through this scene were rainbow-coloured with petroleum products. About 200 metres from the base, we looked over the side of the precipice to see the whole hillside covered in a river of waste that flowed down into the gullies, where it collected in a mass.

'At the second Argentinian base, Esperanza, I found a huge "off-limits" waste dump. When I was spotted they went up the wall. I don't speak Spanish but I didn't need to – they were mad! They told us the dump was "designated for official treaty inspectors only" and that we were not allowed to see it.'

Another of the expedition's aims was to draw world attention to the Antarctic fishing industry. All the fishing boats the *Gondwana*'s crew spoke to

Opposite: Greenpeace inflatable between catcher vessel and factory ship. The idea is to prevent the offloading of the kill onto the factory ship (above); Greenpeace helicopter worries a whalechaser, two of its victims already slung alongside, (below).

'Mactown', the US McMurdo base.

reported very poor catches. They were often leaving established fishing grounds after only two or three days, which indicated that fish stocks might already be almost exhausted in some areas.

'When we spotted the *Mikhail Verbitzkiy*, a Soviet factory trawler fishing for *Notothernia guntheri* (Antarctic cod),' recalls Maj, 'we launched three inflatables. The crews, in survival suits, fought three-metre swells in near-zero temperatures to carry across placards reading "Stop the Plunder", "Stop Overfishing" and "Plunderers Stop!" (this last one in Russian). The boats closed in on the stern of the trawler, and two of the Greenpeace crew jumped onto the stern ramp to prevent the ship from launching its nets again. They stayed there for three hours. During this time the Russian fishermen gave thumbs-up signs to the Greenpeace crews, cheered and clapped, and even asked us if we'd like "one big fish" – it wasn't accepted!

'Later the *Gondwana* herself took over the protest, steering close to the *Verbitzkiy* with a banner reading "Antarctic Fisheries Is Russian Roulette". We followed the ship for more than twenty-four hours until noon the following day. It did no fishing in that time, and had in fact left the Shag Rock fishing area when we called off the protest.'

In an effort to regulate Antarctic and Southern Ocean fisheries the Antarctic Treaty nations set up the Convention on the Conservation of Antarctic Marine Living Resources (CCAMLR) in 1980. It was then considered something of a breakthrough, since for the first time it gave recognition to the entire Antarctic marine ecosystem rather than addressing single species in isolation. However, despite its fine principles CCAMLR has proved a dismal failure in conserving marine species.

'While Greenpeace has been calling for a moratorium on finfishing in the Southern Ocean to allow depleted populations to recover, CCAMLR allows for virtually uncontrolled fishing in Antarctic waters,' says Maj. 'Not only are the fish stocks themselves threatened, but the whole ecological balance in the

Greenpeace action during IWC conference, Auckland 1988.

Southern Ocean is put at risk, as these fish are the staple diet of penguins, seabirds, seals and whales. The great whales that once populated this area are gone, and now the fish are threatened. Greenpeace will not simply stand by and watch.'

On 28 December the *Gondwana* arrived back at Auckland, docking directly in front of the *Rainbow Warrior*. Two weeks later she headed south again to resupply the Greenpeace World Park Base in the Ross Sea, while the *Rainbow Warrior* left for the Tasman and the driftnet fishing protest.

During that year's Antarctic expedition, while New Zealand campaigner Janet Dalziell was busy lobbying in Wellington, campaign assistant Arani Cuthbert was organising the 'Rolling Snowball' Antarctic campaign tour of New Zealand. 'Greenpeace's first national speaking tour on the Antarctica issue had been made the previous year by Vicki Getz and Cornelius Van Dorp. The Antarctic was still not that much of an issue then, so Vicki and Cornelius toured twenty-five towns around the country to talk about the issues and encourage the setting-up of local support groups. In 1990 I followed up Vicki's work while she went back on the *Gondwana*. It was election year, so we had a focus for the Rolling Snowball tour. Phil Doherty and I tried to make it an election issue and targeted marginal electorates as well as the towns we had visited the year before.

'I hoped for something more than just a single-issue tour, and kept quoting Margaret Mead's adage: "Never doubt that a small group of thoughtful, committed citizens can change the world." The idea was to empower people, and the response was great. It seemed that passive membership, the days of simply donating $20 to Greenpeace, was over. We were inundated by people who wanted us to point them towards useful action. I think the Greenpeace television ads running at the time really got through to people, because a lot of them sat up and said, "Give me something to do."

'We also visited schools where environmental groups were being set up.

They were really keen on the Antarctic, as it combined wildlife and scientific issues. One school in Napier sent 1,700 letters to the Prime Minister during Conservation Week, urging the Government to abandon the mineral negotiations on the Antarctic Treaty. I was really blown away by the energy and enthusiasm on the tour, but I realised that follow-up was crucial too. Greenpeace's role is in resourcing and networking for the public. A lot of people are prepared to do things; we have to make sure that the information and direction gets through to them.'

Janet Dalziell had joined the campaign in 1989. 'We had been told by MPs that their constituents weren't especially interested in the Antarctic issue, so the two national speaking tours were an effort to change this. Meanwhile I concentrated on direct lobbying in Wellington, using the increased public interest generated by the tours. We were able to use the *Exxon Valdez* and *Bahia Paraiso* oil spills, and France's about-face on the minerals convention, to vastly increase pressure on the Government.

This two-pronged approach proved effective. Among the lobbyists, ASOC, in which Greenpeace is an active member, achieved an unusual degree of input into government policy-making on the issue, and several Labour ministers, including Prime Minister Geoffrey Palmer, showed particular interest. Between ASOC's Cath Wallace, Auckland University lecturer Alan Hemmings, Janet Dalziell and others, during 1989 and 1990 the Government was brought round to a change of policy. 'Antarctica had developed into an election issue,' explains Janet, 'and the National Opposition had already said it would not ratify CRAMRA, so the Government was under considerable pressure. Once it had finally officially abandoned its commitment to the minerals convention, we continued our negotiations with the Government in order to participate in the process of developing new policies. Today New Zealand is an ardent proponent of the new environmental protocol. And now, with the Antarctic Treaty nations having agreed to a minimum fifty-year mining ban, the Antarctic campaign has come close to achieving its central goal.'

Greenpeace began campaigning for a world park in 1984. Since 1985 Greenpeace has conducted five major expeditions to Antarctica, which have visited and evaluated thirty-six national scientific bases. Wide support for the world park regime now comes not only from environmental organisations and private citizens, but increasingly from governments too. More than one and a half million people, including scientists and politicians, signed Greenpeace's international 'Antarctic Declaration', in which the concept for a world park was embodied. Environmental groups around the world have worked closely to develop the practical aspects of the regime. The world park concept serves as a model of co-operation among private citizens, environmental groups and governments to develop sensitive and effective means of managing the last wild places on earth.

In retrospect, Roger Wilson puts down the campaign's success to three vital components: a sound political strategy, protest action and scientific back-up. Vicki Getz points to the grassroots pressure Greenpeace's and ASOC's work has encouraged. 'In New Zealand the Government has been persuaded to reverse its support for CRAMRA and has called for a mining ban.

Antarctic sunset.

'When I was driving through Rotorua in the painted Antarctic campaign van this older guy came up to me to say he supported us all the way on the Antarctic. He was a pretty conservative type who had lost his brother in the Mount Erebus plane crash, but he knew the Antarctic was unique and that we had to save it from exploitation. That's the bottom line for me. The Antarctic inspires people and our work there has got many more people involved. That is our real success.'

In June 1991, after three of the main pro-mining countries, Japan, Britain and Germany, reversed their positions on the issue, the Antarctic Treaty nations finally agreed on a minimum fifty-year ban on all minerals activities. The ban comes as part of a new environmental protection agreement, which commits the Treaty parties to 'the comprehensive protection of the Antarctic environment and dependent and associated ecosystems', and designates Antarctica as a 'natural reserve, devoted to peace and science'. At the last minute, the United States, anxious to remove the power of veto over any future mining, saw to it that the agreement was severely weakened. The ban can now be lifted after fifty years by a three-quarters majority of the existing Treaty parties. Nevertheless the agreement stands as an encouraging and important advance, bringing World Park Antarctica a large step closer.

CHAPTER TWELVE

You Can't Sink a Rainbow

AT THE AGE OF FORTY-EIGHT, after sixteen years' total commitment to Greenpeace New Zealand, and with her family pretty much grown up, Elaine Shaw decided to treat herself to a holiday. She went to Australia, bought a van and started travelling, but she never was much good at taking holidays, and in a few months she found herself working as a Greenpeace canvasser in Adelaide. Soon afterwards she was diagnosed as having lymphatic cancer and returned home to spend the time she had left in a little house she bought on Waiheke Island. While her health deteriorated, she continued to keep in touch with her many Greenpeace and Pacific friends while working on her house and on the revised edition of her French testing *Chronology*.

All through 1990 a small group of her closest women friends – the same core group from the 1984 office 'coup' – and her own remarkable children maintained close support. Characteristically, Elaine was incapable of giving up her work entirely, and while she was able she remained a regular visitor at the Auckland office. This book was conceived in July 1990 in part to maintain and channel her restless energy. On 16 October 1990 Martin Gotje and Stephanie Mills, on their way to join the new *Rainbow Warrior* en route to Moruroa, joined Elaine's other visitors at her bedside. She died the following morning. For Greenpeace New Zealand it was the end of an era.

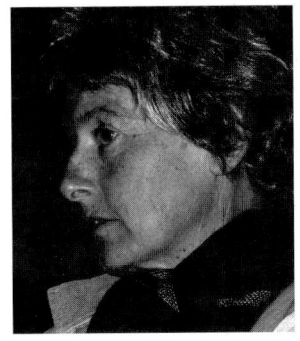

'I first met Elaine at the 1980 Nuclear Free and Independent Pacific conference in Hawai'i. Later she came and stayed at my home in Tahiti. She was interested in local politics in Tahiti, but I sensed that her interest stemmed from her concern for the people rather than any political ideology. She went to many islands and saw for herself what people in the Pacific wanted. She was a warm person who had a "feel" for things here. She looked so straight, like a housewife, and to look at her, you'd never believe she was an anti-nuclear militant. People here liked her for that, and remember her for it. Elaine was unique. She was an ordinary person who did extraordinary things.' *Tea Hirshon*

By 1990 France's Moruroa nuclear tests had been reduced to six a year. Politically it was more important than ever to keep up the pressure on the French Government over the issue, now part of the broader Pacific campaign. In late 1985 Martini made a speaking tour of Europe. As he saw it, two new elements in the Pacific anti-testing case were called for: first, authoritative

Opposite: The *Rainbow Warrior* in Papeete.

independent scientific expertise; second, an effort to focus more on the human dimension of the testing and the experience of today's nuclear victims.

In 1985 France was still conducting an average of eight nuclear tests a year at Moruroa, but after a series of accidents on the atoll in 1979, fears of radioactive leakage had increased. On one occasion a 150-kiloton nuclear device jammed halfway down the test shaft. Unable to dislodge it, the technicians detonated it where it was, tearing out a huge slab of the atoll's flank – assessed as at least one million cubic metres of coral and rock – and causing a tidal wave that swept across the lagoon. French authorities initially denied that any mishap had occurred and claimed the tidal wave was of natural origin, but in 1985 an official publication at last acknowledged 'the accident of 25 July 1979'.

The shroud of secrecy surrounding Moruroa remained a source of deep anger in the region. Official claims that the tests were completely safe carried little credibility given the French Government's track record of deceit and disinformation on the subject. Greenpeace persistently called on the French authorities to allow an independent team of scientists to monitor Moruroa. If radioactivity were leaking through the cracks in the atoll, it would ultimately accumulate in the marine food chain.

Further information about the impact on human health also came to light. Since the seventies there had been stories about Polynesians coming to New Zealand for cancer treatment, but most of French Polynesia's cancer patients have always been sent to France. According to French journalist Luis Gonzales-Mata in *Actuel* magazine, large groups of Polynesians had been secretly sent on military flights to Paris for treatment of cancer. Fifty Tahitian cancer patients, all of whom were aged under thirty-five and suffering from brain tumours, were flown to Paris on one occasion alone; at the time of the atmospheric tests these people would have been between ten and twenty years old.

Gonzales-Mata claimed records held by the State Secretary of Health's office in Paris showed that fifty patients were sent there in 1976, about seventy in 1980 and seventy-two in 1981. More than half of them had cancer. Tahitian activist Charlie Ching told a nuclear-free Pacific hui in Auckland in 1983 that more than 200 Tahitians had died from radiation-linked illnesses in five years. Because of the secrecy surrounding all health statistics in French Polynesia, these figures remained impossible to confirm, but the twin threats to human health and the environment increased the urgency for an independent and comprehensive scientific survey.

In 1983 the French Government permitted a mission comprising scientists from New Zealand, Australia and Papua New Guinea, and led by Hugh Atkinson, director of New Zealand's National Radiation Laboratory, to spend four days on Moruroa under CEA supervision. The ensuing Atkinson Report found parts of the atoll cracked and unstable, repeatedly expressed frustration over the restrictions imposed on the survey and emphasised the need for further study. Despite these reservations, France seized on other statements in the report – in particular, the estimate that radioactive leakage would not occur for 500 to 1,000 years – to claim that the report proved that testing was safe.

'Twice the French authorities had manipulated and misrepresented the scientific evidence [the 1982 Tazieff and Atkinson reports], and we knew we

'Since nuclear testing began in the land of the Maohi, the people have never been consulted. Practically all our political, religious and trade union leaders have repeatedly called for the testing to stop. Today we note that nothing has been done.'
Statement by Tahitian hunger-strikers outside Papeete Cathedral on the 1989 anniversary of the first atomic test over Moruroa

'Te Hotu o te Fenua', the Tree of Life, by Bobby Holcomb. 'The traditional spirit of Polynesians is that the land is like our mother. People come from the land. We must respect our mother, not explode bombs in her belly. Our good way of life comes from the land. Destruction of the land will lead to the destruction of life and the way of life of Polynesian people.'
Jacques Ihorai, president of the Evangelical Church of Polynesia, Tahiti

needed a more authoritative scientific voice,' recalls Martini. 'But we also wanted to apply the lessons of Rongelap – that the real human costs of nuclear testing were being hidden. The 1986 Chernobyl nuclear accident brought the issue home to people in Europe. At last they had a taste of what many people in the Pacific have experienced for forty years.'

The Moruroa campaign was stepped up in 1988, when Rebecca Johnson, who had lived for five years at the Greenham Common peace camp and had been a leading activist in the British CND, was appointed international co-ordinator of Greenpeace's nuclear test ban project. Working with Bunny McDiarmid and Julie Miles in the New Zealand office, Rebecca set about building a new campaign against French testing and preparing for the 'return' of the new *Rainbow Warrior* to Moruroa. This time the campaign would have a greater international dimension. In January 1991, a comprehensive test ban treaty would be on the United Nations' agenda, and this would provide a focal point for Greenpeace's international campaign against nuclear testing.

While Greenpeace was busy preparing for a return to Moruroa, the French authorities had drawn up their own plans to deflect criticism of the tests. In June 1987 the famous French marine biologist Jacques Cousteau had paid a visit to Moruroa.

A Cousteau expedition diver examines a fissure in Moruroa's coral crown.

Cousteau was permitted five days on Moruroa – three for filming, one for meeting officials and one for a limited sampling expedition under the direction of the CEA. His preliminary findings, released in June 1988 and supported by convincing underwater film footage, revealed evidence of potential leakage at Moruroa. Yet once again the French authorities managed to present the report to the world's media as a reassuring vindication of their claims. The film, shot only to a depth of 200 metres, showed cracks in the coral crown, but the basalt rock beneath, the French Atomic Energy Commission claimed, remained secure. There is no independent evidence to confirm this.

Cousteau's conclusions were in fact far from reassuring. His team found significant levels of artificially produced caesium-134 in two separate water samples nine kilometres apart. 'No satisfactory explanation for the presence of caesium-134 has been furnished,' commented the report. 'Even if the measured quantities pose no danger at this time the presence of this radioelement should be explained.' According to American scientist Norm Buske's analysis of the Cousteau findings, this new data clearly indicated radioactive leakage into the lagoon at Moruroa. Promotion of Buske's analysis of the Cousteau data, refined through peer review over many months, was to be a key component in Greenpeace's new French testing campaign.

Martini, Bunny and Rebecca Johnson were determined that the *Rainbow Warrior* should this time include a goodwill and educational visit to Papeete on her itinerary as a preparation to the return to Moruroa. Their first problem was to find someone to do the essential groundwork in Tahiti, as Jane Cooper and Elaine Shaw had in the past.

New Zealander Stephanie Mills, a former journalist, had been working for CND in London and already had a background of working with the NFIP network both in Europe and New Zealand when she decided to return home. She had been back barely two weeks when she received a phone call from Sydney, where Rebecca had been discussing the year's plans with the Pacific campaigners.

Stephanie flew to Tahiti to meet Greenpeace contacts. 'I found Papeete a political minefield with an extensive rumour mill and a particularly anti-Greenpeace press. It's virtually impossible for a Greenpeace campaigner to remain invisible there. While making a phone call at the post office on my very first day, I was photographed by a mysterious man – the Danielssons thought he was probably with the secret police. Even the chambermaid at the small hotel I was staying in knew who I was and warned me that her boss was very pro-French and had already been visited by the police about my stay there. On the other hand, I was warmly welcomed by our contacts there – Dr Patrick Tahiata Howell, Oscar Temaru, Vito Maamaatua and Tea Hirshon, Philippe Siu and Jacqui Drollet and members of the Eglise Evangelique.'

Stephanie returned to New Zealand after the visit to organise French material for the trip and to brief the crew of the *Rainbow Warrior,* preparing to depart for Tahiti, about the situation there. On board were Alain Connan, president of Greenpeace France, and Roger Spautz, director of Greenpeace Luxembourg and a fluent French speaker.

'We all recognised the importance and delicacy of our visit to Papeete,' says Stephanie, 'which is why so much effort was put into the preparations. We wanted to present the French testing issue in the context of all Greenpeace's campaigns in the Pacific on driftnetting, coral reef protection, energy use and waste issues.'

In the humid and draining heat of Papeete a few weeks later, the *Rainbow Warrior*'s crew showed hundreds of people around the ship, explaining in 'Franglais' Greenpeace's objectives in the Pacific. The theatre in the ship's hold was regularly packed for the Pacific slide-show. Alain, Stephanie and Roger, meanwhile, were busy ashore making political contacts and giving press briefings that would pave the way for the yet-to-be-announced trip to Moruroa later in the year.

In 1987 and 1988 Andy Biedermann, the Swiss doctor on board the first *Rainbow Warrior,* had made two extended visits to the islands around Moruroa. Andy returned with a dossier of interviews with Moruroa workers and people living on neighbouring atolls. The account was published by GPNZ, as *Testimonies,* shortly before the second *Warrior*'s Tahiti visit, which was followed up by international promotion of *Testimonies* and of the Buske Report on Cousteau's findings. The two publications received extensive coverage

Stephanie Mills and Oscar Temaru, at the French Embassy, Wellington, commemorate the fifth anniversary of the *Rainbow Warrior* bombing.

Tavini Huiraatira (Polynesian Liberation Front) protest during the *Rainbow Warrior*'s visit to Papeete, May 1990. 'Militarism pervades the entire fabric of life in Te Ao Maohi – political, economic and social.' *Ben Teriitehau, Tavini Huiraatira*

throughout the Pacific, and Greenpeace was asked by the South Pacific Forum secretariat to circulate copies of the Buske Report to all its members.

On the basis of this work, Norm Buske was employed by Greenpeace as a consultant and joined Rebecca, Stephanie, Bunny and Martini for a planning meeting in Auckland. 'Norm arrived from Seattle on a cool August morning,' recalls Stephanie. 'I was expecting a boffin type in beige strides; instead, Norm was wearing what I was to learn was his "uniform": purple reflective wraparound sunglasses, a tie-dyed T-shirt and safari shorts. Rebecca had told me about his famous giggle, but I was still a little unprepared for some of his idiosyncracies. Norm is utterly unique. He has an amazing brain and a sometimes exasperating tenacity for detail, which for this campaign was vital.' Everyone crammed into Stephanie's Grey Lynn kitchen for a wet winter week, poring through detailed scientific, political and logistical scenarios for the planned voyage to Moruroa over copious amounts of coffee.

Included in the *Rainbow Warrior*'s complement for the Moruroa voyage were Martini, Stephanie and Alain, Philip Pupuka and Sue Ware, with Pete Willcox, the original *Warrior*'s skipper, as captain.

3 November, 1100 hours Pacific Standard Time. Stephanie: 'The *Rainbow Warrior* has just passed under Golden Gate Bridge, leaving San Francisco bound for Moruroa. We had a great send-off, with champagne and cheers from the San Francisco office. We're all excited and looking forward to some interesting times ahead.'

Norm had his own problems with ship life, as shipboard journalist Alison McCulloch wrote: 'Buske works in a laboratory the size of a large closet deep

French warships, Papeete 1990.

in the ship's bow, next to what used to be a fishhold in this converted Scottish trawler. At least the closet is air-conditioned, but the adjacent workspace gets stinking hot. Buske can be seen emerging from the hold at all hours of the day and night dripping with sweat… They aren't ideal conditions for a laboratory … Buske says it's like setting up a lab on a dog sled.'

26 November. After a three-week voyage, the *Rainbow Warrior* arrives at Tahiti. The ship is met by Oscar Temaru, Jacqui Drollet, Bengt and Marie-Thérèse Danielsson, Patrick Howell and truckloads of Tahitian supporters. A dance group and band on the wharf welcome the crew. Oscar Temaru comes on board with literally a ton of fruit for the onward voyage – bananas, taro, pawpaw, mango, babaco, grapefruit, pineapple… The bananas are strung up in great heaps on the deck, while the other fruit is loaded into the hold.

The crew is wined, dined and shown around the island, meeting new crew members, Tahitian representatives of the Federation of Ecology Groups (Gaston and Thierry Bernardino) and the Eglise Evangelique (Pastor Remuna Tufariua).

Nearly two months before, on 8 October, Greenpeace International had submitted a scientific proposal to French Environment Minister Brice Lalonde, Greenpeace's old ally whose opportunistic political career had seen him enter the French Government in 1988. Now, instead of responding to the proposal, the High Commission in Papeete contacted the *Rainbow Warrior,* and on 28 November Alain, Stephanie and Roger met with the chef de cabinet of the Commission. Greenpeace representatives were invited on a one-day visit to Moruroa to meet with scientists and officials, see their equipment, discuss safety procedures and view an old test site on the atoll. This 'tourist invitation' had been cleared through the offices of the President, the Prime Minister and the Ministry of

Bengt and Marie-Thérèse Danielsson.

Rainbow Warrior, Papeete, May 1990.

Rainbow Warrior crew, December 1990.

Defence. Greenpeace replied that they were not prepared to be treated as tourists. They were all too aware of how such a visit could be misrepresented in the French media.

29 November. On the day the *Warrior* leaves Papeete for Moruroa the Ministry of Defence presents another, amended proposition to Greenpeace International negotiator Remi Parmentier in Paris. Remi writes: 'The "offer" is: one day at Moruroa (and/or Fangataufa) for as many crew as want to visit; the opportunity to confer with officials, scientists, etc., and go "anywhere you want with very few exceptions". This basically conforms to the deal offered by the High Commisioner in Papeete yesterday, but with the addition that the authorities would undertake to negotiate a protocol for sampling and monitoring, to be effected in the first half of 1991.'

30 November. Greenpeace tells the French Government they are interested in the offer but under certain conditions: They would want safe anchorage for the *Rainbow Warrior* at Moruroa, the right for Greenpeace to use its inflatables for transporting crew, and permission to sample in the lagoon. France refuses to permit these conditions and withdraws an earlier offer permitting a Greenpeace scientific mission to Moruroa in 1991, proposing instead a mission organised by the French Atomic Energy Commission, 'which will take into account the suggestions from Greenpeace'.

Papeete welcoming party.

2 December. In Tahiti Roger Spautz is responsible for monitoring the media and liaising with the High Commission and local groups. 'For the moment all is quiet here. The press reporting yesterday was as usual: *Les Nouvelles*, good; *La Dépêche*, bad (I think their journalist is angry we haven't offered him a place on board). When the ship left Papeete there were many Army and Secret Service personnel on the quay. Saw Alain's interview on TV last night – pretty good. Yesterday I tried all day to phone the boat, but without success. I think the press have better connections at the post office than I do, or they don't want me to contact the boat, as they kept telling me they couldn't get through, though it wasn't a problem for the journalists.'

3 December. The *Rainbow Warrior* arrives at the twelve-mile limit around Moruroa and begins its scientific testing programme. Stephanie: 'Sullen clouds hang over us, matching the oppressive grey of our warship escorts. In contrast to the bright sunshine and blur of colour and noise in Tahiti, Moruroa seems a strangely silent and ominous place. There are three ships circling us – a frigate, *Lieutenant de Vaisseau Lavallée,* a fast attack patrol boat, *La Railleuse* and a supply ship, *Rari*. Our crew have launched inflatables to begin drogue studies to measure current movements around the atoll.'

5 December. Remi Parmentier responds to the French Government: 'It was Greenpeace who first approached you with a proposal to undertake a preliminary study as the first step towards a definitive evaluation of the radiological impact of the nuclear tests. Your own proposal to establish a mission under the Atomic Energy Commission, which could then consult with

Greenpeace inflatables on the twelve-mile limit.

Greenpeace, is far more limited, and I fear it would be difficult for it to really cast light on the consequences of the nuclear tests.' To the *Warrior*, he writes: 'We are all aware that we have been successful because, in a way, we took them by surprise. What we are achieving has potential as the starting point of the final push to end French nuclear testing at Moruroa and Fangataufa.'

6 December. The *Rainbow Warrior* finds traces of radioactivity in plankton outside the twelve-mile limit. Martini: 'Norm ran a scan over the plankton we towed last night, and the bloody thing started to tick. We didn't expect this at all.' Norm's preliminary analysis reveals indications of both caesium-134 and cobalt-60.

7 December. Greenpeace releases these findings to the media. Stephanie: 'The phone has rung every five minutes for the past twenty-four hours – during the day the Pacific, New Zealand and Australian press, during the night the Europeans. I sleep in the radio room, or rather sprawl uncomfortably on the seat, closing my eyes briefly between phone calls.'

French scientists are invited to visit the *Warrior* to discuss the Greenpeace evidence. The invitation is rejected. Stephanie: 'After a glorious sunset, we have put two inflatables in the water to do some more sampling. We are about twelve miles off Moruroa and can easily see the lights of the village and airport there. The two inflatables go in opposite directions, which agitates the *Lavallée* captain no end. First of all he warned us we were right on the twelve-mile limit, then that our inflatables were about to go over it... They are obviously very nervous.'

Scientific team heads into the zone (from left): Alain Connan, Remuna Tufariua, Norm Buske, Beth Higgs, Martin Gotje.

Rebecca writes from Paris: 'Although the French Government haven't responded formally to our invitation for their scientists to come on board, Agence France Presse [AFP] has a wire story that someone on Moruroa says it wouldn't be possible to measure the cobalt, and that plankton does not retain caesium-134. Unfortunately for him, Cousteau also found traces of caesium-134 in his samples of plankton! We rang AFP to direct their attention to the relevant page in Cousteau's report. The fun continues...'

Norm: 'It's incredible, the difficulty they have trying to keep up with what's happening. They're not used to confrontative science. We throw in a drogue, a $5 piece of equipment made out of pegboard and a float and a little wire and string. We put it in the water to see where the currents are going and you have three gunboats, a ship and a couple of Zodiacs out keeping track of this thing. It's the theatre of the absurd – extremely entertaining. I just love that aspect of it... this absurdity has a real good feel to it.'

9 December. International media coverage of the *Warrior*'s findings is good. Rebecca writes to the crew: 'It's a cold Sunday in Paris. The story got very good coverage on two of the main evening news broadcasts on French TV. The Government said we couldn't possibly have found what is claimed – it's all a Greenpeace publicity stunt. But since the shots that followed were of Cousteau's divers alongside large underwater cracks in the coral beneath Moruroa, the overall impression gave credibility to our claims.

'Then Greenpeace were accused of jumping to unscientific conclusions. This is pretty silly, since all along we have emphasised that conditions for

Alain Connan, on the *Warrior* bridge, talks to the French Navy.

sampling are hardly ideal. We have in fact been fairly cautious, stressing that the main conclusion to be drawn from our positive indications of caesium-134 is that there is an urgent need for further, thorough investigations in the lagoon.'

11 December. Greenpeace launches an inflatable with a scientific team on board. Stephanie to Rebecca: 'We are readying the ship for "phase one": hiding film in survival suits, faxing Norm's results to Auckland in case the ship is seized, preparing the Avon inflatable for the scientific team's incursion into the zone. The inflatable, towing its plankton net behind it, is proceeding slowly across the twelve-mile limit, her progress punctuated by warnings from the rather uptight captain of the *Lavallée*.'

After an hour of tense waiting, the military make their move: forty masked commandos in four high-speed inflatables converge on the Greenpeace Avon. The five are seized and taken on board the *Lavallée*. Four hours later, after interrogation on board the frigate, they are returned to the *Warrior*.

12 December. Early in the morning the scientific team crosses the twelve-mile limit a second time in a further attempt to collect samples. Three miles into the zone they are again arrested, and this time taken to Moruroa. Stephanie: 'Although the inflatable has been returned to the *Warrior*, we've heard nothing of the crew.'

In fact, the five crew are taken to Moruroa and held incommunicado and under guard for three days. But their efforts to collect samples continue. One of the five, Tanya Popp from Coromandel, describes one of their more unconventional techniques: 'We were given bottled water to drink, and on the second day we were sent to a little hut by the lagoon. I asked if I could go and sit on the water's edge and read a book. Every time I went down I'd take a bottle of water under my arm, tip the fresh water out, and sitting there looking as though I was reading, try to fill it with my feet. I filled three bottles that way.'

'Then we decided to try getting samples of trees, leaves and fruit,' adds Martini. 'The head of the place, an admiral, came out to meet us in the middle of this. We were shaking hands with him and trying to swap our samples from one hand to the other at the same time... so they caught on and took the samples from us.' Eventually, all the samples taken by the five on Moruroa are confiscated, and all their film exposed. As scientist Norm Buske points out, 'They confiscated everything, which seems to indicate they have everything to hide.'

Meanwhile, Roger keeps up shipboard morale with tales from Tahiti: 'This afternoon at the military airport I met the journalist from *La Dépêche* off a plane from Moruroa. He told me he was sick all last week while he was on one of the warships. Maybe that's the reason he wrote such bad articles about Greenpeace! But here's the big story: On Tahitian TV they showed all these big scientists from Moruroa around a table. In front of them was the Cousteau report opened at page twenty-nine and caesium-134 is marked with a circle around it. They claim the reference to caesium-134 is a TYPING error!'

13 December. French Government disinformation again. Bunny writes from Auckland: 'Radio and TV3 both ran stories this evening claiming the five have been released or are "in a state of freedom" on Moruroa. I told them we

'The military make their move...' The scientific team is seized inside the zone.

have not been contacted at all regarding the status of the five, and that if they were free they would have contacted the ship. Apparently the story is coming from the French Embassy here.'

14 December. A banner hung from Nôtre Dame in Paris calls for an end to nuclear testing. A delegation from Greenpeace France visits the Ministry of Defence to demand a meeting with Chevènement, the minister. Support actions also take place in San Francisco, Vancouver, New Zealand and Australia.

Meanwhile, the five on Moruroa are finally released. Roger informs the *Warrior,* 'They arrived at Faa'a airport at 7.30 pm. They were taken out of a back door of the airport to the Gendarmerie, then transferred to the court, where I finally had a chance to talk to them. They were all fine and in good spirits, though very tired.

'At 10 pm the Prosecuter arrived. Apparently he had been negotiating with Paris in the interim. He informed the five that, judicially, they were free. Then they were taken by a Gendarmerie van under police escort to the High Commissioner's office, which is just across the road! I was not allowed to enter that building. Tanya came out for a minute to tell me they would probably be expelled. An hour later, Alain and Gaston were free. Norm, Martini and Tanya were driven away in a police van to the airport, where all three were put on a flight to Los Angeles.

'After Gauguin', by Andre Marere.

'The whole day I have been supported here by local Tahitian activists, including Oscar Temaru. On Saturday there will be a big anti-testing demonstration here.'

17 December. Bunny reports to the *Warrior* crew: 'Martini and Tanya arrived back in New Zealand today at 7.30 am. They walked out barefoot, carrying black plastic bags for their luggage and wearing their anti-testing T-shirts. We started cheering and the whole airport joined in clapping.'

With the campaign's leading scientist deported, the *Rainbow Warrior* returned to Papeete, and from there sailed to Auckland, to spread the news of the findings and to get the samples analysed further. Meanwhile another Greenpeace boat, the *Fand,* the yacht Chris Robinson had been building in Australia, maintained a vigil at Moruroa. On 5 January, while thousands of people joined a Greenpeace action at the US Nevada test site, Chris radioed a message to the captain of the warship shadowing his yacht. The *Fand* crew then handed across a letter, addressed to President Mitterrand, calling on France to sign the 1963 Partial Test Ban Treaty and the 1970 Non-Proliferation Treaty, the most important multilateral treaties governing nuclear testing and the spread of nuclear weapons. It asked France to work constructively for a complete test ban, and to implement an immediate moratorium on nuclear tests at Moruroa and Fangataufa while an independent environmental audit was carried out and a test ban negotiated. The French warship later confirmed that the message had been transmitted to Paris, and acknowledged they were aware that the United

Nations conference on a comprehensive nuclear test ban was about to open in New York.

Greenpeace meanwhile was urging delegates to the United Nations conference to support a comprehensive test ban. Greenpeace's immediate political objective was realised: not only was nuclear testing back on the international agenda, but it was also agreed to convene another meeting 'at an appropriate date' to discuss further a comprehensive nuclear test ban.

Stephanie: 'Greenpeace's opposition to nuclear testing is not based solely on environmental concerns. Nuclear warhead and missile testing is the "engine" of the nuclear arms race, driving the nuclear weapons states to develop and refine new generations of weapons of mass destruction. If there were a ban on all testing in all environments, the arms race itself could be short-circuited. A comprehensive ban would check the "qualitative" escalation of the arms race while also inhibiting the development of a nuclear weapons capability by new nations.

'Greenpeace New Zealand's campaign against French testing in the Pacific has concentrated on its environmental impact for several reasons. We have seen the consequences of the testing on our neighbours, the forgotten people of French Polynesia, and have felt a responsibility to bear witness to their plight. We also know the importance of the marine environment, under threat from radioactive contamination, to Pacific people. But it has also been a tactical approach, which we felt more likely to succeed than a head-on attack on strongly held notions of nuclear deterrence and military security in France.

'Nonetheless the role nuclear testing plays in the arms race has always been the backdrop to our campaign. Nuclear testing at Moruroa does not occur in a vacuum. Current tests aim to refine warheads for France's nuclear strike force of submarines, long-range bombers and land-based missiles – and of course the threat of their use continues to endanger us all.'

CHAPTER THIRTEEN

Turning the Toxic Tide

'Greenpeace suggests New Zealand should:
* Avoid repeating the environmental mistakes made in the industrialised nations.
* Cease to operate on the assumption that the environment has an infinite capacity to absorb hazardous substances.
* Adopt a "preventative, precautionary approach", which involves "clean production".

This all sounds very reasonable, but be warned, Greenpeace is duplicitous. Greenpeace may talk sweet reason in public, but it is as absolute in its opposition to waste pollution as it is to nuclear testing, driftnet fishing and whale hunting.'

NZ Chemical Industry Council circular to Greenpeace-targeted member companies, 31 January 1991

ON A WINDY JANUARY afternoon in 1991 the *Rainbow Warrior* sat at anchor off Matata Beach in the Bay of Plenty. Gordon Jackman, GPNZ's pulp and paper campaigner, was in the first inflatable with Philip Pupuka and Carol Stewart. 'It was difficult to judge what sort of sea was running, and by the time we hit the beach we were soaked. My guitar took some retuning once I'd poured the water out!' The *Warrior* delegation sloshed along the sand to the mouth of the Tarawera River, a little apprehensive of the Maori welcome and the crowd of onlookers awaiting them. The challenge was laid down for the *Rainbow Warrior*'s new skipper, Joel Stewart, and after his acceptance the meeting ground rang with speeches and singing.

The *Rainbow Warrior* had left Auckland two days earlier to begin a tour of New Zealand. On board were fifteen crew straight from the Moruroa voyage and eight GPNZ staff, most of them new to this kind of campaigning and shipboard life. For co-ordinator Lesley Stone and the rest of the toxics campaign team, the tour had required several months of meticulous planning. For six weeks the *Rainbow Warrior* would circumnavigate New Zealand, drawing attention to the growing toxic waste problems facing the country and highlighting New Zealand's main toxic waste producers, the widespread acceptance and use of hazardous products in the home and workplace, and the country's dependence on vast quantities of hazardous toxic imports.

Opposite: Manukau sewage outflow pipes.

'The prevailing image of New Zealand overseas is of green pastures, fluffy sheep and fat trout – great tourism publicity, but dig a little deeper and

Matata welcome: wero from Paul Warbrick (Tuwharetoa ki Kawerau).

things don't look so clean and green,' Lesley suggests. 'On the tour we will be working to increase public awareness and debate on toxics issues, particularly the dispersal of toxic contaminants into the environment. We want to alert people to the threats to our environment and to generate community action now to save it from further harm. Too many countries have left it too late to take effective action. It's our hope to propose clear, practical steps for members of the public and the Government to consider so as to avoid some of the pollution problems of other industrial nations, where the environment has been treated as if it had an infinite capacity to absorb hazardous waste. The logical course for New Zealand is to adopt a preventative, precautionary approach to waste management.'

Known locally as the Black Drain, the mouth of the Tarawera River at Matata was the first stop, the nearby Tasman pulp and paper mill the first target. Before dawn four inflatables set off from the *Warrior,* riding the waves in darkness, negotiating the sand-bar, everyone getting soaked in the process. For two hours they made their way up the stinking, discoloured and sometimes foaming river before reaching the mill's settling ponds.

According to the six o'clock television news that night, there were two newsworthy events on 16 January: US forces launched a massive air attack on Iraq, and Greenpeace protesters blocked off the outflow pipes at the Tasman mill in Kawerau. When the mill was closed down by strike action during the early 1980s, locals had observed how the river would clear, revealing the bottom, in some places for the first time since the mill was established. By blocking off the outflow for a day, Greenpeace could demonstrate graphically the impact of the mill on the river.

The pulp and paper issue is one of an interlocking set of projects within the overall toxics campaign, spotlighting this industry as a major polluter of New Zealand's rivers. The pesticides project targets the import, export and use of agricultural chemicals and raises the issue of corporate responsibility in New Zealand. Completing the triad is the 'Ban, Don't Burn' project, which focuses on the contamination that results from private waste incinerators and the barrier they present to clean production. The national campaign also aims to highlight local environmental problems in co-operation with local groups.

Gordon Jackman was returning to Matata nearly ten years after he had first campaigned in the area. 'Greenpeace was relatively unknown then. We didn't have anything like the resources we have now, and I was viewed as a bit of an oddball. Today there's so much more support from all sectors of the community, and it goes without saying that we have the backup of a large, well-resourced office.'

Gordon began working for Greenpeace as a volunteer in the late 1970s, when he did much of the newsletter work. Like his friend Michael Taylor, he had a special interest in archaeology, and it was when he was returning from

Natasha Perry prepares to be chained to the Tasman outflow valve.

Gordon Jackman (right) addresses local protesters outside the Tasman mill.

an archaeological dig near Whakatane in 1981 that he first realised the extent of the pollution of the Tarawera. 'I was flying back to Auckland from the dig when I looked out the window and saw a huge dark plume coming out of the river's mouth into the ocean. You couldn't miss it. My parents lived in the Bay of Plenty and I had always thought of it as an area where I'd like to live.'

The Tarawera River, fed by Lake Tarawera, runs more than fifty kilometres to enter the sea in the eastern Bay of Plenty. In 1955 the Tasman pulp and paper mill was built to process the large pine forests of the volcanic plateau. Kawerau was developed as the mill's service town. While the upper reaches of the river are still famous for their trout fishing and natural beauty, the river below Kawerau has been heavily polluted for thirty-five years, its water unfit for safe human or agricultural use and supporting only a limited range of life. It is effectively a dead river, a sewer for the Tasman and neighbouring Kawerau mills.

In the early 1950s many Maori families living near Onepu ran small dairy herds. After the mill was established their cattle became sick from drinking contaminated water, and dairying had to be stopped for lack of an alternative clean water supply. Ironically, local dairy farmers were then forced to seek work at the mill that had destroyed their livelihoods.

Soon after the mill began operations trout were wiped out in the lower Tarawera, so when the Ministry of Agriculture and Fisheries declared the river unfit for watering stock, Pakeha farmers, through the local Federated Farmers organisation, persuaded Tasman to sink wells for them. The company's generosity, however, did not extend to the neighbouring Maori farmers at Onepu. Local Maori were so angry at their treatment by the company that one Tuwharetoa elder lay down in front of a bulldozer moving onto her land to build a work camp for the mill. Her protest was successful and the camp was sited elsewhere.

As he learned more about the river and the mill's impact on it, Gordon determined to work to put a stop to the destruction of the river. Determination has been a dominant trait in Gordon's life. As a ten-month-old child he had contracted polio, which left him with partial paralysis in both legs, but with stubborn application and hard work he overcame his disability and went on to excel in athletics, for which he holds several New Zealand records and medals.

With the aid of a few hundred dollars from Greenpeace, Gordon's first task in 1981 was to research river pollution and assemble a file of local information. 'I was able to incorporate my research into the biology degree I was doing at university. From my own sampling I discovered that pollution levels were above legal limits at least 50 percent of the time. When I tried to find out why the mill was not being prosecuted, I discovered the Enabling Act that exempted them from the normal pollution regulations.'

Gordon's 'Waiora – Living Waters' campaign set out to persuade Tasman, a subsidiary of Fletcher Challenge, to clean up its act so that the Tarawera would once again be fit for human and agricultural use and free of toxic pollutants. Specifically, this meant repealing the Enabling Act, enforcing the normal environmental regulations of the local catchment board, persuading the mill to install clean production equipment, and applying the 'user pays' principle to the monitoring of the river and waste disposal.

'Given our small budget, we had to rely on the support of the local people. At about that time they started up their own group, Riverwatch, to keep an eye on the mill, and I came to spend a lot of time with Isobel and Jackie Fox, elders of Ngati Tuwharetoa ki Kawerau, who were especially concerned about the fate of their sacred waters. I also met Bill Marr, of Matata, who remembers whitebaiting at the rivermouth in the 1930s, when the river teemed with fish of many species.'

A heavy environmental price was being paid to keep the mill's profits up. Water sometimes flowed blackish brown from the mill, and the long-term effect of the chemicals on the food chain and local ecosystem had never been comprehensively researched. Future generations would inherit land and water that had been polluted for short-term gain. But in spite of the visible pollution, Tasman continued to claim that the river was 'no more discoloured than a glass of white wine and no more harmful than a cup of tea'. In a lengthy press statement, the company accused Greenpeace of 'wildly exaggerating the case'. Gordon responded by circulating a leaflet refuting Tasman's claims, calling on the Government to set up an inquiry into the ecological effects of the mill effluent, and asking Fletcher Challenge shareholders to give Greenpeace their proxy votes so shareholders' meetings could be used as a forum for public discussion on the condition of the river.

Isobel and Jackie Fox

By 1983 Tasman had opened communications with Greenpeace. They admitted there were problems and were even prepared to see the Enabling Act repealed. However, instead of repealing it immediately the Muldoon Government chose to set a cut-off date in 1995. 'In hindsight, the campaign was a limited success,' says Gordon. 'Tasman claimed that they had spent around $10 million cleaning up their operation, which at least demonstrated that they were sensitive to public concern. I think ultimately the media coverage led the mill to change its ways, but only once their public image was compromised.'

It was an encouraging start to the local campaign, but the pollution of the Tarawera River was merely the tip of New Zealand's toxic iceberg. The work needed to be extended to other waterways and mills, and there were still all the pesticide, fertiliser and other toxic waste issues to be tackled. In Gordon's view, the National Government had been encouraging multinational corporations to set up exporting industries, increasing New Zealand's involvement in the petrochemical industry. On top of decades of continual chemical use in agriculture, forestry and horticulture, the specific toxic time-bombs facing New Zealand included the Marsden Point oil refinery, the Manukau Harbour (long used as Auckland's toilet and toxic waste dump), the Taranaki ammonia plant, the heavily polluted Hutt and Waikato Rivers, and the Ivon Watkins-Dow dioxin plant in New Plymouth. 'New Zealand was ripe for a campaign against multinational companies on the toxic waste issue as more New Zealanders became aware of the dangers to their health and environment. People started to write to Greenpeace, asking us to do something about their

Bare hills, dead trees – *Pinus radiata*. A woodchip factory near Nelson.

local pollution problems, but we just didn't have the resources then.'

Gordon had learned something fundamental from his Tarawera experience. 'I saw how the water level of the river dropped because the pine forest was absorbing more of it, thus threatening the ecosystems downstream, ecosystems that had evolved over millions of years. Less water meant higher temperatures, a vicious circle that had its origin in single species forest monoculture. Pine forests exhaust the soil quickly, and felling a pine forest destroys an already limited ecosystem. Today I'm even more convinced that sustainable forestry with diverse species is the answer. This would also create sustainable communites instead of boom and bust towns dependent on one resource, whether gold, coal or pine logs. Our first priority needs to be balance, not profits at any cost. On the toxic tour we always saw the land from the perspective of the sea, and the evidence of all those years of plunder, in the form of scarred and eroded hillsides, was all too apparent.'

After Gordon's departure in 1984, a chance event drew Greenpeace back into toxics work. As Carol explains, the campaign to stop the production of the pesticide 2,4,5-T in New Zealand was Greenpeace's first against a specific toxic substance.

'Though other groups like Friends of the Earth had been campaigning for a ban for some time, Greenpeace New Zealand didn't have a specific toxics campaign at the time. In fact, we became involved almost by accident. Renate Kroesa, a chemist working for Greenpeace Germany, happened to be in New Zealand on holiday. She had worked on toxics issues in Germany and had researched dioxins for Greenpeace in Canada. Then came the fire in ICI's Mt Wellington warehouse, which released chemicals like chlorine, paraquat and 2,4,5-T into the atmosphere.'

The fire presented a major toxic hazard. More than fifty tonnes of chemicals were burned, and the toxic cocktail created exposed people working in the emergency services to dangerous chemicals that had serious health effects on many of them. Four hundred tonnes of contaminated effluent was discharged into the Tamaki estuary, whose marine life was also severely affected. For three weeks parts of the estuary ran clearer than a swimming pool, having been chlorinated and sterilised of all life by the discharge. Further toxic debris was simply dumped at a local tip.

'Renate contacted the Fire Service and was horrified to learn that firemen attending the blaze were not given proper protective clothing or any information on the effects of dioxins produced by burning a mix of chemicals,' says Carol. 'She immediately got in touch with the firemen's union, warned them they should wear protective gear on the site, and explained just how dangerous dioxin can be and what sort of health effects they could expect if they didn't protect themselves. Unfortunately, Renate, Elaine and two of her kids and I were leaving that day for a hiking trip round Lake Tarawera, so we frantically called in Gordon Jackman and Michael Taylor to go to the site and get samples and other information that could be used later.'

Following the fire, ICI denied there had been any toxic danger. By the time Carol and Renate got back to Auckland the issue was already being discussed in the media and Greenpeace was receiving a steady flow of inquiries about dioxin, so they asked Renate to spend the rest of what would have been her holiday helping them.

After contacting a world-renowned dioxin expert and laying the groundwork that led to the ICI firefighters' being tested for dioxin exposure, Renate turned her attention to the Ivon Watkins-Dow plant in New Plymouth, then the world's last producer of 2,4,5-T. All such plants overseas had ceased production after accidents that left workers and, as in the case of the notorious explosion at Seveso, northern Italy, residents heavily exposed to the lethal carcinogen. IWD had maintained that its production process did not create dioxins as a byproduct. Renate insisted that it must. A few months later IWD was forced to concede that dioxin wastes were indeed stored at the plant.

Anneke, Jude, Onno and Renate cordon off the front gate of the IWD plant.

Renate had spoken at public meetings organised by the local IWD action group. When GPNZ decided to mount a protest action at the plant in June 1985, the local group was not consulted for fear of a leak to IWD. Given how things worked out, this was a doubly regrettable omission. 'As usual,' Carol recalls, 'we tipped a quiet word to the media, but the local TV stringer apparently went straight to IWD to ask them what they thought about Greenpeace doing an action against them, so the staff at the plant were forewarned and waiting for us!

'The team for the New Plymouth 2,4,5-T action were Peter Whitehouse, a fireman involved at the ICI fire who was now a Greenpeace volunteer, Renate Kroesa, long-time volunteer Anneke Ursem, her husband Jan and their two teenage sons, Coen and Onno, Jude Seaboyer, Chris Robinson and me. The theory was that everyone except Chris and I would drive up to the gates and try to block off as many as possible with chains. Meanwhile we were to be driven to the back fence, which we would scale, then run like hell for the storage tanks, scamper up the ladder and chain ourselves and the banner to the top and sit it out. Fine theory, and during the training sessions it all seemed relatively simple!

'The day dawned – and what a rotten day it was! Pouring with rain and the wind howling – I didn't even want to get out of bed at the motel. We soon discovered that the plant staff were waiting for us, but for some reason the main gate was still open. While Chris and I were being dropped off by Peter at the rear of the plant, the others chained themselves across the main gateway and made sure the other gates were locked.

'Chris and I could see the workers wandering around inside the plant with their walkie-talkies. Trying to heave a large, weighted banner over a two-metre fence in wet and windy conditions is no easy task – especially when the fenceline is built on the edge of an incline covered in blackberries and gorse. Then it was our turn, Chris first and me struggling after. Have you ever tried climbing a wiremesh fence that heaves and sways, buffeted by wind and rain – and fast so as not to be spotted? Well, it was my first time, and probably my last. Chris made a gallant run and made it to the foot of the storage tank before the plant staff nabbed him. I tried a diversionary tactic and headed off in the opposite direction, but was also soon caught. A police car arrived to take us back to the main gate, where four of the others were still chained across the gateway. The police obviously didn't want to arrest us, but IWD insisted, so the padlocks were cut and we were all duly arrested and taken to the police station.

'Though our comical misadventure didn't quite go to plan, the extra publicity paid off, and after several false starts, various inquiries into dioxin contamination around the plant were ordered by the Health Department. Soon afterwards IWD announced it would cease manufacture of 2,4,5-T, having first offered all their stock to agents around the country at a specially reduced price. Renate left for Canada in August, and Peter Whitehouse took over as our toxics campaigner.'

For Jude, the action illustrated an important and sometimes misunderstood aspect of Greenpeace protests. 'The IWD protest showed us yet again that the strength of Greenpeace's direct actions lies first of all in securing TV

footage and radio coverage, whether or not the immediate goal is achieved. The truth is that media coverage at the time focused public attention on the plant, and over the next year footage showed up several times on TV. At the time we were disappointed, but the net result was just the kind of public exposure of the dangers of 2,4,5-T production we were after. Yes, we are keen on publicity, but in order to draw the spotlight to the issue, not simply to promote Greenpeace.'

As Peter Whitehouse became more involved in the international Greenpeace pesticides project, Lesley Stone, who had been working on GPNZ's school speakers project, came in as a second toxics campaigner, to work against the threat of hazardous waste incineration in the Pacific.

'After the burning of hazardous waste on ships in the North Sea was banned by north European countries through the London Dumping Convention,' Lesley explains, 'the waste industry turned to the Pacific as the next waste disposal site. My first role in the toxics campaign in 1988 was to solicit Pacific support for a global ban on the incineration of hazardous wastes at sea. When the Convention agreed to a global ban in October 1988 my work expanded to cover the Pacific region. Gradually the toxics campaign has developed into an integrated set of projects concerned with clean production, solvents, incineration, pulp and paper, pesticides and solid waste.'

Lesley soon had an opportunity to put these new ideas into practice. When the Marshall Islands Government received a proposal involving the dumping of seventeen million tonnes of waste from the United States in a

The Pukeuri meatworks at Oamaru has been discharging into the sea for seventy years and provided one of the most graphic examples of environmental abuse seen during the tour. The effluent falls about seventy-five metres over a cliff, then runs in a river down the beach and out to sea, drifting south towards the town.

lagoon as landfill, they asked Greenpeace to investigate. 'It didn't take us long to conclude that this would have been an environmental disaster for the islands, leading to pollutants leaching into the marine environment and jeopardising their all-important marine resources,' Lesley says.

'In trying to stop the waste trade we came up against the problem of local waste disposal and the impact imported goods were having on the Marshalls. In the Pacific there is no landmass in which to bury waste as occurs in New Zealand or the United States. This led us to search for alternative methods of domestic waste processing, and that's how we came up with our waste awareness project.'

Lesley Stone

This project developed as a co-operative venture between the Marshallese and Greenpeace's Pacific waste trade campaign, as a way for local people to deal with local issues. A series of educational resources in Marshallese, based on the 'Reduce, Reuse, and Recycle' themes were produced and are now being translated for wider use around the Pacific region. Bunny McDiarmid has been closely involved in this project since the beginning, and when she returned to the Marshalls on the *Rainbow Warrior* in 1991 she was able to deliver a commercial can-crusher to the local people as a practical gesture of support.

The focus of the toxics campaign had now shifted to the source of the problem, to waste production rather than its disposal. In 1989 Greenpeace began promoting 'clean production' – that is, production without the use, or generation, of hazardous wastes. 'Clean production makes sense from both an environmental and economic point of view. It's possible to keep producing polluting plastics economically only as long as the environmental costs are not included in the production budget,' explains Lesley.

'Most waste in New Zealand and the Pacific is a byproduct of the region's imports, so establishing viable alternatives in New Zealand could provide useful models for elsewhere in the Pacific. 'Sometimes Greenpeace is the only alternative, independent information source to the US Government or the World Bank. It is common for studies by these institutions to advocate more energy, more tourism and more mining without much regard for the environmental impact.'

With Greenpeace New Zealand's expansion in the late 1980s, local toxic waste problems were identified as a priority campaigning area and funds were set aside to employ new campaigners on related issues.

'In the past,' says Lesley, 'production and waste management systems have taken little account of their impact on the environment and human health, and environmental policies have always been subservient to the vested interests of industrial development, with "safe" levels of emissions or discharge into the environment often later proving to have been unsafe. Greenpeace wants to see this traditionally permissive attitude replaced with a precautionary approach. In essence, this would put the burden of proof on the "polluter" to demonstrate that their practices are not causing environmental damage, rather than on the ecologist to prove that they are.'

During 1990 the toxics campaign set about planning a detailed strategy addressing the full range of toxic problems in New Zealand. The central idea was to promote the concept of clean production for New Zealand industry.

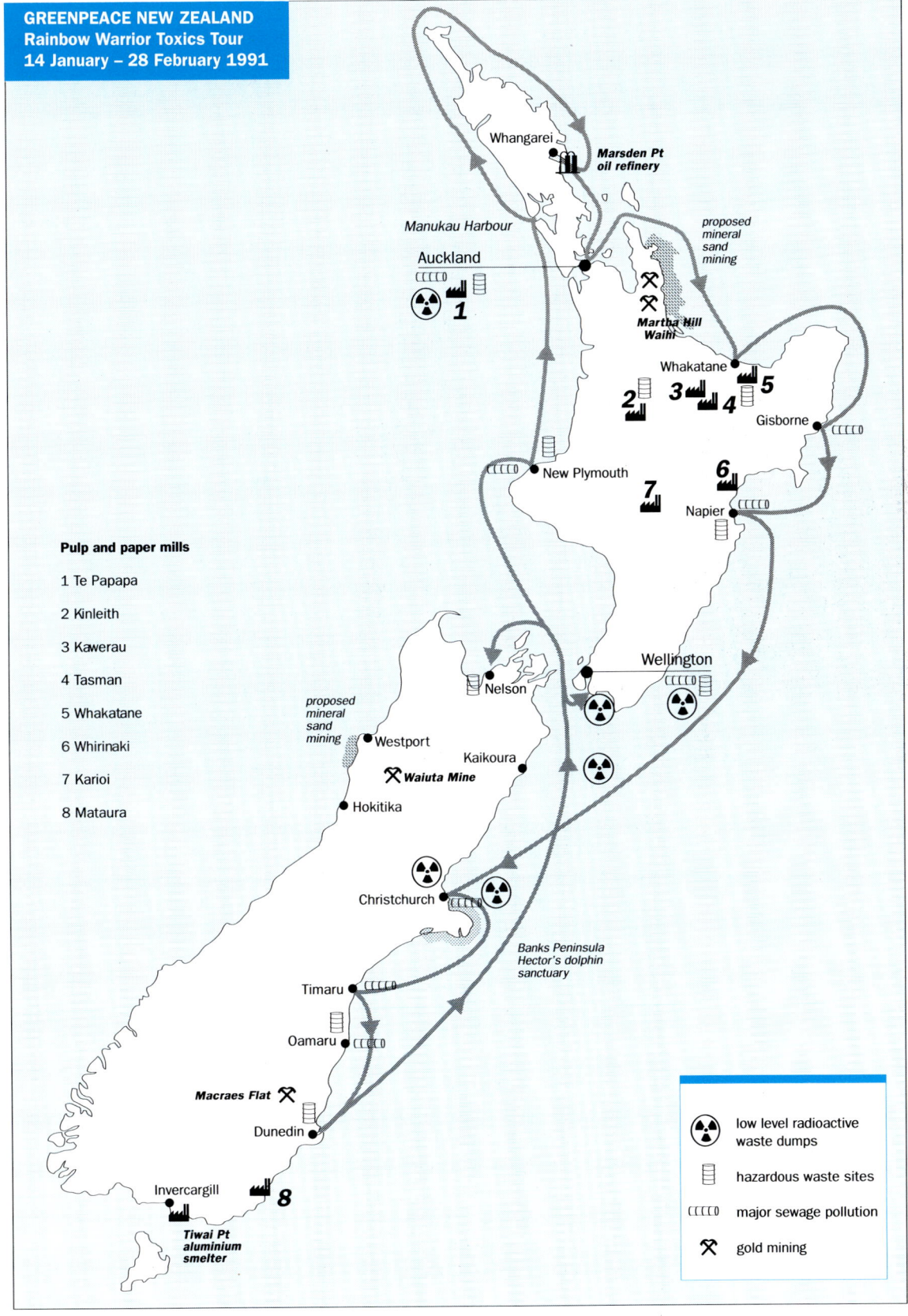

Given the size of the country, and with a determined and well-planned campaign, it was thought substantial goals might be achieved here in a relatively short time, and New Zealand could then offer the world a model for clean production.

The plan involved building up a new team bringing together pesticide, pulp and paper and solid waste campaigners. To complement the political lobbying work for which the *Rainbow Warrior* tour was to be a catalyst, Lesley also strongly advocated establishing a grassroots network to encourage local groups to work in their own communities.

First in line among the new campaigners was Gordon Jackman. Since he had left GPNZ in 1984 Gordon had travelled through the Pacific to work on an archaeological dig in Papua New Guinea, and returned to work in the Waipoua Forest. 'Later I taught science and music in Gisborne. I was ready to settle there when out of the blue, around Easter 1990, I got a letter from Carol Stewart in which she suggested I apply for the new post of pulp and paper campaigner. I must admit it was the last thing on my mind, but I went up to Auckland for an interview, got the job and started in May. The *Rainbow Warrior*'s New Zealand toxics tour was fast approaching, so I spent as much time as possible in the Bay of Plenty renewing old friendships and making new ones.'

In the Bay of Plenty Gordon got together again with Isobel and Jackie Fox. 'I have to say, Isobel gave me a bit of a roasting about how Greenpeace had come and gone the last time, and that now she wanted to see a long-term commitment. All the time Jackie, sitting next to me, kept saying, "Don't mind her," but I sat there feeling pretty bad. It was a powerful reminder of the impact of the mill on the local community, who were the ones who had to bear the environmental costs. As Isobel said, "We live here. We can't go away because we've nowhere else to go."'

The next addition to the campaign was Tony Lindsay, who had been brought into Greenpeace by Bev Cormack in 1987 to develop the computer system and look at organisational structures, and who went on to become GPNZ's trustee. In 1990 he joined the toxics campaign and now works as 'Ban, Don't Burn' campaigner. Apart from work on incineration, Tony is also concerned with hazardous waste-generating products such as chlorinated solvents. 'Every year thousands of tonnes of hazardous substances are imported into the country. Once their useful life is over, these substances are dispersed as waste into the environment, poisoning our land, water and air, and posing serious health risks. No one seems to know how much hazardous waste New Zealand generates – estimates range from 25,000 tonnes to 200,000 tonnes each year.'

Meriel Watts was brought in to work on the pesticides issue in New Zealand and the Pacific region and joined the toxics tour in the North Island. 'I grew up in Auckland with parents with unusual views. Our diet always included raw and home-grown food, and my mother fought hard to spare us the usual innoculations and drugs children are subjected to. So I've been something of a greenie all my life.

'I did a degree in agriculture, then I worked in plant disease research for a while, but my interest in biological control was discouraged, and I was very reluctant to use pesticides, so that came to an end. It was my experiences in the alternative health care field, as a naturopath and homoeopath treating people – casualties of pollution – who were continually becoming ill from chemical exposure, that led me directly to Greenpeace. I wanted to do something to stop the poisoning of people and the land.

'Here our goal is to promote "ecological agriculture" – land use that is ecologically sound, economically viable and socially just. In many parts of the Pacific traditional methods of agriculture are still used that sustain the people and replenish the earth without sapping it of its goodness. In other places, such as the monoculture plantations in Fiji and Papua New Guinea, imported agricultural systems using pesticides and other chemicals poison the land, leach into the rivers and pollute the lagoons and marine environment. The Pacific is becoming a dumping ground for pesticides that are recognised as too hazardous for use in the countries that developed them.

'In New Zealand, too, we are looking at the wider issue of land use and ecological agriculture. We've targeted the import, export and use of all agricultural chemicals and hope to achieve bans on selected chemicals. Current agricultural practices in New Zealand, along with global warming, are probably the most serious threat to our environment. Soil is being lost all the time and, as in many Third World countries, we are trading our environment down the drain in order to pay off our overseas debt.

'Some agricultural chemical products banned in other countries are still used widely in New Zealand. An example is the fungicide Captan, a known carcinogen that is banned in Australia and severely restricted in the United States but freely available here. Then there is the continued use of pesticides such as 2,4,5-T that have been deregistered in New Zealand, or of products whose registration has been banned, such as Dieldrin. Although 2,4,5-T was withdrawn from sale in 1988 and the manufacturer claimed that stockpiles of the pesticide would be exhausted by the end of that year, we found that it was still being used – by the Wellington Regional Council, for example – in December 1990, and was even being advertised for sale in the classified section of a Wellington newspaper.'

After January's action at the Tasman mill, the *Rainbow Warrior* headed south, following the parched Bay of Plenty coastline, whose denuded and eroded hillsides were a far cry from most of the foreign crew members' expectations of New Zealand as a land of fresh green pastures. As the *Warrior* approached Gisborne, the stench of the meatworks greeted those on board. Greenpeace canvassers arrived from Wellington, and thousands of locals came for the open day, for tours of the ship, for the stalls and to listen to the band playing on the wharf. Again a Maori welcome opened the way for the crew, and the local Greenpeace group and the tour's shore support party had organised the whole visit ahead of the *Warrior*'s arrival.

'The ship received Maori welcomes wherever she put in around the country,' reported Margaret Baker, who had worked as press officer for Greenpeace in London before returning to her native New Zealand to take up a new job as media co-ordinator. 'In Napier, a magnificent waka came out to welcome the ship. As the canoe came alongside the ship, the paddlers' haka rose

Tamatea-Ariki-Nui, a massive thirty-metre-long totara waka built in 1989 for the Ngati Kahungunu iwi, during the *Warrior*'s visit to Napier.

up to us strong and clear in the bright morning sunshine.

'The tour concentrated on making local contacts and investigating local problems. National coverage wasn't the goal; the local perspective was what counted. Councillors and local business people attended the receptions and public meetings alongside tangata whenua and environmental activists, some of them talking directly to each other for the first time.'

The pattern of the tour was beginning to emerge, and the wheels seemed to turn surprisingly smoothly, largely through the organisational skills of the local support groups. 'We pull into port and prepare for the open day – all hands on deck to unload the displays and merchandise from the hold and set them up on the wharf and around the ship. Briefings follow for the canvassers and the local support group, and media interviews were organised for the campaigners. At about four o'clock we roll everything back into the ship's hold and prepare for the receptions, and at seven we head off into town for the public meeting.

'After crossing the heavy seas of the Cook Strait, the *Rainbow Warrior* travelled down the cooler South Island coast. Dolphins dance around the ship, surfing on the bow wave, even the occasional whale slides past, and albatrosses wheel about the mastheads.'

Christchurch was cold and rainy. Greenpeace campaigners joined local activists in a protest against pollution of the Waimakariri River. The next day a truckload of street theatre mutants in 'toxic waste' drums set off from the ship through the Lyttelton Tunnel to the city's Arts Centre to dramatise the dangers of toxic ingredients in a range of products for sale in the local supermarket. Also that day the *Gondwana* berthed at Lyttelton on her way back from the World Park Antarctica base. A soccer match and party were called to mark the unusual occasion of two Greenpeace ships sharing port facilities. The following morning the *Warrior* sailed into the Sunday sunshine, bound for Timaru and points south.

On her ports of call down the east coast of the South Island the *Warrior* was greeted by large enthusiastic crowds. But the tour wasn't universally well received, and targeted companies were now beginning to show their displeasure. At the end of January the Chemical Industry Council had circulated a guide for targeted companies on how to deal with and discredit Greenpeace. 'Discount the Greenpeace claims,' the circular advised, 'as being unproven, hypothetical, false or based on a genuine misunderstanding! Do not question the motivation or morality of the Greenpeace activists. Patronise them if you must, but don't get in a position where the public has to decide who is the most moral.' In fact, Greenpeace was relying on more than moral arguments to support its case against toxic contamination of the New Zealand environment. Now it could draw on a formidable resource of scientific expertise, giving it a widely recognised authority that clearly worried the chemical industry.

North of Timaru, the *Warrior*'s crew helped in a long-term Department of Conservation Hector's dolphin population survey. 'The DOC research team welcomed the offer of help from the *Rainbow Warrior,* a larger boat than they had available, to count Hector's dolphins in an area around Banks Peninsula,' says Diana Pipke, of the ocean ecology campaign. 'Along 200 miles of coastal transects, independent observers backed by *Warrior* crew recorded the location of each dolphin seen. The results confirmed that nearly all Hector's remain close to the coast in the summer, where they are seriously at risk from coastal setnets, which suggests that the present marine mammal sanctuary needs to be extended.'

Street theatre toxic 'mutants', Christchurch.

At Port Chalmers engine trouble interrupted the flow of the tour. Water was found to be leaking into the drive shaft, so to everyone's disappointment the trip up the West Coast was cancelled. Instead the *Warrior* sailed back up the calmer east coast to the warmth of Nelson and back across the Strait to Wellington.

Throughout the tour the Gulf War had been a constant distraction for the crew and the staff back in the Auckland office. Continuous news broadcasts were monitored in the radio room, while computer mail from Greenpeace offices all round the world churned out information on everything from chemical weapons to commentaries on the reporting of the war. Information packs on the war produced in the Auckland office lay on mess tables next to clippings of leaching dumps and polluted streams. With so many staff away on the tour, Stephanie Mills and Kirsty Hamilton in Auckland had been frantically collating information on the environmental aspects of the war as tens of thousands died in the carnage and millions of tonnes of crude oil bled onto the coral reefs and beaches of the Persian Gulf. Wellington offered an

New Plymouth schoolchildren welcome the *Warrior*.

opportunity to use the *Warrior* as a symbol of peace, and to press for peaceful solutions to the Gulf crisis. A special Gulf War briefing for MPs was organised, and the ship flew a large banner proclaiming 'The War Will Cost the Earth'.

After Wellington, the green dairylands of Taranaki offered relief from the familiar dull brown coastline. At New Plymouth a Maori cultural group from a local school welcomed the *Warrior*, and tangata whenua were joined by mayors from all the surrounding councils at the subsequent public meeting. Up at Cornwallis on the Manukau Harbour the reception was similarly stirring. Hundreds of Maori from communities around the harbour turned out to welcome the Greenpeace ship into their waters, many of them spending a chaotic afternoon on board the ship.

The tour was winding down as the *Warrior* rounded Cape Reinga, passing from the Tasman into the Pacific. Repairs could wait no longer and the ship checked in for drydock at Whangarei. To everyone's disappointment, further engagements in Northland and the Coromandel had to be shelved, though a joint protest involving GPNZ and Coromandel Watchdog at the Waihi goldmine tailings dam went ahead successfully.

On Bikini Day, 1 March 1991, the *Rainbow Warrior* sailed back into the Waitemata Harbour as quietly as she had left. The same day a new Greenpeace New Zealand publication was released: *Chronology: The French Presence in the South Pacific, 1838-1990* marked a decade of Elaine Shaw's commitment to the French nuclear testing issue.

Two days later fifty protesters chained themselves to cement-filled barriers, blocking the entrances to the Auckland hazardous goods wharf, to highlight the importation of toxic chemicals. 'New Zealand spends almost $1 billion a year on chemical imports,' says Lesley. 'But the costs don't end there. All hazardous chemicals eventually find their way into the environment and they need to be cleaned up. Then there are the environmentally induced cancers and other diseases.

'The tour has opened up new opportunities as well as a lot of areas where we will have to make sure we deliver the goods. We have to continue to impress on people that it is local activities that count. We can provide support, but people have to act locally.'

It had also been an opportunity to share the *Warrior* with a range of local community and environmental groups. Indeed, without the work of many volunteers, support groups and other environmental groups, along with the Department of Conservation, it could not have been a success. 'It was also the most concrete way for us to channel GPNZ's resources into local issues,' says Tony Lindsay. 'In the Manukau, for instance, the *Warrior* was used by the local Kawerau and Tainui people and the local Manukau coalition to highlight the pollution of the harbour.'

One consistent feature of the coastal New Zealand towns visited was the discharge of raw sewage into the sea. In Wellington untreated and screened sewage, industrial waste, landfill leachate and stormwater is discharged from the Pencarrow and Moa Point outfalls. The Pencarrow outfall contaminates Wellington's coastal waters with heavy metals and persistent toxic organics. A range of industries – producing paints, plastics, chemicals, batteries, detergents – jostle for position along the Lower Hutt River, some discharging straight into the sewer.

In towns like Napier, Lyttelton, Oamaru and Dunedin, little is being done about the readily identifiable, and easily solvable, problems associated with sewage disposal. In other towns solutions tend towards the cosmetic and politically expedient. Milliscreening, the treatment used in Gisborne, Timaru and at Wellington's Moa Point, for example, only removes solids, but the wastes that pour from the outfalls into the sea are still loaded with pathogens and other toxic materials. While the Manukau is amongst New Zealand's most damaged, other harbours suffer similar pollution and are unfit for food gathering or swimming.

'Meatworks effluent is another big problem,' says Tony. 'The old approach to the treatment of meatworks effluent in New Zealand is: Don't bother treating it; contaminate it, render it useless, then discharge it into the sea. Meatworks release thousands of tonnes of effluent daily, often contaminated with tannery wastes including sulphides and chromium, both of which are harmful to marine life. Up to 20,000 cubic metres of partially treated effluent is discharged every day into the Waimakariri River. Little wonder that recreational users of the river report gastrointestinal disorders and infected sores.

'Little expertise exists to identify or separate hazardous wastes in local dumps,' says Tony. 'Many small tips continue to accept all wastes, no questions asked. In Oamaru, a dump from an old timber treatment facility on the foreshore contaminates a nesting site for little blue and yellow-eyed penguins with copper, chromium, PCPs and arsenic. Where councils have started refusing industrial or hazardous wastes, no one seems to know where the hazardous materials are going.'

Compounding the dumping problem is the practice of on-site incineration. Many dumps are still routinely burned. Tip burning releases contaminants, such as dioxins and furans, into the air, yet from Northland to Bluff the practice continues, though local action is starting to get results. For instance,

'One of the Greenpeace techniques is to pillory your company publicly and then ask for a meeting with you. To this meeting they invite the media, Maori groups, local body officials and the like. You would be unwise to participate in such a meeting. Agree instead to meet with them privately at another time. In this way you will be seen (by the public) to be open to dialogue, though in reality the meeting will achieve little, because the Greenpeace position is predetermined and not open to reason.' *NZ Chemical Industry Council* following the disclosure of serious health problems among tip workers, and concerted local protests, the Mareiri dump in Nelson is no longer burned.

Stockpiles of hazardous materials are a problem everywhere. The country's large industries dump and disperse significant quantities of hazardous wastes, including sulphur dioxide, fluoride, aluminum, cyanide, hydrocarbons, organochlorines and other often unspecified pollutants. Sources of these pollutants include stack emissions, effluent outfalls to rivers and the sea and sludge or other waste disposal to local dumps, mines or excavated pits. The Marsden Point oil refinery disposed of sludge and solid wastes in an unregulated tip in mangroves at Uretiti, for many years resisting efforts by the Department of Conservation to shut the tip down. Though the practice has now stopped, there are as far as Greenpeace knows no records of what was dumped at Uretiti. The New Zealand Refinery Company at Marsden Point discharges 30 tonnes of sulphur dioxide into the air daily.

The law permits the continuing pollution of New Zealand's waterways and coastal areas. Other major polluters, who are operating at currently accepted 'safe' levels, include Comalco's aluminium smelter at Tiwai Point (fluoride discharge), the Waihi Mining Company (heavy metals, arsenic and cyanide) and New Plymouth's Dow Elanco, formerly IWD (dioxins).

The *Warrior*'s toxics tour exposed the shocking legacy of favouring short-term economic growth over long-term environmental viability. 'But the great thing is that this is preventative campaigning,' explains ship's mate Dave Theoren. 'We've seen bad things, but there's time to clean up and implement regulations that will stop this from totally ruining the country. Usually we're protesting as a last-ditch measure, but here there is still time to catch things before it's too late.'

'The implications of the tour are huge,' believes Tony Lindsay. 'We have begun to bring together a broad-based green coalition – from trade unions to tangata whenua, health professionals, recreational organisations and councils to environmental and peace groups. During the ten open days of the tour some 14,000 people visited the *Rainbow Warrior*.

'Now, drawing on scientific peer review and a coherent media strategy, the toxics campaign has moved into a new phase. We are ready to take on the multinationals in a way that we were not able to before 1987. The tour was the first step for the newly reorganised campaign – the best is yet to come. If there are any companies out there that think, as the industry response to the tour suggests, that we are just a motley collection of hippies to be patronised, then they really better think again.'

'There's still a lot of educating to be done,' says Gordon. 'With driftnetting or Moruroa, support is safe because those issues exist at a distance. This time we've taken the issues home. Now people have to face a lot of questions they haven't heard before, and some don't like to be confronted with things about themselves that need changing.'

The relatively low-key approach of the tour surprised some of the *Warrior*'s crew, used to more dramatic activity. 'There was some disappointment at first,' says skipper Joel Stewart. 'But it was soon apparent that what worked in other places wasn't necessarily appropriate in New Zealand, and that the low-key approach was proving very successful. It did a lot of the

Kaikorai estuary, Dunedin.

groundwork for the toxics campaign. Now many more people know the issues, and the campaigners know the people.'

It was also an important learning time for the office staff, many of whom had never been to sea, had no experience of campaigning from a ship and knew little of this side of Greenpeace's work. The trip helped bring home to Carol the importance of getting away from pushing paper round in the office. 'It put us in touch with the day-to-day, practical problems facing people, and it's given us the personal contact we need.'

But it is the *Rainbow Warrior* herself that will remain the tour's enduring image. 'We have something very precious in the *Warrior*,' Lesley Stone feels. 'Above all, she's a symbol of hope.' As Gordon puts it, 'So many people wanted to see and touch and feel this ship, this phoenix they had heard so much about.'

CHAPTER FOURTEEN

New Horizons

AT FOUR O'CLOCK in the morning of 10 July 1987, the second anniversary of the *Rainbow Warrior* bombing, a Greenpeace team of twelve crept up onto the Auckland Harbour Bridge from Northcote Point, using a ladder to reach the maintenance catwalks running along the underside of the bridge. As the sun rose over Rangitoto nothing unusual could be seen from the harbour. Then, at about seven, a twenty-metre banner began to unfurl beneath the bridge's central arch.

Barbara Fruth, an experienced climber with Greenpeace Germany, led the action, while five volunteers from the Auckland University climbing club contributed their skills and expertise, hauling up the twenty-kilo banner, securing the ropes to the girders and pre-checking each abseiler's gear. Soon after dawn the two heaviest abseilers dropped over the edge and slowly

Opposite: Tarawa Atoll, Kiribati – the first victims of global warming?

Launching the Nuclear Free Seas Campaign.

unravelled the banner from each end, then three more abseiled down to take the weight at the bottom of the banner.

Three of the abseilers were novices, but the training sessions had prepared none of them for the strong south-westerly wind that gusted under the bridge that morning. Even the experienced climbers found it hair-raising to be swinging free, twisted and buffeted about like rag dolls some thirty metres above the water. They had their work cut out disentangling ropes, and it was Barbara, the lightest of them, who was blown across the wrong side of the banner. As she tried to climb back up, her karabiner caught in the banner. The initial small hole, caught by the wind, rapidly became a large rip, as the banner billowed and bucked on its moorings. After two nerve-racking hours the banner party abseiled down to the water and two waiting Greenpeace inflatables, while the support team above hauled the banner back up to the catwalk, and the action was over.

Meanwhile, on the harbour below, Greenpeace nuclear campaigner Jacqui Barrington had been explaining the significance of the occasion to a receptive gathering of journalists on board the *Greenpeace*.

In 1985 the Labour Government had refused entry to the destroyer USS *Buchanan* after the United States invoked its 'neither confirm nor deny' policy over whether or not the vessel carried nuclear weapons. In retaliation, Washington suspended its Anzus Treaty obligations to New Zealand, denied New Zealand access to high-level government-to-government contacts, and took various other punitive measures intended both to force New Zealand to abandon its nuclear-free policy and to deter others from attempting to imitate the New Zealand example – the nuclear allergy or 'Kiwi disease', as the US military called it. This day had been chosen to launch Greenpeace's new international Nuclear Free Seas Campaign. The banner, which read 'Spread "Kiwi Disease" – Nuclear Free Seas', made it clear that while the Labour Government still found it politically expedient to insist its nuclear-free policy was not for export, Greenpeace was keen to see the 'allergy' spread.

For the New Zealand peace movement, after its long crusade, the election in August 1984 of the firmly anti-nuclear Lange Government was a cause for deep satisfaction. The signing of the South Pacific Nuclear-Free Zone Treaty on 6 August, Hiroshima Day, 1985, less than a month after the bombing of the *Rainbow Warrior,* by eight of the thirteen South Pacific Forum nations was also heartening. For all its limitations, the pact gave further expression to the resolute determination of New Zealand and her South Pacific neighbours to rid the region of nuclear weapons. But the treaty's limitations were crucial, for while it prohibited the testing of nuclear warheads, nuclear waste dumping and land-based nuclear weapons in the region, it continued to sanction uranium mining, the testing of nuclear weapon delivery systems and the operation of commercial nuclear reactors. And worst of all, it did not prohibit the passage of ship-borne nuclear weapons, the greatest nuclear threat in the Pacific. What's more, the two main nuclear powers operating in the region, the United States and France, have refused to sign the pact.

One-third of the world's nuclear weapons are deployed at sea, while 500 nuclear reactors, more than exist on land, power the world's five nuclear navies. Ship-borne nuclear weapons and reactors are necessarily much more vulnerable and dangerous than their land-based equivalents. Nuclear weapons based at sea can be launched without consent of heads of state, multiplying the chances of accidental nuclear war. Many people would be surprised to learn how frequently nuclear vessels have run aground or sunk, collided with other ships, or have suffered fire, floods or mechanical breakdowns. In June 1989 Greenpeace released a report revealing that the world's navies experience an average of one major accident each week. There are known to be at least forty-eight nuclear weapons and nine nuclear reactors already littering the ocean floor.

Responding to Greenpeace's allegations that the US military had covered up a string of nuclear submarine accidents, the US ambassador accused them in a letter to the press in mid-1986 of 'deliberately misleading' the public. Jacqui Barrington was able to reply with detailed evidence to support Greenpeace's claims. Research for Greenpeace by Owen Wilkes had found that sixty-eight of the American ships that had visited New Zealand had suffered a total of ninety accidents during active service. In particular, he found that the nuclear-armed ship USS *Henry Wilson* had collided with a New Zealand vessel some 150 kilometres off Great Barrier Island in 1968, the same year that the USS *Caliente* ran aground while entering Auckland Harbour. The goals of the Nuclear Free Seas campaign were to generate public and political opposition to naval nuclear weapons, spread New Zealand's 'nuclear allergy', maintain the freedom of the high seas for non-military vessels and bring about a ban on naval nuclear reactors.

Jacqui Barrington took over the nuclear campaign in 1987, though her involvement with Greenpeace went back much further. 'I was a Greenpeace supporter when I lived in London in 1978. I had read about the *Rainbow Warrior* and her work and went down to London Bridge to wave her off on her maiden voyage. I'd also visited the London office in the vain hope of getting a job on the ship, and I remained a supporter.

'During the early 1980s I went to the CND demos in Hyde Park and visited the women's peace camp at Greenham Common. The cruise missiles and the Thatcher Government finally drove me away from England. I arrived in New Zealand in late 1982 and began working in Napier at the Rudolf Steiner Hohepa Centre, teaching people with disabilities.'

In Napier Jacqui joined the local Hawke's Bay peace group. 'About 500 of us turned out to protest the visit of the USS *Wadsworth* in 1984. I was active in that group until 1986, when my life went through a big change: I left my job and my husband. I wasn't sure what I was going to do until I saw an advert in the Dominion. Greenpeace New Zealand needed a nuclear campaigner, and this time I got the job.

'I had expected the work to focus on French nuclear testing, but at the interview I learned that GPNZ's Pacific campaign covered this issue. What, I wondered, would I be doing now that the peace movement had succeeded in stopping nuclear ship visits and had made New Zealand nuclear-free? The main answer was the new Nuclear Free Seas campaign. At the time, the hull of the *Rainbow Warrior* was still tied up at the wharf downtown, so we decided to launch the New Zealand end of the new campaign with the banner-hanging off the nearby harbour bridge. Photos of the banner were seen next day around the world.'

Jacqui saw this country as offering a nuclear-free model for others to follow. 'It was only logical that the New Zealand example be exported, particularly to Australia, which hosts several very important US military bases as well as supplying uranium to the international nuclear industry. Within New Zealand the thrust of our work involved co-operation with groups like Peace Movement Aotearoa and Votes for Peace to persuade the National Party, then still opposed to the nuclear-free policy, to change their policy.'

The first National MP Jacqui visited was the doggedly pro-nuclear Deputy Leader Don McKinnon. 'He spent much of the time drumming his fingers on the table and staring out of the window, and insisted Greenpeace was overestimating the importance of the nuclear weapons issue in New Zealand. He also promised that the National Party would overturn the nuclear-free legislation when it was returned to office, and that they would welcome American nuclear ship visits on the same "neither confirm nor deny" basis as before.'

But McKinnon's views were out of step even with many in his own party. Labour's election wins in 1984 and 1987 had owed much to their commitment to the anti-nuclear cause, but now the nuclear-free 'allergy' had spread among National voters too. In June 1989 a public poll revealed a steady rise in support for Labour's nuclear-free policy across the political spectrum – from 75 percent in 1985 to 84 percent, including an extraordinary 73 percent of National voters.

Three Auckland Peace Squadron yachts join nuclear ships protest during the Australian Bicentennial Naval Review, Sydney Harbour.

Greenpeace supplied all its members with a postcard to send to National Party leader Jim Bolger, urging him to heed the 84 percent of New Zealanders who supported the nuclear-free policy. Bolger's response was to circulate a letter criticising Greenpeace's 'irresponsibility'. His letter fudged the issue and claimed National had always been anti-nuclear, so that they had no need to change their stance. In December 1989 Jacqui travelled to Wellington to speak to the National leader. 'After twenty minutes' listening to a summary of his party's policy, I told him in no uncertain terms that portraying his party's policy as 'nuclear-free' would not wash either with Greenpeace or the New Zealand public. If nuclear ships were permitted back into New Zealand, I predicted there would be a public outcry and a mobilised opposition on the scale of the 1981 Springbok tour.'

Jacqui's comments upset Bolger, who took offence at 'someone coming into my office and threatening me'. 'It was a difficult issue for the National Party. Clearly the overwhelming majority of voters supported a genuine nuclear-free policy, and by now most National MPs were unhappy with their party's stance – Winston Peters and Denis Marshall spoke out strongly against it. They knew it would be political suicide to enter the next election without a change of policy, and they saw the risk of losing their third election in a row because they had allowed Labour to monopolise a popular policy.'

Within three months the National Party had changed its policy to an unequivocal endorsement of the standing nuclear-free legislation. Their U-turn gave New Zealand the world's first bipartisan nuclear-free policy backed up by legislation, while it effectively deprived Labour of its strongest policy advantage in the upcoming election, which National won easily.

As part of its campaign to spread the 'Kiwi disease', in September 1988 Greenpeace New Zealand sponsored a trans-Tasman voyage by three yachts from the Auckland Peace Squadron, *Dawn Mist, Friendship* and *Metaphor*.

Three weeks later this trio joined a chaotic assemblage of other vessels out on Sydney Harbour to confront four US and three British nuclear warships arriving to participate in Australia's Bicentennial Naval Review. An estimated 700 demonstrators in craft ranging from tugs and ferries hired for the occasion to yachts, kayaks and surfboards joined them in the largest demonstration of its kind ever seen in Australia.

First of the nuclear ships into Sydney was HMS *Edinburgh*, at one point brought to a standstill by *Dawn Mist*. While all four of the American ships were nuclear-armed, only the USS *Ingersoll* carried Tomahawk cruise missiles, whose armoured launchers squatted conspicuously on the iron-grey foredeck.

So the *Ingersoll* was singled out for special attention by the Greenpeace team, deployed in four fast inflatables, weaving their way through the melée to fix nuclear symbols to the ship's hull.

To celebrate the anniversary of New Zealand's legislation banning nuclear ship visits, and to salute the role played by the Peace Squadrons in bringing about the reform, GPNZ's nuclear campaign decided to sponsor an annual yacht race on

The Greenpeace Cup is carved in a traditional style by Guy Moana from a piece of salvaged kauri given to him by his grandfather, a former carving tutor in Rotorua. The figures of Tangaroa, god of the sea, a marakihau (sea spirit) and a mermaid feature on the cup. Forming the handles are Tane Mahuta, god of the forest, and Rongo, god of the moon, peace and agriculture. Pictured below: Guy and the cup.

Auckland's Waitemata Harbour. On 4 June 1989 the inaugural Greenpeace Cup nuclear-free yacht race was held.

To close GPNZ's nuclear campaign, Jacqui and Lynx Henderson organised the 'Nuclear Free Sheep' tour of New Zealand in August 1990. For this occasion Greenpeace brought out English farmer Maurice Steele to speak to farmers and rural community groups about the devastating impact of the Chernobyl nuclear accident on his and other sheep farms in Cumbria, northern England, 1,400 miles west of Chernobyl. In 1986 four million sheep on about 900 British farms were classified as having dangerous levels of caesium-137 contamination. Four years later 600,000 sheep on 700 farms, including Steele's, were still too contaminated for human consumption. Indeed, given caesium-137's thirty-year half-life, the restrictions on his farm are expected to remain for many years. Also on the tour was Marvin Hendrickson, a former health physicist with the US nuclear industry.

The month-long tour made such an impact on New Zealand's farmers that the traditionally conservative Federated Farmers, who had previously lobbied for an end to the nuclear ships ban for fear of its adverse effects on their export markets, had within a year voted for a ban on all land-based nuclear reactors in New Zealand as part of their new environmental policy.

In 1990 Prime Minister Geoffrey Palmer fired the starting gun at the Richmond Yacht Club for the second annual Greenpeace Cup race before joining the 54 competing yachts on the water in the coastguard's search and rescue vessel. Pictured here with Jacqui Barrington and the cup.

By the late 1980s, with the decline of the Cold War and the consequent easing of the nuclear threat, the predominant international environmental issues were global warming and the destruction of rainforests. The discovery in 1987 of the 'hole' in the ozone layer over Antarctica brought home to New Zealanders the global nature of the new environmental threats. Jacqui Barrington has now set up a New Zealand-based rainforests campaign, aiming to integrate her work closely with the atmosphere and energy and toxics campaigns. 'With global warming, energy and transport issues are only half the problem,' she says. 'The other imperative is to halt the destruction of the rainforests.

'The rate of destruction of rainforests has increased dramatically in the past decade. Today they cover just 6 percent of the world's land surface, yet tropical rainforests are the habitat for half the earth's life forms. The protection of these remaining rainforests is among the most urgent and crucial ecological issues we face, and is now a top priority for Greenpeace.

'My area of concern will cover mainly Malaysia and Indonesia, possibly extending to the Philippines – all areas where massive deforestation is devastating the environment. Here in New Zealand I'll be supporting the grassroots work of the Rainforest Coalition, a broad spectrum of rainforest action groups, in working to enforce a total ban on the export of New Zealand native woodchips and for the maintenance of the ban on native log exports. We will also be campaigning against tropical hardwood imports unless they are proven to be from sustainable plantations and are extracted with the consent of the local indigenous people.

'I believe there is a neglected sector in our international work where several concerns overlap in the area of terrestrial ecology and integrated land use. The advent of a new Greenpeace International tropical rainforest campaign has thrown up the whole question of land use and degradation. Our efforts here in New Zealand in the areas of pesticides, pulp and paper, atmosphere and energy and native forests are all linked to the issue of land use. We look to promoting ecological agriculture and integrated land use systems.

'Deforestation and intensive chemical farming using nitrogen-based fertilisers are big contributors to global warming through the emission of carbon dioxide and nitrous oxide. New Zealand is the second largest user of nitrogen-based fertilisers in the world, at over 1,000 kilograms a hectare. Chemically farmed soil is lacking in the micro-organisms that enable living soil rich in humus to absorb carbon, while livestock emit extraordinary quantities of methane, a potent "greenhouse" gas. New Zealand's economic mainstay, farming, is therefore contributing directly to steadily worsening global problems.

'One of our long-term goals must be to change New Zealand's current agricultural and forestry practices so that the land and the climate on which farming and the prosperity of the nation depend are protected, and their damaging impacts minimised. In a nutshell, we want to see economic planning recognise the importance of environmental concerns. This means public education on the hazards of forest and scrub clearance, which leads to flooding, siltation and climate change. It also means promoting native reafforest-

The tyranny of *Pinus radiata*.

ation for aesthetic, cultural and wildlife values. We need native trees to provide permanent watershed protection and hold together fragile, erodable areas. We also need to see forestry diversification into exotic hardwoods and agro-forestry, where food or timber trees are planted on land grazed by livestock. These measures are essential elements in slowing down and eventually halting global warming and will give New Zealand the best chance of survival as the climate changes and the globe warms up.'

In the 1990s the planet earth faces a new set of challenges. These newly identified environmental problems require new approaches and solutions. 'Applying the lessons learned in the Pacific and Antarctic campaigns,' says Kirsty Hamilton, GPNZ's atmosphere and energy campaigner, 'we are determined to be more than the whistle blower. Now we have to be part of the solution.'

Kirsty Hamilton

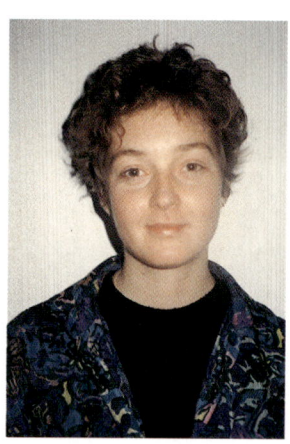

'For the first time ever, humans have damaged part of the earth's atmosphere on a global scale. Average annual ozone levels have already fallen 5 percent in New Zealand since 1985. Increased incidence of skin cancer in the last decade, including a doubling of melanoma, the most dangerous form, may be due to the greater ultraviolet B light reaching the earth's surface. This also affects plant growth and nutrition, and could affect up to half of all marine life.' *The NZ Meteorological Service, 1990*

Kirsty comes from a conservation-minded family and grew up near Edinburgh in Scotland. After university she travelled to Australia. 'I was appalled to learn how much of the forests in Queensland and Tasmania would be felled to be turned into woodchips for the Japanese market. First I got involved with the Wilderness Society as a volunteer, helping the campaign to protect the Tasmanian forests as a world heritage park. Though we had some success here, many other important forest areas are under increasing threat of clear felling. Next I decided to come to New Zealand and it was while I was in Wellington, active on energy and global warming issues, that I applied for and got the Greenpeace campaigning job.'

Kirsty represents a new generation in Greenpeace, too young to remember their early actions, yet with much the same concerns and determination. But now the issues are more complicated than they were twenty years ago. 'Take global warming,' Kirsty says. 'Everyone has heard about it now, along with the hole in the ozone layer. Ozone depletion is already affecting the amount of ultraviolet light that New Zealand gets. But it's our job to make these concepts understandable to ordinary people, to break down the jargon and also to propose ways in which people can address these problems in their everyday lives. We need to divert people away from doom and gloom, to motivate them and channel their concern towards positive solutions. Sometimes that's as simple as saying, take the bus, cycle, or walk, insulate the roof and don't create waste. It's also essential to persuade governments of the importance of the issues, so that they introduce appropriate policy initiatives and institutional frameworks.

'These issues also touch on all our other campaigns. Recognising this interrelatedness helps to reveal a path towards a more holisitic approach to life. This perspective will help convince people that we need to redefine economic thinking to include the environmental costs of development. Our present economic system is distorted by the so-called free market, which does not allow for the costs to the environment and to future generations. Until we take account of the costs of, say, exploiting non-renewable resources like fossil fuels and rainforests, and recognise the rights and needs of the next generation, the developed world's economic systems will continue to aggravate global environmental problems.'

The atmosphere and energy campaign started out targeting air pollution but has increasingly focused on energy issues. Scientists now agree it is vital to reduce radically carbon dioxide and 'greenhouse gas' emissions from the burning of fossil fuels. With the industrial nations producing the bulk of these emissions, this means, for instance, changing our attitude towards our cars – by using public transport or bicycles or walking more, or at least by developing and using alternative fuels rather than petrol. 'But here we're taking on the vested interests of the multinationals, so we still need responsible government intervention on issues of national and international importance,' says Kirsty.

'Greenpeace is helping with research on the global warming problem, spreading awareness and suggesting sustainable alternatives. We will continue to blow the whistle when it's needed, but we also have positive things to say, and we're now in a position to be able to participate in the search for solutions.'

In October 1989 Greenpeace New Zealand began a controversial six-month pilot programme of door-to-door canvassing, sending trained canvassers to selected neighbourhoods in and around Auckland. It was not a uniformly popular move within Greenpeace, but the idea has steadily gained ground. The pilot scheme brought in many new members and much-needed funds, and canvassing is now a fully integrated part of GPNZ's activities, with offices devoted to the programme in Wellington and Christchurch. There are now fifteen canvassers in Auckland, who take to the streets each weekday evening between 5 pm and 8.30, talking with people about Greenpeace campaigns, signing up new supporters and collecting signatures on petitions.

'To me, the most important function is to raise awareness; fundraising is secondary,' says the director of the programme, Michele Nanni. 'Raising awareness is the first step. From there we hope people will be galvanised into action, whether it's writing a letter to a newspaper or their MP, or making a change in their own lifestyle.

'We go out to reach people and to show that Greenpeace has a human face. We don't want to be seen as some faceless group "out there". The follow-up is important too – we ensure that people are kept informed about things they're interested in; we don't just take the money and run. That's one advantage over just sending impersonal packages by mail.

'If people relied on the mainstream media for news on green issues, they'd only get the simplistic view – either the world is beyond saving or there was no problem in the first place. I know we can't suddenly change attitudes on the doorstep, but we do offer an alternative source of information; we can plant a seed.'

For Bev Cormack, it's important for Greenpeace to use a range of different approaches in its work. 'Having the resources and the money has made all the difference for some issues; we can't shy away from that. Take Antarctica, for instance: sure, we're not the only organisation campaigning on the issue, nor are we solely responsible for the current environmental reforms. But the world park idea didn't really take off until we had established our permanent base there and exposed many of the pollution problems associated with the national bases on the ice. Now a world park is within our reach. All this was

possible because we had the money.

'But in spite of all the changes, I think people still support us for the same reasons they did ten years ago – that we don't compromise, we still accept no party political or corporate associations, and we continue to adhere to a strict code of non-violent protest to publicise environmental abuses.

'Greenpeace New Zealand now has more than 130,000 paying supporters, many of whom have become active in our local Adopt-a-Beach or Antarctica groups, in our toxics campaign network or with other local environmental groups. I'd like to think our experience – our mistakes as well as our successes – can be shared with community and grassroots groups to empower people to act locally.

'Over the years, our team of public speakers have given slide shows, videos and talks on Greenpeace campaign issues to many thousands of New Zealanders. We have also corresponded with thousands of young supporters. The focus of our education work has been to empower young people to act for themselves. We're keen to share the skills we have learned collectively over twenty years of researching, lobbying and non-violent direct action. We're now creating a unit that we hope will help children, indeed anyone, to find ways to take personal or collective responsibility for environmental problems in their own communities. We began this programme in 1990, testing out an ocean ecology model in an Auckland intermediate school, where the children

Under the kauris, Manginangina, Bay of Islands Maritime Park. New Zealand's heritage – a balanced ecosystem that single species forestry cannot replace.

responded enthusiastically. The important thing is to be able to offer a range of practical skills to schools and community groups; it will be up to them what issues they choose to apply them to.

'Volunteers have always been the mainstay of Greenpeace New Zealand's work. In the early days, of course, it was all volunteers. Most of our long-term staff began by helping out in their spare time whenever they could, and over the years there have been many who have worked for us quietly and selflessly without thought of reward or recognition. Many stayed with us after 1985 and became part of the larger office family. In 1989 we were able to create the position of volunteers co-ordinator, with the objective of giving more supporters the opportunity to contribute practically rather than simply financially. In 1990 alone, Greenpeace volunteers contributed 14,400 work hours, equivalent to $144,000, to support our campaigns.'

Informal support groups around the country have played a role in Greenpeace activities since the early years. In 1989 it was decided to formalise this arrangement, and by 1991 there were five official support groups outside Auckland. Each group had signed a contract that authorised them to raise funds, give school talks and otherwise support existing GPNZ campaigns. In order to protect the organisation's credibility, however, they were not empowered to use Greenpeace's name to become involved in local environmental issues without the express permission of Greenpeace campaigners. Soon after the toxics tour, when the Dunedin group found they would not be authorised to make submissions to the council on a local issue, the main movers resigned in protest. This unfortunate incident highlighted a persistent drawback in the support group system. Communication in both directions had been unsatisfactory and the local groups had often been poorly serviced. The arrangement was restrictive and unsatisfactory for both parties. Then the Tauranga group found itself unable to replace its active members, who had moved on. Finally it was decided to dissolve the system and work out a new, more open relationship with local allies. Now GPNZ encourages independent local groups to pursue their own local concerns, while offering them Greenpeace's resources and support where it fits into an existing GPNZ campaign area. An example of this arrangement is the Millwatch group, which works quite independently but sometimes turns to Gordon's pulp and paper campaign for specific support.

Greenpeace has carved itself a niche through the 1970s and 1980s as a leading independent pressure group on environmental and peace issues. But the Greenpeace of the 1990s is in many ways a far cry from the pioneering group of the 1970s. In today's world of green consumerism and multinational corporations, environmentalism has become far more complex. Today oil company giants are as likely to fund green projects as they are sports events, even while persisting with their own environmentally destructive practices. The world is

Native bush and vegetation, Mangarakau Scenic Reserve, Golden Bay.

constantly changing and, like everyone else, Greenpeace has to change with it.

'It's easy to forget that twenty years ago so many people felt powerless to change the world. Perhaps Greenpeace has played a part in breaking down that barrier,' says Irene Petersen. 'The way we did things was also important. When Greenpeace New Zealand was set up we were determined to work co-operatively. For all our hard work, we had fun. I remember Bette Johnson once told Elaine that her time with Greenpeace New Zealand was the most fun she'd had in all her years of activism.'

In 1985 the office had just six full-time staff. By 1990 GPNZ was employing fifty-nine full-time and five part-time staff along with forty-one canvassers, with 150 volunteers on call. Perhaps inevitably, this extraordinary growth brought both positive and negative changes. There are those who feel that somewhere along the line Greenpeace lost some of its passion. For Stephanie Mills, Greenpeace's strength lies in its blend of diverse outlooks and skills. 'There has always been a tension between the anarchic and professional sides of the organisation. Sometimes that creates problems, but mostly it's a healthy thing. There are areas of Greenpeace's work, such as fundraising, which makes all our campaigns possible, that have to be more "professionalised" and money-oriented. And inevitably there are disagreements. Everyone gets frustrated by some aspect of the organisation they don't like, but it's the combination of passion and professionalism that makes the whole thing effective. As long as we strike a balance between the two, and keep fine-tuning it, I think we'll remain effective.'

'GPNZ has never operated according to some grand design,' says Carol Stewart. 'It responds to the ever-changing issues. We have to change with the issues while always placing the responsibility for solving environmental problems back on the community. With the growth of our resources and public image, there's a danger that people will simply turn to us for ready-made answers. But Greenpeace is really only a bunch of ordinary people like me. Finally, it's up to each individual to do what they can to bring about changes in their own lives and communities, not wait for someone else to do it for them.

'Greenpeace New Zealand used to be just a tiny group of hardworking volunteers, but now we've evolved into something different. Where once our people freely gave their energy and time because of their personal concern and commitment, GPNZ staff are now employed, and paid decently, on the basis of their skills, qualifications and experience. There's a danger that Greenpeace will become too precious, the organisation becoming more important than the issues. If we cannot stay in touch with our roots, we'll have lost the sense of whanau we always had, which meant valuing personal beliefs and mutual support over notions of professionalism. We can all learn to respect each others' opinions more, to listen more and work towards an ideal of consensus – that was our aim in Greenpeace in the early 1980s, and we tried to export the idea. Once we showed those in the international organisation that we could be both effective and "laid back" in our approach, I think we earned their respect.'

Success in Greenpeace's brand of activism is elusively hard to quantify. Scattered through this story are examples of changes in government policy

GPNZ, 1991.

and industrial practice for which GPNZ can take some of the credit. More often, though, their contribution has been subtle and intangible and relates to slippery notions like raising public awareness of issues and ideas. The current popularity of green ideas owes much to the long years of persistent campaigning by Greenpeace and other environmental groups, and GPNZ's authority today rests on the dedication and stubborn commitment of a whole generation of Greenpeace supporters. The last word goes to Martini:

'Everything Greenpeace New Zealand is today has only been made possible because of past achievements. We have to be committed to the long term. The French nuclear testing issue brought us into existence, and it's the issue from which all the others have grown. The fact that the French are still testing at Moruroa should remind us of the enormity of the opposition we face and save us from delusions of grandeur. No one ever said it was going to be easy to save the planet! The problems are not going to just go away, and we can't afford to let success go to our heads. Crucial decisions affecting the future of our planet continue to be made in secret by the rich and powerful, and it remains our job to ensure that these are exposed to full public scrutiny. Sometimes the task has seemed beyond us, but we know now that people like you and me can make a difference. It's this positive vision that will enable us to create a green and peaceful world for our children.'

Photo Credits

The following have kindly provided photographs for this book:
Brian Brennan (73), Paul Bruce (70), Bengt Danielsson (3, 30, 32, 84, 105, 134), Grant Davidson (11), Steve Dawson (172), Department of Conservation (169a), Noel Fuller (23), Bruce Gabites (198, 207, 208), Gil Hanly (83, 92, 93, 96, 97, 98, 100, 101, 102, 104, 122, 128, 129, 139,140, 143, 150, 154b, 160), Hiroto Kiryu (48, 49), Brice Lalonde (31), Tony Lilleby/Department of Conservation Design Centre (244/5, 246), Lincoln Potter (24a, 51b), David Robie (title page, 41a, 46, 114, 117, 120, 125), Ted Rutter (21, 24b, 25, 26, 27), Orietta Sloth (prelims, 44, 47, 50, 51a, 52).

Greenpeace photographers include Tim Baker (prelims), Michael Chechik (82), Brian Coffey (162), Jane Cooper (85), Diewa (252), Tom Donahue (72), Michael Dean (234, 240, 250), Lorette Dorreboom (18, 112, 158, 159b, 164, 204, 205a, 206, 209, 210, 212, 214, 216, 217, 220, 223, 228, 229, 230, 233, 241), Leith Duncan (170), Pierre Gleizes (60), Roger Grace (69, 142, 144/5, 159a, 161, 165, 166, 167a, 263), Henk Haazen (151a), Rik Hakaart (175, 203), Sebia Hawkins (132), Anna Horne (34), Gordon Jackman (219), Andi Loor (181, 184), Martinez (131), Chris Mauger (248), Bunny McDiarmid (151b, 152, 153, 154a), Steve Morgan (178, 185, 188, 189, 190a, 191, 192, 205b), John Paton (58, 59), Fernando Pereira (55/6, 110, 111, 115, 116, 118, 119), James Perez (186), Naomi Petersen (65, 66, 67), Jonathan Sligh (174), Lesley Stone (168), Keith Swenson (183) Mike Taylor (77), Grenville Turner (238).

For those photographs that are uncredited, we apologise to the photographers who we were unable to identify. Copies of most are held in the GPNZ photo library.

Opposite: Greenpeace New Zealand commemorates the 25th year of French nuclear testing in the Pacific. At dawn on 2 July 1991 Greenpeace climbers unfurled this banner from the roof of Auckland's Aotea Centre beside the banner advertising the hit musical *Les Miserables.*

Further Reading

Biedermann, Andy, and Mills, Stephanie. *Testimonies: Witnesses of French Nuclear Testing in the South Pacific*. Greenpeace International. Auckland 1990.

Brown, Vinson, and Willoya, William. *Warriors of the Rainbow*. Naturegraph USA. California 1988.

Caron, Elsa, and the crew of *Fri*. *Fri Alert*. Caveman Press. Dunedin 1974.

Caufield, Catherine. *In the Rainforest*. Picador. London 1986.

Crocombe, Ron. *The South Pacific: An Introduction*. Longman Paul. Auckland 1983.

Danielsson, Bengt and Marie-Thérèse. *Poisoned Reign: French Nuclear Colonialism in the Pacific*. Penguin. Auckland 1986.

Dawson, Stephen. *The New Zealand Whale and Dolphin Digest: The Project Jonah Handbook*. Brick Row. 1985.

de Deckker, Paul (ed.). *The Aggressions of the French at Tahiti and Other Islands of the Pacific*. Auckland University Press. Auckland 1983.

Dibblin, Jane. *Day of Two Suns: US Nuclear Testing and the Pacific Islanders*. Virago. London 1988.

Donoghue, Michael, and Wheeler, Annie. *Save the Dolphins*. David Bateman. Auckland 1990.

Harford, Barbara (ed.). *Beyond Anzus*. The Beyond Anzus Committee. Auckland 1985.

Hayes, Peter, Zarsky, Lyuba, and Bello, Walden. *American Lake: Nuclear Peril in the Pacific*. Penguin. Melbourne 1986.

Heimann, Rolf. *Knocking on Heaven's Door*. Friends of the Earth. Sydney 1979.

Hepenstall, Peter, and Rutherford, Noel. *Protest and Dissent in the Colonial Pacific*. University of the South Pacific. Apia 1984.

Hersey, John. *Hiroshima*. Penguin. Auckland (1985 edition).

Howarth, Jolyon, and Chilton, Patricia. *Defence and Dissent in France*. Croom Helm. London 1984.

Opposite: Fri Liberty Sail, New York 1986.

Hunter, Robert. *The Greenpeace Chronicle*. Picador. Auckland 1979.

Hunter, Robert, and McTaggart, David. *Greenpeace III – Journey into the Bomb*. Collins. London 1978.

Kand, Mikio (ed.). *Widows of Hiroshima*. Macmillan. London 1989.

King, Michael. *Death of the Rainbow Warrior*. Penguin. Auckland 1986.

Krop, Pascal, and Faligot, Roger. *La Piscine: The French Secret Service since 1944*. Blackwell. London 1989.

Lange, David. *Nuclear Free the New Zealand Way*. Penguin. Wellington 1990.

Leggett, Jeremy. *Global Warming: The Greenpeace Report*. Oxford University Press. Oxford 1990.

May, John. *The Greenpeace Book of Dolphins*. Random Century. Auckland 1990.

—— *The Greenpeace Book of the Nuclear Age*. Gollancz. London 1989.

—— and Brown, Michael. *The Greenpeace Story*. Macdonald. London 1989.

Miles, Julie, and Shaw, Elaine. *Chronology: The French Presence in the South Pacific 1838-1990*. Greenpeace. Auckland 1991.

Milliken, Robert. *No Conceivable Injury*. Penguin. Melbourne 1986.

Mitcalfe, Barry, et al. *Boy Roel: Voyage to Nowhere*. Peace Media. Wellington 1972.

Moody, Roger (ed.). *The Indigenous Voice*. Vols 1 and 2. Zed/IWGIA. London 1988.

Newnham, Tom. *Peace Squadron*. Graphic. Auckland 1986.

Robie, David. *Eyes of Fire: The Last Voyage of the Rainbow Warrior*. Lindon. Auckland 1986.

—— *Blood on Their Banner: Nationalist Struggles in the South Pacific*. Pluto Press. Melbourne 1989.

—— (ed.). *Tu Galala: Social Change in the Pacific*. Bridget Williams Books. Wellington 1991.

Rogers, Paul, and Landais-Stamp, Paul. *Rocking the Boat: New Zealand, the USA and the Nuclear Free Zone Controversy in the 1980s*. Berg. London 1989.

Seager, Joni (ed.). *The State of the Earth: An Atlas of Environmental Concern*. Unwin Hyman. Wellington 1990.

Wilson, Roger. *From Manapouri to Aramoana: The Battle for New Zealand's Environment*. Earthworks Press. Auckland 1982.

All these titles available from:

Trade Aid, 74 Pitt Street, Auckland

or by mail order from:

One World Books, P O Box 68 419, Newton, Auckland

Directory

A Directory of New Zealand Environmental, Peace and Development Groups

Antarctic and Southern Ocean Coalition (ASOC)
P O Box 11 057, Wellington
Ph (04) 846 971

Campaign for Nuclear Disarmament (CND)
74 Pitt Street, Auckland
Ph (09) 309 3809

CORSO
P O Box 9716, Wellington
Ph (04) 836 224

Environmental and Conservation Organisations (ECO)
P O Box 11 057, Wellington
Ph (04) 846 971

Friends of the Earth (FOE)
P O Box 39 065, Auckland
Ph (09) 303 4319

International Physicians for the Prevention of Nuclear War (IPPNW)
Auckland Medical School
Private Bag, Auckland
Ph (09) 795 780

Manukau Harbour Protection Society
c/o John McCaffrey
P O Box 109, Manurewa, Auckland
Ph (09) 687 001, ext 8709

Maruia Society
P O Box 756, Nelson
Ph (054) 83 336

New Zealand Foundation for Peace Studies
P O Box 4110, Auckland
Ph (09) 732 379

New Zealand Native Forests Restoration Trust
P O Box 80 007, Green Bay, Auckland 7
Ph (09) 602 933

New Zealand Rainforest Coalition
P O Box 2600, Wellington
Ph (04) 846 971

Nuclear Free Peacemaking Association
P O Box 18 541, Christchurch

Oxfam New Zealand
P O Box 68 357, Newton, Auckland
Ph (09) 358 1480

Pacific Concerns Resource Centre (PCRC)
P O Box 3148, Auckland
Ph (09) 307 5862

Peace Movement Aotearoa (PMA)
P O Box 9314, Wellington
Ph (04) 737 247

Peninsula Watchdog
P O Box 51, Coromandel

Project Jonah
P O Box 31 357, Auckland
Ph (09) 302 3106

Royal Forest and Bird Protection Society
P O Box 631, Wellington
Ph (04) 728 154

Scientists Against Nuclear Arms (SANA)
c/o Bill Peddie
30 Gibbs Crescent, Papakura
Ph (09) 298 4249

Trade Aid
P O Box 18 620, Christchurch
Ph (03) 791 982

Index

Abon, Lemoyo, 46
Achterberg, Rien, 47, 111, 123
Adopt-a-Beach campaign, 173-75
Agar, Janet, 169
Alliance, 135, 136, *136*, 137
Amchitka, 5, 21
Anderson, Hilari, 87
Anderson, Lloyd, 82, *82*, 85, 123
Anjain, Fred, 150
Anjain, Jeton, 111-12, 118
Anjain, John, 46, *46*
Anjain, Nelson, 47, *47*, 48, 49, *88*, 109
Antarctic and Southern Ocean Coalition (ASOC), 180, 196
Antarctic campaign, 92, 104, 180, 182-97, 243
Antarctic Treaty, 178-79, 197; meeting (1987), 186-87, *190*
Antarctica, *176*, 177-78, *197*; bases at, 180, 182, 187, 189, 191-93; fishing around, 193-94; mineral exploitation of, 178-80, 186; world park concept, 178, 181, 196
Armstrong, George, 77
Armstrong, Wendy, 39
Atkinson, Tony, 137
Atkinson Report, 200
Atmosphere and energy campaign, 242-43
ATOM (Against Tests on Moruroa) groups, 42, 43, 44
Auckland Harbour Bridge banner, 235-36
Australian Bicentennial Naval Review, *238*, 239
Australian Government: Labour, 28-29; and whaling, 63
Azores, whaling in, *65-67*, 65-68

Bahia Paraiso wreck, 191, 196
Balos, Ataji, 47
'Ban, Don't Burn' project, 217, 226
Barbary, 26, 28
Barrington, Jacqui, 237, 240, *240*
Barry, Alister, 25, 32

Bartrum, Ken, 40
Bastille Day memorials, 87, *93*
Bataillon de la Paix, 29, 30
La Bayonnaise, 8, 9-10
Bearing witness, 5
Belau, 154
Bell, Terry, 73
Biedermann, Andy, 111, 119, 137, 203
Bikini Atoll, 2, 5, 45, 45-48, *47*, 147
Bikini Day demonstrations, Tahiti, *88*, 133-34
Bland, Michael, 62
Bluenose, 26, 28
Bolger, Jim, 239
Bollardiere, Jacques Paris de, 30, 31
Bone, Chris, 149, *150*
Boy Roel, 14, 15, 16-18
Boyack, Jim, 38, 39
'Bravo' test, 45-46, 118
Breeze, 135, 136, *136*
Bruce, Paul, 68-69
Burch, Pip, *92*, 96, 97, 99-100, 104
Buske, Norm, 202, 203-05, 208, *209*, 209, 212

Caesium-134, 202, 208, 209
Caesium-137, 240
Caillard, Michel, 16
Campaign for Non-Nuclear Futures (CNNF), 75
Campaign for Nuclear Disarmament (NZCND), 1, 6, 7, 13, 76, 88
Campaign Half Million, *74*, 75
HMNZS *Canterbury*, 33
Castle, Jon, 85
Cauty, Karen, 40-41, 42
Cavaney, Joan and Ron, 26, 39, 78
Centre d'Expérimentation Nucléaires du Pacifique (CEP), 3, 10, 12, 33, 82

Charrière, Franck, 136
Chemical Industry Council circular, 215, 229
Chemicals, toxic, 220-23, 226, 227, 230
Chile, pirate whaling of, 68-69, 70
Ching, Charlie, 84, *85*, 112, *113*, *134*, 134, 200
Chu Hoi Yuen, China, 51
Churches, support by, 38, 77
Ciguatera, 137
Claverie, Admiral, 12, *12*
Coastal ecology campaign, 169, 173-75
Coffey, Brian, 164
Conaglen, Kevin, 182, 183
Connan, Alain, 203, *209*, *210*, 212
Convention on the Conservation of Antarctic Marine Living Resources (CCAMLR), 194
Convention on the Regulation of Antarctic Mineral Resource Activities (CRAMRA), 186, 191, 196
Cook Islands and nuclear testing, 16
Cooper, Brett, 14
Cooper, Jane, *83*, 83-84, 103
Coral reef protection, 156
Cormack, Bev, *92*, 101, 104
Coromandel Watchdog, 230
Cortesi, Lafcadio, 156
Cottier, Jim, 15, 135
Couper, Kay, 39, 43
Cousteau expedition to Moruroa, 202, 209
Cuthbert, Arani, 195

Dalziell, Janet, 195, 196
Danielsson, Bengt and Marie-Thérèse, 32, 33, 84, 131-32, 133, 205
Dasler, Clive and Yvonne, 26
Davidson, Grant, 7, 12
Dawson, Steve, 171
Department of Conservation, 63, 173, 229
Doherty, Phil, 195
Donahue, Tom, 70, 85, 87, 92, 169; as co-ordinator, 95, 96, 102-03
Donoghue, Michael, 63, 64, 69-70, 88
Don't Make a Wave Committee (Vancouver), 5
Doom, John, 112
Doudart de Lagrée, 31
Driftnet fishing, 71, *162*, 163-67, *164*, *165*, *166*, *167*
Drollet, Jacqui, 84, 112, 113, 203
Dumont d'Urville (French Antarctic base) airstrip, *178*, 180, 187-89, *188*, *190*
Duncan, Leith, 172, 173
La Dunkerquoise, 31
Ebeye, 111, *112*, 118, 153-54

Ecology Action, 76
Edward, Davey, 123-24
Enewetak, 2, 45, 153
Environment and Peace Information Centre *see* Epicentre
Epicentre, 39, 76, 93
Esperanza (Argentine Antarctic base), 189, 193
Exclusion zones, 3, 6, 30, 135

Fand, 212
Farrelly, Justin, 182, 191
Federated Farmers, 240
Federated States of Micronesia, 44-45
Fiji and nuclear testing, 29, 44, 68
Forestry, 220, 241-42
Fox, Isobel and Jackie, 219, *219*, 226
France: nuclear weapons testing, 2, 19, 29, 33, 35, 83, 138, 147, 199-200
Freedom for the Seas project, 170
French Embassy, Wellington, 81, 130
French Government: and GP at Moruroa, 205-08, 209, 211; and *Rainbow Warrior* bombing, 130-33
French High Commission, Papeete, 205
French Navy, 9, 135, 205
Fri, 20, 21-28, *23*, *24*, *25*, *27*, *36*, *50*, 94-95; at Azores, 65-68; at Moruroa, 30-33, *31*; in 1985, 110-11; and the Odyssey, 37-39, 43-44, 47-53
Friends of the Earth, 58, 62, 220
Fruth, Barbara, 235-36
Fukuryu Maru (Fifth Lucky Dragon), 46-47, 49, *49*
Fur seal campaign, 168, *169*, *170*, 172

Galvin, Tihema, 135
Gaudian, Gudrun, 182-85, *186*
Gentle, Tim, 169, 173
Gerson, Clare, 149, *150*
Getz, Vicki, 191-93, 195, 196
Gfeller, Emile, 44
Global warming, 240-43; and the Pacific, 155-56
Glue, Murray, 25
Goldsworthy, Lynn, 180, 181
Gondwana, 187, 189, *189*, 191, 194, 195, 229
Gonzales-Mata, Luis, 200
Gotje, Martin, 24, *24*, 31, 37, 38, 50, 110, 111, 123-24, 141, 150; at Moruroa, 204, *209*, 211-12; and Pacific campaign, 157
Grace, Roger, 164-65
Great Britain: nuclear weapons testing, 2, 81
Greenham Common, 86
MV *Greenpeace*, 105, 135-38, *136*; in Antarctica, *181*, 182, 187; helicopter, *183*

Greenpeace Cup, *239*, 240
Greenpeace Foundation of Canada, 5, 60-61
Greenpeace Foundation of NZ (GPNZ): campaign conflicts, 94-95, 97, 103; direct action, 222-23; door-to-door canvassing, 243, 247; education work, 244-45; finances, 92, 96, 105, 106; formation of, 37, 38, 39-40; fundraising, 40, 42, 97, 98-99, 130, 247; and GPI, 91-92, 103; Hobson St office, 106; local groups, 85; and local issues, 231; mail-outs, 97, 98; and media, 60, 107, 131-35, 222-23; merchandising, 94, 96, 105; Nagel House office, 95-96, 105, 121-23; and nuclear power, 75; and nuclear-powered ships, 78, 80; official support groups, 245-46; publications, 203, 230; staff, 106, 247, *248*; structure of, 102-03; supporters, 96, 97, 106, 135, 244; volunteers, 94, 100, 245, 247; in Wellington, 81, 88; and whales, seals etc., 60, 62-71
Greenpeace France, 212
Greenpeace International (GPI), 82, 85, 91, 111, 154, 180; structure of, 91
Greenpeace London, 29
Greenpeace (name), 91
Greenpeace III see Vega
Greenpeace Vancouver *see* Greenpeace Foundation of Canada
Gulbransen, Graham, 101
Gulf War, 229-30
Guy, Ross, 62

Haazen, Henk, 110-11, 134, 135; on Mejato, 150
Haddleton, Roger, 7
USS *Haddo, 73*, 73-74, 80
Hager, Nicky, 86
Hagler, Mike, 163, 166, 170, 172, 174
Halkyard-Harawira, Hilda, 87
Hamilton, Kirsty, 229, 242, *242*
Hao Atoll, 32, 132
Harrison, Rodney, 130
Hawkins, Sebia, 154, *154*, 170
Hayes, Peter, 38
Heather, Alice, 136-37
Hector's dolphin, 171, *172*, 229
Hemmings, Alan, 196
Henderson, Lynx, 240
Hennessey, Wayne, 95
Hetherington, Mabel, 6, 21
La Hippopotame, 9, 85, 136
Hiro, Henry, 84, *85*
Hiroshima Day memorials, 39, 49, 81, 87, *90*
Hirshon, Tea, 83-84, *88*, 112, 203
Hoffmann, Benne, 118, 119, 123
Holcomb, Bobby, paintings by, *148, 201*

Holyoake, Keith, 4, 76
Hooker's sea lion campaign, 168-69, *169*, 173
Horn, Kurt, 24
Horne, Anna, 6-7, *33*, 33-34, 87-88
Huahine, 113
Hunt, Jonathan, 37

Iceland, whaling by, 167
ICI fire, 220-21
Independence movements, Pacific, 29, 30, 35, 84, 89, 134
Ingram, Nigel, 7, 12, *12*, *33*, 33-34, *34*
International Court of Justice, 28-29, 30
International waters, annexation of *see* Exclusion zones
International Whaling Commission (IWC), 62, 63-65, 68, 69-70, 167-68; conference action (1988), 195
HMS *Invincible*, 88
Ivon Watkins-Dow plant, 219, 221-22, 232

Jackman, Gordon, 215, 217-20, *217*, 220, 226
Jackman, Paul, 92
Japan, 49, 101; fishing methods of, 163; whaling by, 167-68, 189
Japanese Festival parade, *167*, 168
Johnson, Bette, 39, 41, *41*, 42, 76
Johnson, Giff, 41, 109, 111
Johnson, Rebecca, 201, 202

Kaikorai estuary, Dunedin, *233*
Kakuta, Naoko, 163, *164*, 165
Kearney, Patti, 62, 70, 92, 94
Killi Island, 47, 48
Kiribati, 119, 155, *157*, 234
Kirimati (Christmas) Island, 2, 101
Kirk, Norman, *28*, 29, 30, 39
Kroesa, Renate, 104, 220-22, *221*
Kuboyama, Aikichi, 47, 49
Kwajalein, *108*, 112, 118, *119*, 157, *158*

Labour Party (NZ), 4, 19, 89
Lalonde, Brice, 30, 82, *82*, 205
Lange, David, 132
Lautua, Pio, 150
Lavallée, 207, 210
Leeuwen, Willem and Ann van, 14, 22
Lefale, Penehuro, *155*, 155-56
Levy, Dorothy, 113
Lindsay, Tony, 106, 226, 231
Lini, Walter, 44, 77, 89, *119*, 119-20
USS *Long Beach, 77*, 78-79

Lornie, Mary, 33, 33-34
Lucky Dragon see Fukuryu Maru

McDiarmid, Bunny, 110-11, 119, 120, 134, 135, 141; on Mejato, 150-54, *151*; and Pacific campaign, 154, 160, 224
Mackenzie, Raewyn, 75
McKinnon, Don, 238
McMurdo base, 191-93, *194*
McTaggart, David, 1, 6-13 *passim*, *12*, *33*, 33-35, *82*, 82; as chair of GPI, 91, 92
Mafart, Alain, 130, 141
Magic Isle, 14, 16
Mangarakau Scenic Reserve, *246*
Mangareva, 137
Manginangina, Bay of Islands, *244-45*
Mann, Birdie, 75
Manukau Harbour, 219, 231; sewage pipes, *214*
Marambio (Argentine Antarctic base), 193
Marches and rallies, 81, 86, 87, *87*, *90*, *100*, *101*, *102*, *105*, *106*
Marere, Andre, painting by, *212*
Marine mammals *see* individual species
Marine reserves, 171, 173
Marrett, Graeme, 25
Marriner, Tony, 82, *82*
Marsden Point oil refinery, 219, 232
Marshall, Colin, 25, 31
Marshall, John, 19, 29
Marshall Islands, 44, 47, 109, 147, 155 *see also* individual atoll names
Martin, Peter, 27
Matata Beach, 215, *216*
Matauri Bay, Northland, 139, 141, *143*
Mejato, *116*, 118, 151-53, *151*, *152*, *153*
Metcalfe, Ben, 6, 7-8
Mikhail Verbitzkiy, 194
Mills, Margaret, 123, 125
Mills, Stephanie, 86, 202-04, *203*, 204, 229
Millwatch group, 246
Ministry of Agriculture and Fisheries (MAF, NZ), 59, 63
Missiles testing, US, 112, 157
Mitcalfe, Barry, 13-14, 18-19, 21, 22-23, *23*, 30, 43
Mitcalfe, Jacqui, 13
Mitterrand, Francois, 132, 136
Moana, Guy, *239*
Monroe, Hugh, 33
Moodie, David, 21, 22, 23, 24, 31, 37; at Azores, 65-68; on Odyssey, 38, 39, *47*
Moore, Mike, 37
Moruroa: accidents at, 82-83, 200; appearance of, 12, *17*, 32;
CEP built at, 3; danger zone, 2; radioactive leakage at, 202, 208; scientific survey of, 83; testing at, *1*, *4*, *8*, 83, 113, 199-200
Muldoon, Robert, 39, *39*, 78
Muller, Jean-Marie, 30

Nahodka, Soviet Union, 49, 50, 52
Nanni, Michele, 243
Nevada, 2, 5
New Zealand Government: and Antarctica, 178, 186, 196; and nuclear power (National), 75; and nuclear-powered ships (National), 76, 78, 238-39 (Labour), 76, 99, 236, 238-39; and nuclear tests (National), 4, 7, 13, 15 (Labour), 28-29; and whaling, 62, 64
Nicolas, Gilbert, 25, 30, 31
Northey, Richard, 4-5, 7, 134
Norway, whaling by, 167-68
Nuclear-armed and -powered ships, 236-37
Nuclear fallout effects, 42, 46, 48, 118, 200
Nuclear Free and Independent Pacific (NFIP) movement, 41, 42-43, 85, 89, 147-48
Nuclear Free Pacific campaign, 82
Nuclear Free Seas campaign, 237-40; launching, *235*, 236
'Nuclear Free Sheep' tour, 240
Nuclear power, 75-76
Nuclear ship visits to NZ, 73-89
Nuclear Shipping Code (NZ), 80
Nuclear weapons testing, 213; atmospheric, 2-3, *4*, 8, 35, 45-48; marches, pickets and petitions against, 13, *80*, 81, 86, *86*; underground, 35, 83

Ocean ecology campaign, 169-70
Ohana Kai, 61
Operation Exodus, 113-18, 134
Operation Namibia, 65
Orr, Marjorie, 63
O'Sullivan, Grace, 119, 135, 138
HMNZS *Otago*, 28, 29
Ouvèa, 130
Owen, Susan-Jane, 87, 97, 104, 169, 181
Ozone depletion, 240, 242

Paeamara, Lucas, 137
Pacific campaign, 150, 154, 156-57, 160, 199
Pacific Concerns Resource Centre, Hawai'i, 148
Pacific Peace Odyssey, 37-39, 43-44, 47-53
Pacific Peace Voyage, 111, 149
La Paimpolaise, 10-11
Palmer, Geoffrey, *240*

Parmentier, Remi, 206, 207
Patterson, Walter, 75
Paul, Rua, 24, 25
Peace Media, 1, 13, 14, 19, 22, 37, 38; flotilla plans, 23, 26
Peace movement groups, 85-86, 88, 99; French Polynesian, 133-34
Peace Squadrons, 77; Auckland, 72, 73, 74, 75, 77, *77*, 78-79, *78, 79*, 87, 88-89, 120, *238*, 239; Wellington, 78
Pereira, Fernando, 111, 123-25
Perry, Natasha, *217*
Pesticides project, 217, 227
Petersen, Hugh, 39, 92
Petersen, Irene, 39, 40, *40*, 75, 78-79, 92
Petersen, Naomi, 22, 25, *25*, 26, 32, 38, 94-95; at Azores, 65-68; on Odyssey, 39, *49, 51*, 51-53; and new *Rainbow Warrior*, 158-60, *159*
Petitions, 13, 75
USS *Phoenix*, 87-88
Phyllis Cormack, 5, 60
USS *Pintado*, 79
Pipke, Diana, 168, 229
Pitcairn Island, *26, 27*, 28, 159
Pollution: river, 217-19, 228
Poorter, Maj de, 191
Popp, Tanya, 210-12
Pouvanaa a Oopa, 29-30, *32*, 43, *44*
Prieur, Dominique, 130, 141
Project Jonah, 62, 63
Protest voyages: (1972) 1, 4, 7-13, 14-18; (1973) 25-35; (1981) 82-85; (1985) 135-38
Puhi Hau peace festival, 84, *85*
Pukeuri meatworks, Oamaru, *223*
Pullen, Jane, 97
Pulp and paper project, 217, 246
Pupuka, Philip, 159, 204, 215

USS *Queenfish*, 88

Radio Hauraki, 7, 14
Radio Waikato, 14
Rainbow Warrior: bombing, 123-24, *126, 129*; bombing, effect on GPNZ, 104, 127-30, 135, 149; bombing, media coverage of, 131-32, 133; compensation for, 141; crew, 110, 128; memorial, *143*; Pacific Peace Voyage, 109, 111, *111*; wreck of, 138-39, *139, 140, 142*, 141
Rainbow Warrior (new), 158-60, *159, 160*; crew, *206*; and drift net monitoring, 163-66; inflatables, *208*; at Moruroa, 206-12; in Papeete, *198, 203, 206*; toxics tour (1991), 215, 227-30, *230*

Radiation diseases *see* Nuclear fallout effects
Rainforests campaign, 240
Ralston, Bill, 26
Rara, Charles, 120
'Reduce, Reuse, and Recycle', 224
Reeves, Paul, 38
Rhodes, Bernard, 26-27, 39, 78
Rigg, Kelly, 121, 123, 127, 128
Riini, Augie, 150, *150*
Roach, Mark, *81*, 81-82, 167, *167*
Robertson, Grace, 87
Robie, David, 111, 113, 114, 133
Robinson, Chris, 72, 82, *82*, 85, *85*, 87-88, 135, 137-38, 212, 222
Robinson, Dove-Myer, 15, 37
Robson, Frank, 63
'Rolling Snowball' tour, 195-96
Rongelap, 46, 47, 48; evacuation, 111, 114-18, *114, 115, 116*
Roumieu, Mark, 27
Rowling, Bill, 76
Rutter, Ted, 25

Sanford, Francis, 29, 32, *32*, 38, 43, *44*
Save the Whales campaign, 60
Sawyer, Steve, 101, 106-07, 109; in Auckland, 121-23, 127-30; and Pacific Peace Voyage, 111
Scoones, Peter, 164
Scotford, Phil, *81*, 82, 167, *167*
Seaboyer, Jude, 92, 97, 100, 104, 122-23, 129, 222
Sealing, 61, 71 *see also* Fur seal
Servan-Schreiber, Jean-Jacques, 29, 30, *32*
Sewage disposal, 231
Shadbolt, Maurice, 15-16
Shageyev, Alexander, 53
Shaw, Elaine, 39, *41*, 41-43, 75, 76, 79, 81, 85, 87, 89, 120, *121*, 199; as co-ordinator, 92, 94, 95, 101-02; in Tahiti, 112-13; after bombing, 123, 124, *128*, 141; Pacific networking, 148-49, 150
Sherie, Stephen, *73*, 73-74
Shimizu, Japan, *48*, 49, *50*
Slooten, Liz, 171
Sloth, Orietta (and Tobias), 39, 43, *47*
Smith, Peter, 174-75, *175*
Sorensen, Hanne, 124
South Pacific Nuclear Free Zone Treaty, 101, 236
Sowing the Seeds of Peace postcards, 37-38, 39, 43, 49, 53
Spautz, Roger, 203, 207, 211
Spirit of Peace, 26-28, 33
Spong, Paul, 60
Steele, Maurice, 240

Stewart, Carol, 70, 81, 85, 87; Antarctic campaigner, 182, 187; in early GPNZ, 93-94, 102, 103-04, *104*; and *Rainbow Warrior* tour, 109-10, 123, 134-35, 139, 141; in toxics campaigns, 215, 222
Stewart, Joel, 215, 232
Stone, Lesley, 215, 223-24, *224*
Street theatre, 79, 81, *92*, *98*, *229*
Stutzin, Godfredo, 69
HMAS *Supply*, 29
Swenson, Keith, 187
Swete, Didi, 101-02

Taape, 138
Taero, Guy (Jacky), 85, *85*, 113
Tahiti, 2, 83-84, 202-03, 207; Faa'a tree planting, 43, *44*; and nuclear testing, 29-30; protest march at, 29, *32*
Taiyo Fishery Co., 65, 68
Talcahuano, Chile, 68-69, *70*
Tamatea-Ariki-Nui, 228
Tamure, 14, 15-16
Tarawera River pollution, 217, 218-19
Tasman pulp and paper mill, 217, *217*, 218-19
Tasman Sea, 163, 164
Tavini Huiraatira, 84, 134, *204*
Taylor, Michael, 39, 55, 59, 62, 63, 64, 180; as co-ordinator, 92, 94
Tazieff mission, 83, 200
Teariki, John, 3, 32
Temaru, Oscar, 32, 84, *84*, 113, 134, 203, *203*, 205
Testimonies, 203, 204
Teuruaa, Papa, 150
USS *Texas*, 87, 88
Tizard, Cath, 88
Tooker, Jess, 174-75
Toulat, Jean, 30
Toxics campaign, 215-33
Toxics runoff, 171
USS *Truxtun*, 78
Tufariua, Remuna, 209

United Nations conference on test ban treaty, 202, 213
United States: nuclear weapons testing, 2, 5, 45-48, 147
Ursem, Anneke, 100, *221*, 222

Van Dorp, Cornelius, 182, 185-86, 191, 195
Vanuatu, 44, 89, 119-20, *120*; People's Charter, 148
Varangian, 135, 138
Vega (Greenpeace III): and nuclear ship visits, 72, 87-88; peace voyage ((1986) 149-54; protest voyages, (1972) 1, 7-13, *7*, *10* (1973) 33-35, (1981) 82-85, (1985) 135-38, *136*; whaling, 60
Waiau Pa, Manukau, 55-59
Waihi Mining Co., 232
Waimakariri River, 228, 231
Wallace, Cath, 180, 181, 196
Ware, Sue, 135, 138, 150, *150*, 159, 204
Waste: dumping in Pacific, 119, 223-24; incineration of at sea, 223; local disposal of, 224, 226, 231-32; stockpiles of, 232
Watts, Meriel, 226-27
We Carrier, 166
Western Samoa, 155, 156
Whale strandings, 55-59, *58*, *59*, 63
Whale Walk, Auckland (1984), *95*, *96*, 98-99
Whaling, *54*, 60, 62, 63, 64-71; pirate, 65-70; 'scientific', 71, 167-68, 189, *192*
Whitehouse, Peter, 104, 222-23
Wilkes, Owen, 13, 43, 74, 149, 150, *150*, 237
Wilkinson, Pete, 187-88, 193
Willcox, Peter, 123-24, 135, 138, 159, 163, 204
Williams, Peter, 39
Wilson, Roger, 82, 92, 102, 180, 181, 196
Women Acting for Nuclear Disarmament (WAND), 86
World Court *see* International Court of Justice
World Park Antarctica base, 182-85, *184*, *185*, 187

Yeates, Patchouli and Peter, 23, 25
Yensen, Helen, 103, 123
Young, Emma, 21, 38

Opposite: Penguins on an iceberg near the British Antarctica base Signy, South Orkney Island.

第三日新丸
東京
NISSHIN MARU № 3
TOKYO